HOW THE
HELICOPTER
CHANGED MODERN
WARFARE

Also by Walter J. Boyne

HOW THE
HELICOPTER
CHANGED MODERN
WARFARE

Walter J. Boyne

A GINIGER BOOK

PELICAN PUBLISHING COMPANY
Gretna 2011

Library of Congress Cataloging-in-Publication Data

Boyne, Walter J., 1929-
  How the helicopter changed modern warfare / Walter J. Boyne.
      p. cm.
  "A Giniger book."
  Includes bibliographical references and index.
    ISBN 978-1-58980-700-6 (hardcover : alk. paper) 1. Military helicopters—
History. 2. Air warfare—History—20th century. 3. Military art and science—
History—20th century. I. Title.
    UG1230.B69 2011
    358.4'14--dc22

                                    2010043758

Published in association with The K. S. Giniger Company, 1045 Park
Avenue, New York, New York 10028-1030

Printed in the United States of America
Published by Pelican Publishing Company, Inc.
1000 Burmaster Street, Gretna, Louisiana 70053

This book is dedicated with gratitude to the men and women who have participated in the amazing history of rotary-wing aircraft. In particular, we all owe a debt to those members of the vertical flight fraternity who have engaged in combat defending the United States in strange and hostile places around the world. They have been the point of the military sword, sometimes bursting into enemy positions with courage and panache, sometimes acting as angels of compassion, rescuing the wounded under fire. There is no way to measure their selfless bravery, and one can only admire what they have done with so demanding an instrument as the helicopter.

In the Vietnam War, nothing was more welcome than the sight of a formation of Huey helicopters approaching. *(Courtesy of U.S. Army Museum, Fort Rucker)*

Contents

Preface

The helicopter has profoundly changed modern warfare in many ways, from saving thousands of lives to becoming the very tip of the sword of contemporary combat. It has progressed from a tiny, fragile machine of marginal performance to a swift, elusive aircraft capable of dominating low-threat modern battlefields. It has done so thanks to the genius of a handful of individuals in the industry and the military who believed in the ability of the helicopter to do things impossible for fixed-wing aircraft.

The helicopter succeeded despite formidable obstacles that included the laws of physics, bureaucratic indifference, inter- and intra-service rivalries, budgetary restrictions, and simultaneous improvement in other weapon systems.

Most weapon systems experience similar difficulties. The case with the helicopter is somewhat different in that its development and deployment did not follow a smooth curve but were beset by interruptions and displacements that are unusual in the routine development of weapon systems. While extremely frustrating to helicopter advocates, they are of great interest to helicopter historians, for they make the achievements of rotary-wing aircraft all the more remarkable.

As this is written, the military helicopter is of profound importance to the defense of the United States. Any land operations in Iraq, Afghanistan, and other trouble spots in the Middle East would be impossible without the helicopter as a weapon and a supply vehicle. The United States, committed by force of circumstances to wage war against terrorist elements in all corners of the world, depends upon the helicopters of our armed services. These helicopters are flown and maintained by the finest, best-trained, and most dedicated personnel in military history.

It is an irony and a shame that circumstances have dictated that these

9

same expert personnel are forced to use fleets of helicopters of dated design and, as a result, incur casualties at a rate that is deemed unacceptable for other elements of our aerial forces. The current American fleet of helicopters is composed for the most part of designs dating back to the 1970s and 1980s. Helicopters have come to be regarded as "platforms" that can be updated and made more useful by new software and electronic systems.

This is quite true. The helicopters flying today are far better equipped than the original versions. Fixed-wing bombers, such as the Boeing B-52, are also considered "platforms" and are continually updated. The B-52's mission changed from that of long-range, high-altitude nuclear strikes, to low-altitude delivery of nuclear weapons, to the medium-altitude delivery of massive quantities of conventional weapons, a role it performed with distinction in Vietnam. It has since been updated to use modern precision-guided munitions and has thus retained its utility and comparative invulnerability.

But there is a great and too often overlooked difference between the use of the 1960s-era B-52 as a platform and the use of 1970- and 1980-era helicopter designs as a platform. The difference is that the 1960s B-52 possessed the high-speed, long-range, and altitude capability necessary for its 2010-era missions. The 1970- and 1980-era helicopters did not, being too slow, too short ranged, and too vulnerable for modern combat. Nonetheless, many are still used, for they are all that is available.

And while the B-52 makes a convenient and easily understood comparison, the tragedy of the failure to design and place modern helicopters in quantity production is even more apparent when contrasted with tactical aircraft. Even such aged types as the Lockheed Martin F-16 and Boeing F-15 suffer far fewer losses. As this book will show, the lessons of air combat that were learned at such great cost in the Vietnam War were analyzed, *funded,* and applied to tactical aircraft. This has resulted in a dramatic decline in casualties. In contrast, those lessons were neither funded nor applied to helicopters in the same quantity and with the same timing that were applied to fixed-wing aircraft. Even more distressing, an apparently unquenchable thirst for unachievable performance parameters has resulted in much of the helicopter research and development (R&D) money being wasted in cancelled programs.

As a result, helicopter losses in combat due to hostile action, in combat due to non-hostile action, and in noncombat situations continue to exceed fixed-wing aircraft losses in the same situations. Even worse, noncombat, non-hostile helicopter losses exceed combat losses by a four-to-one ratio.

It is an inescapable fact that the helicopters of the United States military services have not had the increases in speed, range, and operational altitude that innovative R&D could and should have provided. This is not an inference about how helicopters might have developed but a statement of fact. Capable prototype helicopters were developed during this period and then not adopted for production. Had they been adopted, they would have led to still better performing helicopters.

If even 50 percent of the funding for R&D that was applied to tactical aircraft had been applied to helicopters, it would have resulted in dramatic improvements, especially in such vital areas as vulnerability to damage, stealth, operating expense, and ease of maintenance.

The ultimate tragedy is that this failure to invest properly in the systematic introduction of new helicopters over the past forty years has resulted in contemporary casualty rates for helicopters that exceed those of the Vietnam War. This occurs at a time when casualty rates for tactical aircraft, employed in the same theater against the same enemy, have declined radically. It cannot be said that there is a direct one-to-one relationship between inadequate R&D and these losses, for there have been changes in the battlefield and in helicopter tactics. Nonetheless, helicopter losses per sortie have risen, while fixed-wing tactical aircraft losses per sortie have fallen.

There are a number of reasons for this sad state of affairs, with no single smoking gun other than the universal culprit, human nature. In the first half of the more than six decades that the helicopter has been employed as an instrument of war, it was immensely improved in terms of speed, range, and altitude. In the second half, it was "upgraded" with new systems and operated with new and better tactics. In that time, improvements in terms of speed, range, and altitude were marginal.

During the same six-decade period, the nature of warfare has changed radically. After World War II, nuclear weapons assumed primary importance. Throughout the long and difficult Cold War, military and political leaders came to rely on the concept of deterrence. The apt acronym MAD was used for the term "Mutual Assured Destruction," which meant that the full use of nuclear weapons would inevitably lead to the utter destruction of both nations. At the same time, in the wistful hope that somehow war could come and nuclear weapons not be employed, the East and the West maintained large armed forces capable of "high-intensity conflict."

With the end of the Cold War, the nature of war shifted to smaller, regional conflicts and to the war against global terrorism, forcing military planners to provide for different contingencies. Today, there are still valid concerns about the use of nuclear weapons, especially by rogue nations or organizations that do not react to the concept of "mutual deterrence." Concerns about "high-intensity conflicts," in which the major forces of one country contend with the major forces of another, have diminished. They have been replaced with the pervasive nature of the war against terrorism, which takes our armed forces to trouble spots around the world—Iraq, Afghanistan, the Horn of Africa, and elsewhere. Despite the great expense and the tragic casualties of the contemporary style of warfare, it has earned the term "low-intensity conflict."

Those actively engaged in "low-intensity conflict" would call it anything but that. However, it is a convenient term for the U.S. government to use. It diminishes public anxiety, allows for reductions in the defense budget, and permits the nation to be defended by a very small percentage of its population. (During World War II, our population of some 130 million furnished more than 16.3 million for the armed services—about 12.3 percent of the population. Today, with a population exceeding 300 million, we have about 2.4 million in the armed services—about .008 percent of the population.)

There were other great changes, including those in industry, the military, and Congress.

In the early days of the industry, innovation was everything, and the field was wide open to the genius of men such as Igor Sikorsky, Frank Piasecki, Charles Kaman, Arthur Young, and many more. As time passed,

Frank Piasecki, one of the great personalities of the helicopter world—entrepreneur, designer, test pilot, and salesman. *(Courtesy of Piasecki Aircraft Corporation)*

the growth of the industry diminished the possibility of a single individual having the same degree of influence. With size came the usual benefits and drawbacks of the modern corporation. Levels of bureaucracy were introduced, and ensuring profitability took a natural precedence over the sheer joy of invention. During the same interval, helicopters became larger and more expensive. This made the risk inherent in committing to a new design less attractive, especially when costs became a driving factor in government procurement decisions. Incremental improvements that kept an established production line flowing were both easier and more profitable than creating a much more advanced design that might not be adopted. (This lesson was painfully learned by Lockheed with its very advanced Cheyenne and by Boeing and Sikorsky with the Comanche.)

There is nothing evil in this industrial conservatism. It is perhaps inevitable, unless offset by the vision and leadership of first the military services and then Congress. (The term "vision" is often overused, as the familiar aphorism "vision without funding is a hallucination" indicates.)

There have been great leaders within the military services who advanced the cause of helicopters, reaching back to such giants as Army Lt. Gen. James M. Gavin and Marine Gen. Victor H. "Brute" Krulak and Lt. Gen. Roy S. Geiger. Over the years, there have been effective helicopter advocates within each of the military services. Unfortunately, as will be noted later, the military services are led by human beings with different views and priorities, and it has too often been the fate of the helicopter to be accorded a lower priority than other weapon systems. This is less true of the United States Marines than of all of the other services. The Marines have had a single-minded commitment to the helicopter since 1947. And while the relative proportion of the defense budget allocated to the Marines is small in comparison to that of the Army, Navy, or Air Force, they have been able to chart the course in developing vertical take-off aircraft to a surprising degree. It is only thanks to Marine persistence that totally new aircraft, such as the McDonnell AV-8 Harrier, the Bell/Boeing V-22 Osprey, and the Lockheed Martin F-35, have eventuated.

As with every other aspect of government, the failure to make the correct decisions regarding investment in R&D and production of advanced helicopters rests with the Department of Defense but even more so with Congress. There are many problems, but the most important are Congress's continuous effort to reduce defense spending, its desire to see that procurement contracts provide jobs in congressional home districts, and the growth in size of congressional staffs, with the resulting layers of bureaucracy.

Congress should have listened to the various military briefings and then committed funding to whatever was necessary to maintain American defenses. It has failed to do so in a systematic manner, so that today the United States not only is depending upon a relative handful of aged fleets of aircraft for its defense, it has no viable plans to produce modern aircraft. This statement applies across the board to fighters, bombers, tankers, transports, electronic countermeasure aircraft, command and control aircraft, and, for this work, helicopters. There are ephemeral exceptions to this—since Lockheed F-22 production was capped at 187 aircraft, much has been made of continuing the production of an aircraft designed for a far different mission, the F-35B STOVL (Short Takeoff and Vertical Landing). This production, however, is problematic, for when costs rise, as they inevitably must, cries will go up for its cancellation as well.

This congressional malaise extends also to too-compliant members of the Department of Defense, who for years had adopted the practice of sheepishly agreeing that their original requests for funding were wrong and that the subsequent congressional revisions of those requests were correct. Part of this defensive attitude stems from such procurement disasters as the vital and too-long-proposed production of new tanker aircraft. Some of this can be attributed to the lingering shame and hesitation caused by a 2003 scandal. While working for the Department of Defense, Darleen Druyan facilitated a contract by which the Air Force would have leased rather than purchased tanker aircraft from Boeing, resulting in much greater profits for the aircraft company. She was subsequently employed by Boeing. Ms. Druyan would later plead guilty to a conflict of interest and receive a jail sentence. The scandal tarnished the reputation of both the Boeing Company and the United States Air Force. It placed the acquisition bureaucracy in an almost catatonic state, unwilling to chance offending contractors, the public, or the services and therefore unable to decide how to proceed.

The passage of time and the growth of bureaucracies have created an environment in which it is almost impossible for an innovative helicopter design to enter large-scale production.

A Dual Purpose

This book has a dual purpose. One is to document the remarkable story of how helicopters, by their unique characteristics, have changed modern warfare and to look into the future of rotary-wing aircraft. The other is to paint as accurate a picture as possible of how the United States has allowed its investment in R&D into rotary-wing aircraft to decline to the present sad state of affairs, where we have almost no potential to introduce helicopters of modern design into production. There has been one long-term, highly controversial, and hopefully very productive exception to this statement, and that is the Bell/Boeing V-22 Osprey, a tilt-rotor rather than rotary-wing aircraft.

In telling the story of how the helicopter has had a major effect upon modern warfare, it will become apparent that changes in warfare forced changes upon the helicopter. While this sentence has a paradoxical tone, it is in fact an apt description of the push-pull effect that helicopter and warfare have had upon each other since World War II. One of the most distinguishing characteristics of this push-pull effect can be found in comparing the differences in the changes that modern warfare has had upon tactical aircraft and helicopters.

The losses in tactical aircraft such as the McDonnell F-4 Phantom or Republic F-105 Thunderchief in the Vietnam conflict were so high that huge (and entirely justifiable) sums of money were spent on R&D as well as on changes in doctrine and tactics. The splendid result was the creation of modern aircraft fully equipped with stealth, which permits them to engage in combat unseen by the enemy, and precision-guided munitions, which allow them to engage the enemy at ever-greater distances with ever-greater accuracy. The consequence has been that air warfare in tactical aircraft has become more abstract, a condition enhanced and emphasized when armed unmanned combat aerial vehicles (UCAVs) are employed. In direct contrast, modern combat has thrust the helicopter into the forefront of virtual hand-to-hand combat over distances no greater than those encountered by Roman legions. Battle in a helicopter is a bloody face-to-face combat with an equally well armed enemy. The helicopter is not cloaked by stealth, nor does it operate at ranges beyond the enemy's capacity to respond. It is instead vulnerable to everything from a rifle bullet to the increasingly dangerous shoulder-fired missile and rocket-propelled grenade. Indeed, helicopter combat is more akin to the era of fixed bayonets than to other modes of current warfare, which may be conducted via satellite from thousands of miles away.

Few weapons have had so long a gestation period as the helicopter, and fewer still have had such equally ardent advocates and opponents. Most weapon systems have solid backing from a service, as the battleship had from the Navy, the tank from the Army, and the bomber from the Air Force. While the helicopter always had the full backing of the Marines, it had opponents within the Army, the service that should have been its strongest proponent and that, ironically enough, was tasked with the development and procurement of helicopters. The opposition within the Army was not meanspirited. Most officers clearly saw the value of the helicopter. However, the Army budget was tight post-World War II, and inevitably some officers saw greater value in other weapons, such as the tank or atomic artillery.

But it was the changing nature of warfare itself that continually forced the need for the helicopter to the forefront, and it followed naturally that the helicopter would change modern warfare in far-reaching ways.

This book will have achieved its purpose if it (a) documents accurately the development of the helicopter in combat around the world and (b) points out the dismal failure to fund adequately the R&D effort necessary to provide the nation with the helicopters it could and should have for its defense. I believe that the reader will be disturbed and perhaps even outraged that such a disproportionate amount of R&D has been applied to weapons that are not being used in combat in any way approaching the use of the helicopter. The result is the very tragic high-loss rate in our helicopter forces, one that is accelerating rather than declining.

Please note that this book concentrates on the helicopter and the events that demonstrate how the helicopter changed modern warfare. Its focus is American and Soviet helicopters. While other foreign helicopters performed well, their employment was not of a nature to change modern warfare and they must, perforce, be omitted.

Acknowledgments

This has been a very difficult book for me to write, and it was possible to do so only through the encouragement and help of a large number of people and some very fine institutions. Perhaps the most remarkable thing about this is that all of the individuals who helped were already deeply embroiled in and overworked with their own important projects. This made their help doubly demanding for them and doubly appreciated by me.

The American Helicopter Society was very supportive and encouraging, and I thank its executive director and publisher of its fine *Vertiflite* journal, M. E. Rhett Flater, for his assistance and for copies of his testimony to Congress and briefing papers. Also extremely helpful at the A.H.S. were L. Kim Smith, editor, and Michael Hirschberg, managing editor. Michael provided me with much material and more of his time than he could afford. I am indebted to the gifted director of the National Museum of the Marine Corps, Lin Ezell, who generously introduced me to her staff and made available the limitless resources of her great museum. Many of the talented staff of the N.M.M.C. helped, as did other members of the great educational facilities there. This included, among others, Dr. Robert V. Aquilina, head of the Research Branch, Lena Kaljot, Annette Amerman, Kra Newcomer, and Shelia Phillips. Also very helpful were Dr. Charles Neimeyer and Dr. Fred Allison of the Marine Corps History Division and Michael "Mike" Miller and James Ginther of the Gray Research Center.

Roger Connor, an expert on helicopters and many other things from the National Air & Space Museum, was very obliging, even though I suspect he was dismayed by my approach to the subject. Clif Berry, an editor schooled by Ian Ballantine, did a masterful job in pointing out errors of context, grammar, and so on, and I deeply appreciate his efforts.

A journey to West Chester, Pennsylvania was incredibly useful. I was able to visit the fine American Helicopter Museum & Education Center, headed by Sean Saunders, director, and a helpful staff, including Larry Barrett. In addition, I was privileged to meet with John Piasecki at his Piasecki Aircraft Corporation in Essington, Pennsylvania. Mr. Piasecki was very forthcoming and provided me with valuable insight into the efforts of his father, Frank Piasecki, and also into his corporation's current research.

A visit to the U.S. Army Aviation Museum at Fort Rucker, Alabama was both fascinating and helpful. There I was privileged to have complete access to the archives and photo files, thanks to the director Steve Maxham, Richard Tierney, Ed Gilmore, and especially Ray Wilhite. Ray is a distinguished forensic paleontologist at Auburn University School of Veterinary Medicine and certainly knows more about the Bell UH-1 than anyone else, in part because his father flew the airplane. More important for this book, he digitized almost the entire museum collection of photos and the entire collection of slides. Ray was immensely helpful, and I appreciate it very much, as will any other researcher visiting the site.

There were many others whose assistance was invaluable, including the noted author Darrell Whitcomb, who gave of his deep knowledge of combat search and rescue and MEDEVAC operations. Lt. Col. John Cook, USA (Ret), not only provided me with the information I needed in his fine book, *Rescue Under Fire: The Story of DUSTOFF in Vietnam*, he gave me permission to quote from it extensively. Dennis Jenkins, a master in so many areas, provided excellent insight into past and future helicopters. Dr. Bruce Charnov, truly an expert in the history of rotary-wing flight, was very forthcoming with film, photos, and data. My old friend Fred Johnsen provided many photos. The artist Zaur Eylanbekov provided an enormous supply of photos and drawings from his own collection. Christophe Pierre, of the Circle Aeronautique de l'ESTACA, filled me in on details of the Cornu helicopter and its re-creation. George Mellinger, always helpful, provided key assistance in obtaining and translating invaluable Russian documents. Dr. Philip Meilinger gave me many useful suggestions, which I incorporated into the text. The noted expert David Isby gave me invaluable information and suggestions.

There were many people of goodwill who provided me with material and moral assistance, including the prolific and authoritative author (and amazing seller of his books) Bob Dorr. Also very helpful were the former assistant commandant of the U.S. Marine Corps Gen. Robert Magnus, Barrett Tillman, Robert Chenoweth, John Sherwood, John Ward, Raymond L. Robb, James F. Aldridge, Mike Wilson, Mike Yared, Charles A. Krohn, Dr. John T. Broom, Stuart Krohn, Lt. Col. Wade Hasle, Jake Myers at Sikorsky, and many more whom I will recall later and be filled with remorse because I forgot to include their names.

The staff at Pelican Publishing Company was helpful, as always, and I value the contributions made by Kenneth Giniger, who masterminded the birth of this book.

My dear wife, Terri, put up with my preoccupation and the unending hours at the computer, always comforting and encouraging, and I thank her for all her assistance.

I know that I've omitted many names that should be mentioned, but I hope that those I've missed will understand and know that I do appreciate their help.

Introduction

This book's title, *How the Helicopter Changed Modern Warfare,* covers a wide variety of related subjects, ranging from the use of the helicopter in training to reconnaissance to major operations, such as Operation IRAQI FREEDOM. To me, there is one area in which the helicopter's effect upon modern warfare is far more important than all of the others combined, and that is its role in aero-medical evacuation (MEDEVAC) and combat recovery operations. Many others feel that the most important role of the helicopter has been in revolutionizing tactics and bringing power to distant points in the battlefield. I respect these views but remain wedded to the idea that it has contributed most to MEDEVAC operations.

There are a number of terms for such vital military operations, and some have been made famous through the media. MEDEVACs of the Korean War showed the efficacy of using helicopters for casualty recovery. U.S. Army, Air Force, and Marine Corps helicopters were utilized for this purpose in what was initially called casualty evacuation (CASEVAC). These efforts were highlighted in the wildly successful television series "M*A*S*H." Post-Korea, the U.S. Army adopted larger helicopters for this mission and included medics on board to provide in-flight medical care, thus increasing the survival rates of casualties. This true combination of medical service with aviation assets was subsequently labeled MEDE-VAC and was turned into an art form by U.S. Army MEDEVAC units in the Vietnam War. Those units primarily used the call-sign "DUSTOFF," a call-sign much revered by soldiers to this day.

Paralleling the adaptation of the helicopter to the CASEVAC and MEDEVAC role, the U.S. Air Force and U.S. Navy also adapted the helicopter for rescue operations. The very first rescue was conducted by the U.S. Coast Guard, under the leadership of Cdr. Frank Erickson on January 3, 1944. Erickson,

Rescue teams put their lives at stake on every mission and are famous for their bravery. *(Courtesy of U.S. Army Museum, Fort Rucker)*

who led Coast Guard helicopter activities, flew blood plasma under appalling weather conditions to the survivors of the USS *Turner*, a destroyer that had sunk after an explosion off Sandy Hook, New Jersey.

The earliest use of helicopters in combat took place in the waning days of World War II and will be covered later. However, they were few in number. It was not until the conflict in Korea that helicopters were formed into units dedicated to search and rescue (SAR). Using first-generation machines and primitive communications systems, USAF and Navy helicopters recovered crewmembers from 10 percent of all fixed-wing Allied aircraft shot down in the war. A decade later, those same rescue forces returned to combat in the skies of Southeast Asia and successfully conducted SAR operations for more than four thousand Allied crewmembers, including in some instances special operations forces trapped deep in enemy territory.

It should be noted that MEDEVAC and SAR are overlapping terms, just as the people and equipment participating have overlapping means and techniques in the pursuit of the basic goal: the rescue of an individual or group in need. Air-rescue efforts extend back to the First World War, but the focus of this book is the use of the helicopter in those efforts.

From late World War II on, the Coast Guard and the Air Force used helicopters for rescue missions on an ad hoc basis. The rewards of these efforts, both in terms of compassion and efficiency, were very obvious in wartime, so much so that more and more resources would be devoted to them—as long as a war was going on. Unfortunately, those rewards, as compelling as they are, did not have the same effect on budget considerations during peacetime. All of the armed services failed to devote an adequate amount of attention and funding to such air-rescue services during peacetime interludes. In this new century, with war a familiar and continuing commodity, a jaded public and Congress have not encouraged sufficient financing of R&D in the field. Despite the increasingly difficult conditions under which rescue forces operate in the Middle East wars, there has been insufficient effort to provide the latest and most effective equipment in adequate numbers.

After the long and divisive Vietnam War, almost all our rescue forces returned to duty in the United States. From their home stations, USAF rescue forces were frequently called out to perform SAR missions for both downed military aircraft and civilian emergencies. In the 1980s, while training and organizing our forces to deal with the growing threat of Soviet expansion in Europe, Air Force rescue planners realized that the techniques to perform "peacetime" SAR and actual combat recovery of personnel endangered by enemy forces were really quite different. They began to refer to the latter operation as combat search and rescue (CSAR), a term that much more clearly identified the reality of the mission.

While helicopters may have achieved brilliant wartime results in conducting special operations, their MEDEVAC and CSAR roles have so many dimensions and such an effect upon morale that they stand above all others, no matter how meritorious those might be. The most important of these dimensions is a humanitarian one, in which heroic participants voluntarily place their lives on the line each time they go out to rescue a fellow airman. This humanitarian aspect lifts morale, inspires others, and in general provides the few elevating moments to be found in warfare.

There is also an innately practical side to these efforts. The crewmembers of modern aircraft receive millions of dollars of training over several years and cannot be easily replaced. Saving their lives and returning them to duty provides a very real monetary reward for the effort.

As will be seen, the helicopter has been employed on missions of mercy since World War II, and its role has grown as its capability has increased. Sadly, as with almost everything related to helicopters, funding for the humanitarian role of the helicopter has not been adequate. Nonetheless, the very nature of the role summons the utmost from the people who participate in it, and thus, despite all obstacles, it reaches new heights of efficiency every year.

The helicopters involved in these operations, as well as the fixed-wing aircraft that often accomplish CSAR sorties, require the very best of the personnel flying and maintaining them. They must not only be heroic but wonderfully skilled, able to cope with surprises, and able to innovate as required. The self-sacrifice implicit in the rescue role attracts only the very best and bravest volunteers, and the standards of their service then transform them into accomplished experts in their art. The men and women who perform rescue operations are a unique community, admired and even beloved by all because of their continuing demonstrations of self-sacrifice in peace or war.

The standards established by the military in these humanitarian roles has, fortunately, spilled over to the civilian community, where similar self-sacrifice is an accepted practice in the execution of civilian medical and air-rescue duties.

SAR capabilities increased over time as the capabilities of the helicopter increased, especially during the Vietnam War. For this reason, I've chosen to include material on these duties in separate sections, rather than including it in discussions of the general employment of the helicopter.

Why the Helicopter?

The virtue of the helicopter is its ability to expand and sustain airborne operations in a way that fixed-wing aircraft cannot, that is, taking off and landing vertically, flying at ultra-low air speeds, and even hovering where necessary. As the man who might be regarded as the patron saint of helicopters, the great Igor Sikorsky, said, "If a man is in need of rescue, an airplane can come in and throw flowers on him, and that's just about all. But a direct-lift aircraft could come in and save his life."

The vertical landing and takeoff capability reduced or eliminated the requirement for prepared runways. It thus developed that geography and terrain often determine that helicopters are the weapon of choice, especially in supporting ground combat operations. It was less immediately apparent that vertical-lift aircraft could have enormous effect upon seaborne operations, ranging from rescue efforts to anti-submarine warfare and mine-laying to such modern requirements as combating pirates.

Of all the American services, the United States Marines seized upon the helicopter the most eagerly. The Marine leaders perceived that the amphibious warfare so typical of World War II would have to be fought under far different circumstances in the nuclear age and immediately began tailoring its doctrine, force structure, and equipment to take advantage of the helicopter. The use of the helicopter in MEDEVACs was implicit in Marine Corps doctrine, even though it was sometimes subordinate to the operational role.

The helicopter started out fitfully, as most weapons do, and had a long gestation period. However, even the early models that served in the Korean War proved that while they were sometimes cranky, often vulnerable, and not easy to fly, they were indispensable. As the twentieth century continued its war-torn course, with conflicts erupting all over the world as colonial empires declined, the helicopter became more and more important. Its capabilities increasingly affected the nature of modern warfare, and they continue to do so.

The helicopter eventually and inadvertently reached its first peak of importance during the Vietnam War. There, time, circumstance, politics, and policy converged with technology and adequate funding to create a true "helicopter war" in which rotary-wing aircraft became the symbol of the battlefield. With the helicopter, the American forces could force decisions on whatever battlefield it chose. The North Vietnamese forces also used the helicopter but on a much smaller scale.

While the operational use of the helicopter declined after the Vietnam War, the years 1965 to 1985 saw the introduction of the operating fleets that still define today's active inventories and, sadly, even the production possibilities for the immediate future. Unfortunately rising costs, arguments over roles and missions, and changed operational situations cancelled some potentially great advances in helicopters.

After Vietnam, planners tended to see the helicopter less and less as a war-winning weapon as the perception of future wars changed and it was believed that any conflict would include a nuclear exchange. The loss of emphasis on the helicopter stemmed not so much from any decline in capability or lack of utility but rather from the budget imperatives of other weapons deemed to be more essential to the probable conflict. It is a hard fact that helicopters are inevitably less efficient and more costly than fixed-wing options and therefore are the weapon of choice only when they can do something no other weapon system can. Furthermore, when contemplating the acquisition of a new weapon system, fixed-wing advocates see the world differently than do rotary-wing advocates. The helicopter began a resurgence after Vietnam with the introduction of the Bell AH-1 and new weaponry, such as the TOW (Tube launched Optically tracked Wire guided) missile.

All around the globe, other governments and military services had similar experiences in their use of the helicopter. It was an ideal instrument for the Soviet Union, given its vast expanse of territory, and its development there was carefully nourished. Ironically, the growth of counter-helicopter weapons proved to be a substantial factor in the decline of the Soviet Union's empire.

An absolutely essential element in understanding the development of the helicopter as a vitally important military weapon is recognizing the importance that individuals have had upon its creation and use. In industry, government, and the military, fielding a weapon system inevitably requires the devoted advocacy of individuals who stake their careers upon the success of the weapon system they promote.

Unfortunately for the majority, the process works both ways. Inevitably many more people devote their careers to programs that do not come to fruition and thus don't earn the rewards they sought. Two perhaps extreme examples serve to illustrate this dilemma. On the one hand, there was Gen. Bernard A. "Bernie" Schriever, whose successful advocacy resulted in monumental achievements in both ballistic missile and space programs. On the other hand, the equally devoted but unsuccessful efforts of Vice Adm. Charles E. Rosendahl failed to make the dirigible a mighty instrument for the Navy.

In any career field in industry, government, or the military, an individual has but a relatively short time to make his or her influence felt. This is most true in government, where the tide of politics can shift influence every few years and where diligent staffers, working on projects important to a congressional constituency, can find themselves suddenly out of a job. The case is less severe in industry, but the period of influence is often shorter than in the military, because it takes longer to gain positions of responsibility. There is (or was for most of the twentieth century) more employment stability in industry than there is in politics, but only exceptionally brilliant engineers, such as Lockheed's Clarence "Kelly" Johnson, are able to push past their contemporaries to top positions.

Members of the military have relatively longer periods in which to make their influence felt, but even these periods are too short given the length of time required for the development of modern weapon systems. A nominal, full-term service career is thirty years. Those who become flag officers, and thus reach positions of the greatest influence, may serve for another four, six, or eight years. The last ten to fifteen years of a flag officer's career are naturally the most important in terms of the effect of his or her advocacy upon future weapon systems. In almost every case, the mindset of the flag officers will have been established by their earlier experience in the field.

In a similar way, although their career length might be more extended, earnest individuals in government and industry sought to improve the capability of helicopters. In industry, young engineers often develop ideas for weapon systems, and they naturally seek out their counterparts in the military services. The same is true in government, although, as noted, the determining factor is often the relative economic effect that a proposed weapon system has upon the constituency of the congressman or senator.

The three centers of advocacy are government, industry, and the military, and they are the nexus of the infamous term "military-industrial complex." Despite the invidious connotation imparted to the term by Pres. Dwight D. Eisenhower in his farewell address, no modern weapon system could exist in any nation without the willing cooperation and exchange of information among the members of the three groups. And while there are inevitably abuses of the relationship (usually well reported upon), the system works for the most part in the nation's interest. There were many who commented on the irony of President Eisenhower's adverse characterization of the very establishment of which he had been so important a part in two of the three categories.

Given that any successful weapon system must have advocates in each of the three categories, and that the effective careers of each of the advocates is often very short, it is something of a miracle that a complex weapon system such as the helicopter can ever be fielded. This is all the more true because in almost all nations, helicopter advocates have always had to swim upstream, fighting three major and sometimes contradictory battles.

The first of these battles was the usual problem of adapting to advances in technology. From its birth, the helicopter was relatively fragile, inherently vulnerable to mechanical failure. In combat, its slow speed and susceptibility to battle damage resulted in high loss rates. Yet it benefited greatly from many advances, including the introduction of the turbine engine, suitable armament, in-flight refueling, and an enhanced ability to operate at night. Unfortunately, advancing technology also worked against its employment, especially with the introduction of radar-guided anti-aircraft guns and surface-to-air missiles.

The second battle was the internecine strife it occasioned not only among the competing arms of the military—Army, Navy, and Air Force—but within those arms as well. This was true to some extent in all nations but particularly in the United States. The U.S. Army, the primary user of the helicopter, had to go hat in hand to Congress for many decades to gain a lesser part of the budget, because the U.S. Air Force was tasked with the principal defense of the nation. But even within the Army itself, there were many conscientious leaders who had priorities other than vertical flight. This is not to say that the contribution of the helicopter was not appreciated at all levels. The difficulty was that its contribution was not always appreciated as much as that of other weapons, ranging from atomic cannons to the tank. And as in all of these services, the cost of any weapon had to be balanced against ever-increasing personnel costs.

The third battle was the most difficult, for it was the very nature of warfare itself, which seemed to change modes each time the helicopter appeared to be on the point of asserting itself as a primary weapon. In its early days, the helicopter was perceived as a rotary-wing version of the familiar liaison plane, able to get in and out of small spaces and to carry a small load. Many regarded its MEDEVAC role as its most important duty, and it is true that in this field the helicopter had the greatest effect upon modern warfare.

As we will see, the helicopter began to come into its own in the counter-insurgency role, reaching a peak of effectiveness in the Vietnam War. In the twenty years of Cold War that followed, concepts of employing helicopters in combat changed drastically. (Only later, in the interminable wars in the Middle East, would the helicopter once again become a principal player.)

During the Cold War, the helicopter was still used on an almost daily basis as a counter-insurgency tool. Nonetheless, the world's major powers saw it as a component of totally different kinds of warfare. These ranged from a mid-intensity conflict to one in which nuclear weapons were exchanged.

In the "mid-intensity" conflict, helicopters were seen by the Western Allies as a counter to the massive number of tanks that would be employed by the Warsaw Pact nations. Yet the vast difference in the scale of conventional forces between the West and the Soviet Union was such that most leaders, on both sides, believed that any "mid-intensity" war could quickly escalate to a nuclear war.

Nuclear weapons, whether delivered by aircraft, rocket, or artillery, made it mandatory to reduce the numbers of soldiers per square mile in the huge battle area. The coordinated employment of those soldiers, with their armor and artillery, could only be accomplished by air vehicles, and the probable nature of the battlefield meant that these air vehicles would be helicopters rather than fixed-wing transports. Again, there is no little irony in the fact that in either the mid-level intensity war or a nuclear exchange, the importance of the helicopter was diminished and not because it was any less useful. Quite the contrary, helicopters were even more valuable in either type of warfare. But in such conflicts, other weapon systems demanded enormous funding, and the helicopter advocates inevitably lost in the budget battles.

Things change. The collapse of the Cold War and the rise of the terrorist threat have once again placed the helicopter in the forefront of modern warfare. The current importance of the helicopter can best be understood against the background of the development of rotary-wing aircraft and their employment in a globe-spanning variety of wars. At this writing, the emphasis is on the war on terrorism and on counterinsurgency, but the tide may change at any time to include the possibility of a large-scale conventional war.

We thus find the helicopter in an unusual position. Over the years, combat experience and advances in technology brought about excellent helicopters well suited for their tasks. But for the last twenty years, and for the foreseeable future, American helicopter technology has fallen behind to the point that it now offers no new designs for aircraft. It is for this reason that a foreign helicopter was selected to serve as the Lockheed Martin VH-71 presidential helicopter, a decision that was later reversed.

Understanding helicopters in modern warfare requires an understanding of the development of the helicopter over time. The stunning advances in helicopter technology have permitted equally great leaps in its employment. And it should be emphasized again that the advances in technology and employment have come about as a result of the insight of certain individuals or groups. These will be identified wherever possible by name, but naming an individual may be a necessary substitute for naming all the members of the team the individual headed.

HOW THE
HELICOPTER
CHANGED MODERN
WARFARE

Chapter One

The Helicopter Goes to War

While it may not be a scholarly comparison, the world's military services have treated the helicopter the way a family might treat an amiable but very troublesome rich uncle. As devoted as helicopter proponents are, and as enthusiastic as the various military services purport to be about its capabilities, it is a sad fact that the helicopter as a weapon has often been neglected until a dire emergency requires its use. This has never been more true than today.

The mission, technology, budget, and service attitudes relating to the helicopter tend to be at variance until guns begin to fire in distant places. Then logistic issues are resolved—most often in a costly and sometimes counter-productive way—doctrinal differences are overcome, and the existing helicopter technology is flogged far beyond its intended capability to achieve the desired results. If these circumstances are sustained for a considerable period, there are improvements in every area, including logistics and doctrine but most importantly in technology, and the helicopter comes into its own. This occurs because the helicopter is usually underfunded in peacetime budgets but gets massive infusions of money when war comes. Unfortunately, once the emergency is overcome, the old conditions reinstate themselves, for a large number of reasons that are ingrained in the economics, culture, and differing doctrines of the military services.

The first of these reasons is the very nature of warfare, in which the cruelest system of arbitrage determines which weapons will be used where. The relative importance of the military helicopter increases in direct proportion to the difficulty of the terrain and the expertise of the enemy in guerilla-style operations. Helicopters were deemed of great importance in Vietnam, given the terrain and the enemy. They are absolutely indispensable in Iraq and Afghanistan for the same reasons. They will in all probability be indispensable in future "low-intensity conflicts" around the globe.

Helicopters are expensive to build, buy, and use. They are difficult to maintain and vulnerable to damage from enemy operations. Therefore, common-sense economics dictate the use of fixed-wing aircraft first, wherever and whenever they can do the desired job.

The tendency to rely on fixed-wing aircraft in most situations stems from several causes. The first of these is the fact that helicopter operations against most enemies are possible only when air superiority is established by fixed-wing aircraft, which means that fixed-wing aircraft are already in the theater and available. The second is the latter's greater speed, range, and resistance to damage and the fact that they are relatively less expensive to operate. A dismal third factor—less recognized because it is shameful—is that aviators in most services not only prefer fixed-wing aircraft to helicopters, but they discriminate against their rotary-wing colleagues.[1]

It is a sad truth that the operators of fixed-wing aircraft are treated better in the vital career terms of prestige, rank, and promotion than are the operators of helicopters. This occurs in spite of the brilliant success that the helicopter has achieved in so many of its varied missions, from CSAR to assault operations far behind enemy lines.

Another reason for the repeated failure to synchronize helicopter development and employment is ingrained in the nature of the military services. As an example, we can briefly compare the attitudes of the United States Army and the United States Marine Corps toward the helicopter.

The United States Army gave birth to American airpower. Initially, a few balloons and a few airplanes were allocated to the Signal Corps, but over time, larger establishments came on the scene, such as the Army Air Service, Army Air Corps, and Army Air Forces. All were dedicated to providing support to Army ground forces. Unfortunately, it is the nature of people operating systems to wish to expand their use. In the case of aviation, it is almost irresistible to wish to go beyond the grunt duties of close air support to the more attractive (and in fact often more productive) mission of air interdiction, that is, the longer-range suppression and destruction of the enemy transport, supply, and personnel. Then there is the siren call of air combat, which always has greater appeal to pilots than dropping bombs at low altitude in a very hostile environment.

Marine Corps aviation followed a similar path and a similar goal, but with the intensity, focus, and adherence to the mission that characterize the Corps.

Doctrinal differences, politically muted as long as the air arm was part of the Army, came into the open when the United States Air Force became a separate service on September 18, 1947. While ostensibly still committed fully to the close air support of ground troops, Air Force leaders genuinely believed that air interdiction was more effective. In contrast, the Marine aviators remained committed to close air support and became exemplars of its conduct.

As will be seen later, the course of world events affected all three of these services. By 1949, it was clear that there were going to be two superpowers armed with nuclear weapons—the United States and the Soviet Union. In the United States, the Air Force began to receive the preferred budgetary support that the United States Navy had enjoyed prior to World War II. The Air Force was now seen as the first line of defense and the Strategic Air Command (SAC) became the symbol of power, deterring the Soviet Union from fulfilling its stated desire to expand its influence.

These events were powerfully important from all viewpoints but had a particular effect upon the development of rotary-wing aircraft. Within the United States Army, three adverse conditions affected the helicopter. The first was the fact that budget cuts and the acknowledged priority of the Air Force forced the Army to go hat in hand to Congress, well aware that it would not receive adequate funds. The second was that many Army leaders liked the helicopter and welcomed its use but preferred to spend the limited budget on other weapons such as armor and atomic artillery. The third element was the inevitable fight that developed between the Air Force and the Army over roles and missions. The Air Force felt that it provided sufficiently for both interdiction and, when and where *necessary,* close air support and was determined to keep the Army from once again creating its own aerial striking power. The Army felt that it could better define when close air support was *necessary* and therefore always wanted to develop its own organic air power. Unfortunately for the Army, it had to defer to circumstances.

The Marines had always been indoctrinated with the value of close air support, dating back to the experience gained fighting insurgent forces in the pre-1941 Dominican Republic, Haiti, and Nicaragua. There the early techniques in dive-bombing were developed, and the concept of ultra-close air support became doctrine. After World War II, the Marines believed that close air support was still their main aviation mission and that helicopters could be adapted brilliantly to the role. The effort became well-defined when Lt. Gen. Roy S. Geiger, then commanding general of all Marine forces in the Pacific, observed the nuclear tests at the Bikini Lagoon in 1946. He wrote a letter stating, "It is quite evident that a small number of atomic weapons could destroy an expeditionary force as now organized, embarked, and landed." General Geiger urged the commandant to "consider this a very serious and urgent matter" and that the Marine Corps "use its most competent officers in finding a solution to develop the technique of conducting amphibious operations in the Atomic Age."[2]

Geiger saw that future operations would have to be conducted from farther at sea, from more widely dispersed forces, and must necessarily be done with far greater speed and with much more ability to create rapid concentration of the forces that landed. The Marines have maintained this viewpoint, strengthening it over time, while the Army has vacillated, despite its own splendid demonstrations of expertise with the helicopter as a weapon system.

It must be emphasized that the very nature of warfare at land and at sea led to the development of specialized types of helicopters along with specialized doctrines for their use. The Navy saw enormous utility of vertical-lift vehicles, now extended to unmanned aerial vehicles (UAVs), from small ship decks and aircraft carriers. This had important implications for the Coast Guard and the Navy for rescue, anti-submarine operations, mine-laying and mine counter-measures, and even for use against a surface combatant such as the modern-day drug runner or pirate. These duties bring about many specialized design requirements, such as folding rotor blades, and add to the complexity of helicopter procurement.[3] The Bell Boeing V-22 Osprey is a perfect example of this almost runaway growth in complexity. The other services that use it must accept these compromises despite their cost in utility and capability for their own missions.

Other nations followed somewhat similar paths in their development of the military helicopter and were affected by the experience gained in aerial warfare in both World Wars I and II. It is helpful then to sketch briefly two concepts of aerial warfare that emerged prior to 1945, both of which foreshadowed and influenced the future use of helicopters.

The first of these is the previously mentioned close air support, which was developed to a surprisingly sophisticated degree in World War I, given the general lack of radio communications. In World War II, close air support was vital in all theaters. It became the signature of the Luftwaffe and the German army in the early part of the war and was recognized by Joseph Stalin as being as vital as "air and bread" to Soviet soldiers. The Royal Air Force, and later, the U.S. Army Air Force (USAAF), for reasons we shall see below, had to learn about close air support the hard way when World War II started in 1939, and, amazingly enough, twice had to relearn the same lessons years later in the war.

The second important concept is the rise, at the very end of WWI, of the idea of "vertical envelopment," that is, the use of airborne troops deployed behind enemy lines, and its subsequent use in WWII. While vertical envelopment never reached the importance of close air support during that war, it was an impressive, useful, but sometimes costly discipline.

Perhaps the most important result of these two concepts is that they combined to create within most services a small cadre of leaders who saw the value of the helicopter but who could only occasionally bring their ideas to the forefront. It also created doctrinal divisions among leaders that were often tinged more with emotion than pure reason.

The Promise of Vertical Envelopment

The very first manned balloon flight was made by Jean-François Pilâtre de Rozier and François Laurent d'Arlandes in a Montgolfier balloon on November 21, 1783, in Paris. On the following December 1, Benjamin Franklin, comfortably ensconced in his carriage near the Tuileries, observed Jacques Alexandre Charles and Marie-Noel Robert carry out the first manned flight in a hydrogen balloon. One year later, Franklin, astutely watching the balloon mania sweeping Europe, made this prescient observation: "Where is the prince who can afford so to cover his country with troops for its defense, as that ten thousand men descending from the clouds, might not, in most places, do an infinite deal of mischief before a force could be brought to repel them?"[4] Continually frustrated by the English Channel, Napoleon Bonaparte is said to have considered using a fleet of 2,500 balloons to invade England and, as Franklin suggested, "do an infinite deal of mischief." Fortunately for the would-be vertical envelopers, the wife of a pioneer balloonist, Sophie Blanchard, persuaded Napoleon that the winds were too fickle for such an endeavor. But the idea was there and remained through the years, especially to innovators such as Winston Churchill and Brig. Gen. William "Billy" Mitchell.

Churchill embraced a commando-style conception of the use of airborne warriors, envisioning dropping a handful at key places to disrupt communications and obtain information. Mitchell, fresh from his superb handling of airpower during the St. Mihiel offensive, had a larger vision.

At St. Mihiel, the largest air battle of World War I, almost 1,500 Allied aircraft were under his control. He used them effectively against about 500 German aircraft during the battle that raged for four days in mid-September 1918. Mitchell's success gave him the credibility to propose on October 17 an even more imaginative plan to the commander of the American Expeditionary Forces, Gen. John "Black Jack" Pershing.

Pershing knew that the Germans were near collapse but did not want to offer an armistice that would end the war with the enemy still controlling much of France. Against the views of his French and British colleagues, Pershing wanted to continue the fighting by driving forward to campaign in the German heartland. He felt that this was the only way to avoid another war with Germany twenty years later.

Pershing knew that it would not be easy, particularly when the Germans reached their own territory, where their defense would be bolstered by their strong, long-established fortifications. He was particularly concerned that the retreating Germans might make a stand at the fortress city of Metz, and, although the term was not current at the time, the last thing Pershing wanted was to engage in "urban warfare."

There is anecdotal evidence to suggest that Pershing was thus more receptive than he might ordinarily have been to Mitchell's idea. His concept was to use parachute troops to open what he termed "a new flank" but would later be called "vertical envelopment." Mitchell proposed that veteran troops of the First Division, the "Big Red One," be swiftly provided with parachutes and large numbers of machine guns and parachuted behind the lines in the Metz sector from Allied bombers.[5] Their task would be to seize the fortress of Metz and hold it until advancing Allied troops arrived.

The British and French, already bled dry, were exhausted and overruled Pershing, accepting the German request for an armistice. The war thus ended before his idea could be carried out, but he maintained his interest in the subject. Some small-scale U.S. Army parachuting experiments were carried out in the late 1920s. Mitchell also advocated the creation of powerful attack aircraft such as the very unsuccessful Boeing GA-X twin-engine, cannon-toting triplane that would have been used to support vertical envelopments.

The fiery, controversial Mitchell also backed R&D at McCook Field in Dayton, Ohio. There, under the guidance of a man whose contributions to aviation have been vastly overlooked, Maj. Edward L. Hoffman, development of the American parachute began.[6] At McCook, Leslie L. Irvin designed a parachute using a ripcord to open the device. While this was satisfactory for individual bailouts, in a mass drop, the differences in timing when deploying the chute resulted in spreading the force over too large an area.

The first unofficial paratroop exercise in the United States was conducted at Kelly Field, Texas in the fall of 1928. Harking back to his 1918 idea, Mitchell had six fully armed parachutists dropped from a Martin bomber in a demonstration. But with Mitchell's 1925 court-martial for insubordination and subsequent resignation, interest in the tactic declined. The United States would not begin an official paratroop program until 1940.

Italy was the first nation formally to adopt vertical envelopment as a tactic, and a 1927 Italian innovation, the "Salvatore" parachute, set the stage for more meaningful developments.[7] The Salvatore parachute was deployed by the use of a static line attached to the parachute just prior to bailout. This was much safer and concentrated the grouping on the ground. The parachutists' mobility was aided by a new development from Great Britain—the quick-release harness. By 1930, spurred by Benito Mussolini's aggressive foreign policy, Italy trained some elite battalions in the art and carried out mass drops in North Africa.[8]

The Soviet airborne forces were born in 1930 with exercises that would excite the interest of military men all over the world. The initial mass jumps were so successful that, by 1931, an airborne brigade had been created in the Leningrad Military District. In true Soviet style, the program was aggressively developed, with some 10,000 men being trained for use in twenty-nine airborne battalions. A positive doctrine of isolating and controlling the battlefield was developed simultaneously. In 1935 the Red Army made a mass jump of 1,200 men at Kiev; the vehicle was the Soviet four-engine bomber, the Tupolev TB-3 (ANT-6). The world was quickly deluged with film and photos of the "sky soldiers" sliding off the corrugated-skin wings of the huge bombers.

The exercise at Kiev was extolled by a future head of the Soviet state, Marshal of the Soviet Union Kliment Voroshilov, who said, "The use of paratroopers is a fine and intricate art, which is being developed by the Red Army not as a sport, but as a means of steeling personal courage, and as an important basis of our military power."[9]

Voroshilov proved to be wrong in this as he did in so many of his later military actions, for the Soviet Union used paratroops infrequently and sparingly during World War II. There were probably many reasons for this, including a shortage of aircraft, training difficulties, and the like. But it is more probable that there was a basic conflict between the initiative and independence required of a paratrooper and the brutal conforming discipline of the Red Army.

Germany, smarting under the terms of the Treaty of Versailles, was casting about for new ideas to level the playing field. These ranged from maintaining only casually disguised quasi-military units to investigating rocketry as an alternative to the artillery that the Versailles treaty limited. It was natural, then, that the concepts of vertical envelopment initiated by Mitchell and demonstrated by the Soviet Union would have appeal.

A man much admired for his courage, but derisively maligned for his slow speech (and, implicitly, slow thought processes), Kurt Student fought in World War I as a pilot. In 1934, he worked with Walter Wever and others in creating Hermann Goering's pride, the Luftwaffe. As a major general, he developed Germany's first parachute unit in 1938. This became the 7th Air Division, a closely guarded secret that became famous in April 1940, when Germany began an offensive that would eventually include Norway, Denmark, Belgium, the Netherlands, and France. Some four thousand paratroopers were dropped in a series of very successful operations. Student personally led the assault and was wounded in the head in the Rotterdam operation.[10] The fit, well-equipped German paratroopers became symbols of Nazi prowess, but their losses were so high in the invasion of Crete in May 1941 that they were never used in large-scale parachute operations again.

As the war continued, the United States and Great Britain developed the concept of vertical envelopment on a greater scale. They used parachute troops, supplemented with men and equipment landed by gliders, in large-scale operations in the Mediterranean and European theaters.

As the Germans had found to their dismay in Crete, conducting large-scale vertical envelopment operations often resulted in high casualties. The United States employed both paratroops and glider forces during the invasion of France, in the abortive Operation MARKET GARDEN attack at Arnhem, and in the March 1945 Operation VARSITY. The latter, intended to secure the Rhine crossings, was the largest airborne operation in history, employing more than sixteen thousand paratroops. While the troops fought well and caused the Germans much harm, there were many casualties. Further, the troops were landed over a wide area and had difficulty concentrating as units.

It will be seen later that, as important as these operations were historically, they led indirectly to the formation of opposing opinions as to the value of the helicopter. Before examining this phenomenon, it is necessary to relate the extent of actual helicopter operations during World War II.

The Helicopter Goes to War

As may be seen in Appendix One, the progressive development of autogiros was key to the successful development of the helicopter. Historians now generally credit the Bréguet-Dorand 314 Gyroplane as the first successful helicopter, flying on June 26, 1935. It apparently lacked development potential and was soon superseded by the work of Heinrich Focke in Germany and Igor Sikorsky in the United States. While autogiros were tested extensively by many armed forces around the world prior to 1939, they were, with very minor exceptions, still not sufficiently developed to be useful in active combat. The war greatly accelerated helicopter development, and there were dramatic instances of their use that forecast their future utility. (*Autogyro* is the generic term; *Autogiro* is the Cierva trade name. *Autogyro* was rarely used at the time. It was mostly pushed by E. B. Wilford, who had his own gyroplane that he didn't want to be confused with Cierva and his licensees. It didn't work. A few publications used *autogyro,* but *autogiro* was a near-universal term at the time.)[11]

In Germany, the resurgent Luftwaffe found time and money to develop a wide series of helicopter types that ranged from the Nagler-Rolz series of portable, one-man helicopters through the imposing Focke-Achgelis Fa 223 to the successful but complex and perhaps overemphasized Flettner Fl 282 series. There were many other types proposed, including the jet-powered Wiener Neustadt Flugzeugwerke WNF 342 designed by Friedrich von Doblhoff. The late years of the war saw a flowering of exotic paper designs that included convertaplanes and vertical takeoff aircraft such as the Focke-Wulf Fw *Triebflügel,* which has become a favorite of speculative television documentaries on Nazi secret projects.

Considered by some to be truly the first successful helicopter, the Focke-Wulf Fw 61 gained international fame when it was demonstrated in Berlin's *Deutschlandhalle* by renowned test pilot Hanna Reitsch in February 1938. The Fw 61 was a benchmark design, but Heinrich Focke was already at work on its successor, the Fa 223.

Focke had been forced out of Focke-Wulf, the company he had founded, for both political and business reasons. The German Air Ministry was interested in his helicopter, however, and assisted him in forming a new firm, Focke-Achgelis, with Gerd Achgelis, Focke-Wulf's former chief test pilot. Together they created the larger Focke-Achgelis Fa 223, which used the same side-by-side rotor layout as the Fw 61.

A much larger aircraft, powered by a 1,000-horsepower BMW engine, the Fa 223 performed well and was considered by Adolf Hitler to have great promise for mountain warfare.[12] While as many as 332 aircraft were ultimately ordered, only 47 were produced. The program had the usual development problems and was hampered by Allied bombing. During its testing, the Fa 223 set eight records for speed, altitude, endurance, and distance and in September 1945 became the first helicopter to fly the English Channel. The type was also made in limited numbers in Czechoslovakia and France after the war.

The most successful German helicopter of World War II was designed by the prolific inventor, Anton Flettner, who had conceived a 2,200–pound, wire-guided, air-to-surface missile for Siemens-Schuckert during World War I. He was also distinguished by the fact that he was befriended by Heinrich Himmler and survived the perils of Nazi Germany even though his wife was Jewish.

Flettner experimented with helicopters during the 1930s and in 1935 created the Fl 184, which was a hybrid autogiro and helicopter design. Testing the Fl 184 led him to adopt a new rotor system termed the synchropter, consisting of twin contra-rotating intermeshing rotor blades, similar to the type now used by Kaman helicopters. This led in turn to the successful Fl 265 and then to the best German helicopter of the war, the Fl 282. Often credited as the first helicopter to go into mass production, the Fl 282 was actually built in small pre-production quantities, with perhaps fifty-four being built and only eleven reaching flight-worthy status.

Called the *Kolibri* (Hummingbird), the Fl 282 had a high top speed (for a helicopter) of 93 mph and a range of just more than one hundred miles. During tests as convoy-protection aircraft in the Aegean and Mediterranean seas, their performance—if not their maintenance characteristics—was so effective that an order for 1,000 production aircraft was placed, but Allied bombing prevented delivery of most.

Surprisingly, tests showed that the little helicopters were difficult for fighters to shoot down because of their ability to slow down and make sharp turns. Anton Flettner survived the war and was brought to the United States as part of Operation PAPERCLIP, the roundup of Nazi scientists and engineers.[13]

While the German helicopter efforts had been hampered by a lack of coordination, underfunding, and over-bombing, the United States was able to build swiftly on the focused efforts of Igor Sikorsky to bring his never-relinquished dreams of vertical flight to a successful conclusion. Sikorsky, as shown in Appendix One, had begun his rotary-flight experiments in 1908 but soon relinquished them to concentrate on large heavier-than-air craft. He distinguished himself by building the world's first four-engine aircraft, the *Russky-Vityaz* (Russian Knight), which first flew on May 10, 1913. This led in turn to the *Il'ya Muromets*, the world's first four-engine bomber.

Sikorsky left Russia after the Bolshevik Revolution, settling in the United States and in 1923 founding the Sikorsky Engineering Company. There he produced large and very efficient seaplanes that were used in a variety of roles, including that of pioneering airline transports. He never lost his interest in helicopters, however, and applied for a patent in 1931 for a helicopter that foreshadowed his VS 300. It featured a single lifting rotor and a much smaller vertical tail rotor intended to offset torque. As with almost every technical achievement in helicopters, the latter development was not without precedent. A Dutchman, Albert G. von Baumhauer, designed a helicopter with a vertical tail rotor, driven by its own independent 80-hp engine. It made unsuccessful attempts at flight for several years in the late 1920s.

In 1938, Sikorsky was backed by the United Aircraft Corporation to begin developing a line of rotary-lift aircraft. The firm he created would become the oldest and arguably the most successful manufacturer of helicopters in the world. Sikorsky later said, "It was most interesting, I would say thrilling, to resume a certain engineering development where it was discontinued thirty years earlier, not only in another country but even in a different hemisphere."[14]

Despite his statement that he was resuming development where he had left it three decades before, Sikorsky had remained *au courant* with helicopter development, traveling to Europe to witness flights of both the Focke Fa 61 and the Bréguet-Dorand 314 Gyroplane.

Sikorsky's new design, the VS 300, was created in the spring of 1939, built during the summer, and ready for tests in the fall.

Although he felt he was clearly on the right track, he had to overcome many problems posed by the VS 300. The design was very similar to his 1931 patent and consisted of a simple steel structure supported by a three-wheel landing gear. The tubular steel frame lent itself to rapid modification, and over the next eighteen months its appearance would be changed many times, sometimes quite drastically.

A four–cylinder, 75-hp Lycoming engine, used by many light planes of the period, was mounted in the center of the structure, powering a twenty-eight-foot-diameter, three-bladed rotor. Sikorsky had opted for a utilitarian truck transmission and a series of belts and pulleys to drive the rotor. The Lycoming also powered the rear two-bladed anti-torque rotor.

Sikorsky had adopted the essential Cierva concept of cyclic control and had a collective control to alter the pitch of the three blades. He was the test pilot, sitting in an open cockpit immediately ahead of the engine. Instead of wearing the traditional leather jacket and white scarf, Sikorsky went to work as a test pilot the way he did as an engineer, in a topcoat and fedora. The first flight took place on September 14, 1939, and as with so many predecessor helicopter experiments, the aircraft was tethered to the ground.

With dogged determination, Sikorsky pressed on, learning to fly the helicopter even as he constantly tried to both improve control and dampen the vibration that threatened to shake the machine apart. In the next sixty days there were improvements, with the tethered flights lasting as long as two minutes, but the program was set back in December when the VS 300 was tilted over by a gust of wind and its rotor blades were smashed.

After appearing in eighteen different configurations, including one that had three tail rotors, the antithesis of Sikorsky's desire for simplicity, the VS 300 made its first free flight on May 13, 1940. The development was marred by some embarrassing incidents, including an occasion when Sikorsky was asked by Eugene Wilson, the vice chairman of United Aircraft, why the aircraft could seemingly fly in all directions except straight ahead. It is not certain how he received Sikorsky's answer that "this was one of the secondary engineering problems on which we are still working."[15]

Fortunately, the problem was solved, and the performance of the VS 300 improved steadily so that by June 1940 it was flying for as long as fifteen minutes at a stretch. Sikorsky often served as the test pilot, setting an endurance record on April 15, 1941, by staying in the air for more than an hour. Two days later, the VS 300 was equipped with large, inflatable rubber floats and operated from both land and water, becoming the first amphibious helicopter.

The U.S. Army Air Corps was interested, assigning Capt. Franklin Gregory as the project officer. A former autogiro pilot, Gregory was at first discommoded by the vibration and control reactions of the VS 300 but soon became an enthusiastic advocate. (By 1944, as a colonel, Gregory would publish *Anything a Horse Can Do: The Story of the Helicopter,* perhaps the first paper clearly articulating the possibilities of helicopters as attack vehicles firing both machineguns and rockets.) He would lead the way in many helicopter projects.

In December 1940, the Air Corps and United Aircraft each put up $50,000 for the development of the first production aircraft, the Sikorsky XR-4 (in company terms, the S-47). On Pearl Harbor Day, December 7, 1941, the first XR-4 was rolled out. It made its first flight on January 14, 1942, with Charles Morris as pilot.

At this point in the helicopter's development, the biggest uncertainty was whether or not it would (as theory indicated) autorotate safely to the ground in case of engine failure. (One of the most important features of the autogiro was its ability to autorotate, landing safely via the lift provided by the rotating blades. In the autogiro, the lift is generated by wind passing upward through the blades. In the helicopter, the lift is generated by the force of air passing down though the blades, and this raised a question about its ability to autorotate.)

Some delicate testing proved that this was possible, which cleared the way for a demonstration on April 20 of its abilities for the armed forces. The prototype XR-4 showed a top speed of 82 mph, an altitude capability of at least five thousand feet, and the ability to maneuver in all directions and hover.

One month later, it arrived at Wright Field, Ohio, for further tests, after having flown 735 miles in stages from Bridgeport, Connecticut in sixteen hours and ten minutes flying time. It was the world's first very long distance flight for a helicopter. Further tests resulted in an initial contract for three YR-4A and twenty-seven YR-4B helicopters for testing and training. This was quickly followed by an order for 100 R-4B production versions. Variants were already designed for multiple missions, including observation, reconnaissance and, presciently, MEDEVAC, with one litter rack fitted externally. Some were equipped with twin pontoons for shipboard use. Before the war ended, Sikorsky had produced more than 400 helicopters for the U.S. Army Air Forces, Navy, Coast Guard, and Britain's Royal Navy.

The Beginning of Helicopter Air Rescue Operations

The R-4 made history in 1944 in association with one of the most efficient—and glamorous—fighting commands of World War II, the 1st Air Commando Group. The 1st Air Commandos were commanded by Col. Philip G. Cochran, whose deputy was the six-victory Flying Tiger ace, then Lt. Col., later Maj. Gen. John Alison.

The 1st Air Commandos had the highest possible backing for an American unit in World War II. The president of the United States, Franklin D. Roosevelt, had been impressed by the eccentric (to say the least) British Maj. Gen. Orde Wingate, who had conducted long-range jungle operations in Burma. Roosevelt indicated to the USAAF commander, Lt. Gen. Henry H. "Hap" Arnold, that he would like to see American air support supplied to Wingate's troops. Arnold created a unit, eventually designated the 1st Air Commando Group, and gave them an unlimited charter to acquire the equipment they deemed necessary. In an unusual move, he appointed Cochran and Alison as "co-commanders," knowing that they were close personal friends. But as Alison knew that a two-commander system would not work, he happily and voluntarily assumed the role of Cochran's deputy.[16]

The two men made full use of their charter, shopping the Air Force inventory as if it were having a fire sale and acquiring an initial 380 aircraft—bombers, fighters, transports, and liaison aircraft. Then, when Alison learned that helicopters were coming off the production line, he asked for four Sikorsky YR-4Bs. This generated a conflict with the R-4 program manager, Frank Gregory, now a lieutenant colonel and fully aware that the pre-production YR-4B was a first-generation helicopter with both reliability and maintenance problems. Alison insisted, however, and the helicopters were flown in Curtiss C-46s all the way to the advance bases in Burma.

The 1st Air Commando Group soon became the vehicle by which

Sikorsky's Model VS-316 served the Army as the R-4 and the Navy as the HNS-1. *(Courtesy of U.S. Army Museum, Fort Rucker)*

Wingate's troops—known popularly as the "Chindits"—made long-range penetrations of the Japanese lines in Burma. Wingate (who was killed in the crash of a North American B-25 on March 24, 1944) set up permanent fortified camps that were resupplied by air. The Chindit attacks disconcerted the Japanese and have been credited with effectively disrupting their planned 1944 invasion of India.

On April 21, 1944, a Vultee L-1 Vigilant liaison aircraft, piloted by T.Sgt. Edward "Murphy" Hladovcak, was shot down sixty miles behind enemy lines in Burma while carrying three wounded British soldiers. The four men managed to evade the Japanese soldiers who rushed to the crash site and eventually were spotted by a Stinson L-5 Sentinel. The L-5 brought word of their plight back to 1st Air Commando Headquarters at Lalaghat, Burma, and subsequently sustained them with air drops of food and water.

At that time, only one of the four YR-4Bs sent to Burma was still operational. 2nd Lt. Carter Harman was assigned the task of rescuing the four men. Harman, who was a reporter for the *New York Times* before the war, had volunteered for the Air Corps. Upon winning his wings in flying class 43-C, he became a flight instructor in primary training before becoming a member of the first class of five helicopter pilots in the United States Army Air Forces.

The YR-4B's low 65-mph cruise speed and short 130-mile range prevented Harman from beginning the rescue operation until he arrived at the forward operating strip code-named Aberdeen, the 1st Air Commando base, on April 25. The jungle's heat and humidity degraded the performance of the YR-4B's Warner radial engine, which already had a dubious reputation for reliability.[17]

Realizing that there was not enough time remaining for him to fly each of the four men back to base, Harman decided to use a liaison plane to do the shuttling. He designated a sandbar in a nearby river as a rendezvous spot. Harman then flew from the sandbar to where Hladovcak was tending to the three wounded British soldiers.

On the twenty-fifth, he made two trips from the sandbar to the rescue site, bringing out a badly wounded British soldier each time. Just as he landed on the second trip, the overheated Warner engine seized, and Harman had to spend the night on the sandbar, hoping that neither he nor Hladovcak and the remaining British soldier would be discovered.

The next morning, the cranky Warner started and Harman ferried out the third British soldier. He returned to get Hladovcak just as what appeared to be Japanese troops began running out of the tree-line about one thousand feet away. Harman made a hasty takeoff and flew Hladovcak all the way back to Aberdeen. They found out later that the soldiers charging into the clearing were friendly Chinese soldiers.[18]

Harman thus established one of the noblest traditions in warfare, that of using helicopters in CSAR operations. And it is quite fitting that this tradition for helicopters would be established in concert with the great tradition of special force operations begun by the 1st Air Commando Group.

Unfortunately, these traditions were unable to overcome the budgetary, doctrinal, and philosophical arguments that would preclude an orderly, structured development of the helicopter and that began in 1947 and extend until this day in the U.S. military services. In the next chapter, we will see how these arguments play out against a historical background of developments related to vertical flight.

Chapter Two

Carving a Combat Niche

The seeds for future contention between rotary-wing-aircraft advocates and opponents were sown even before World War II began for the United States. The rapid growth of the Army Air Corps led to an expansion of capability in both fighters and bombers. However, simulated combat maneuvers led many ground commanders to believe that there was a severe shortage of aircraft devoted to such traditional tasks as artillery observation, liaison between front-line units, and coordination with armored forces.

Brash young officers are often found at the heart of innovation, and so it was with the introduction of light aircraft to the Army Air Corps. An artillery officer, Lt. Thomas M. Watson, took it upon himself to invite the Piper Aircraft Company to demonstrate their already famous Piper Cub at Camp Beauregard, Louisiana in 1939. The Cub elicited much comment—especially from potential competitors—and the upshot was that three manufacturers were asked to participate in the huge 1940 Army maneuvers in Louisiana. According to Stephan Wilkinson, the greatest light-plane salesman ever, William T. Piper, sent Bill Strohmeier to do the demonstrations, which were eminently successful.

As a result, the Army chief of staff, Gen. George C. Marshall, authorized the purchase of 617 "commercial,"[1] light-plane aircraft for use of the artillery in November 1941. These aircraft and those subsequently procured were called "Grasshoppers" and distinguished themselves in all theaters of combat. They expanded their intended roles from artillery spotting, reconnaissance, and liaison to many other important areas. "Grasshopper" was a generic term for light planes built by Piper, Aeronca, Taylorcraft, Stinson, Vultee, Interstate, Porterfield, and many other manufacturers. They were almost all "Cub-types," being high-wing monoplanes constructed of steel tubing, wood, and fabric and equipped with a fixed "tail-dragger" landing gear, fixed-pitch propeller, and Spartan seats for two. Although their primary role was scouting and artillery spotting, the eager young pilots flying the Grasshoppers were pugnacious and often undertook their own form of improvised close air support, dropping homemade bombs and shooting their handguns at the enemy.

The potential success of these aircraft led to the War Department's establishment on June 6, 1942, of Organic Army Aviation. Simultaneous with that action, the War Department authorized two light aircraft, two pilots, and one mechanic for each light- and medium-field artillery battalion, division artillery headquarters, headquarters battery, and artillery brigade headquarters.

This action was very much opposed by then Lt. Gen. Henry H. "Hap" Arnold, who believed it would result in a separate Army Air Force. Arnold was already carrying out a very deliberate policy to suppress any calls for the U.S. Army Air Forces to become independent during the war. His goal was to see that the USAAF supported the Army so well during the war that it would be readily granted independence in the postwar era. Arnold was successful in this, with the independent United States Air Force being established in 1947.[2] Despite Arnold's efforts—or perhaps because of them—there remained within the U.S. Army an inextinguishable desire for its own airpower, and June 6, 1942, is recognized as "aviation's birth date" within the modern Army.[3] During the course of the war, the Grasshoppers, their pilots, and maintenance personnel fulfilled all expectations, proving invaluable right up to the end.

After World War II, many commanders were experienced in the difficulties implicit in vertical envelopment operations. As a result, commanders quickly perceived the utility of the helicopter. Mass landings of troops by helicopters promised a degree of concentration of force and ease of resupply that paratroops or gliders could never provide.

This situation brought about an inevitable tug of war over roles, missions, and the budget for decades to come. During World War II, both the Army Air Corps and Army Air Forces instinctively desired to conduct operations independently of the Army. This was replicated in the independent United States Air Force. What is perhaps surprising is that within the Army after 1947, the proponents of Organic Army Aviation encountered the same sort of problems. As a direct result, helicopter development and employment were never backed by a uniform opinion, common doctrine, or adequate funding within the Army itself. The helicopter debate was part of the larger debate within the Army as to whether or not there should be a separate aviation branch.

This debate persisted even after a separate branch of Army Aviation was created in April 1983 to offset the perception that aviation in the Army was lacking in training, doctrine, and organization. While the formation of this branch ameliorated some of the problems, it created others. Not least of these was the feeling among some in the Army that the Aviation Branch was no longer as ardent an advocate of close air support as desired and that it sought to become a maneuver branch similar to the infantry or the armored branches.

Cold War Balance

When peace finally came in 1945, it was followed by a pell-mell dissolution of the military services that caused immense problems in readiness. The United States was not prepared to defend itself against attack from a major power. It was saved for the time being because the most obvious potential enemy—the Soviet Union—was even more exhausted, although it had not demobilized anywhere near the extent that Western nations had. The truth was that even in the Soviet Union's exhausted state, its armies could have overrun the continent of Europe in just a few weeks from 1946 onward and probably would have done so if the Soviets had not been intimidated by the nuclear power of the United States.

The Soviets overestimated that nuclear power, for the United States had very few nuclear weapons and only a small number of the specially configured "Silverplate" Boeing B-29s with which to deliver them. Fortunately, this proved to be enough to keep the Soviet Union in check as the fragile peace turned into the Cold War.

The emerging Soviet threat had resulted in the newly independent U.S. Air Force and the U.S. Navy contesting for primacy in the defense of the nation. The ill-fated first secretary of defense, James V. Forrestal, tried valiantly to hammer out reasonable agreements that demonstrated his impartiality. In March 1948, he developed a policy paper officially titled "Functions of the Armed Forces and the Joint Chiefs of Staff," more commonly known as the Key West Agreement. A fashionable tourist spot today, Key West, Florida was then more famous for being a favored retreat of Pres. Harry S Truman, who was often photographed there in short-sleeved, multicolored shirts, sitting in front of the "little White House." While Truman was not personally a dedicated helicopter advocate, he had as senator approved suggestions urging the Army to pursue its investigations of rotary-wing aircraft.

The agreement was far reaching but is noted here for the manner in which it allocated aviation duties. They in turn affected both the development and employment of helicopters.

The Air Force, much to its satisfaction, was given the role of strategic air warfare, meaning that it would control all strategic air assets and most tactical and logistic functions as well. This would have profound implications for the later era of intercontinental ballistic missile development. The U.S. Navy was made responsible for control of the seas and would maintain a combat air arm sufficient to accomplish its objectives in a naval campaign. This was a severe and, to the Navy, unfair decision, as it governed budget distributions for the next several decades. But if Navy air power was diminished, Army aviation was set back on its heels, for its stated task was to provide "land combat and service forces, and such aviation and water transport as may be organic therein." By implication, Organic Army Aviation was to be confined to reconnaissance and MEDEVAC duties. This would have adverse effects upon helicopter development.

After Key West, rancor in the ranks increased, and on May 20, 1949, the chief of staff of the Army, general of the Army Omar N. Bradley, and chief of staff of the Air Force, Gen. Hoyt Vandenberg, attempted to alleviate the situation. They agreed that Organic Army Aviation fixed-wing aircraft were limited in weight to 2,500 pounds, with helicopters allowed to weigh up to 4,000 pounds. Duties were reminiscent of those of the Grasshoppers of World War II, calling for liaison work, adjusting artillery fire, and serving as route reconnaissance aircraft. It is interesting to note that no matter how intelligent the proponents were on each side of the

Army-Air Force roles and missions arguments, they seemed able only to come up with decisions that were arbitrarily based on the weight rather than the capabilities of the aircraft involved.

At this particular juncture, the stated weight limitations were still adequate for what the Army saw it needed. In the case of the helicopter, it was also about the maximum the machine could deliver. This would change rapidly as helicopter capabilities developed in the wars in which they would soon be involved in many parts of the world.

In the meantime, while these agreements were being hashed out, the United States Marines were conducting a single-minded approach to a problem that threatened their very existence as a corps—the atomic era.

The previously mentioned report made by Lt. Gen. Roy S. Geiger was immediately acted upon by Marine Commandant Gen. Alexander A. Vandergrift, who created a board of general officers to investigate the matter.

When Vandergrift received the board's report, he reacted with unusual prescience even for a man in his position, concluding that the potential speed and lift capability of the helicopter offered several prospects. The following statement put forth his Vertical Assault Concept:

> With a relatively unlimited choice of landing areas, troops can be landed in combat formations and under full control of the flanks or rear of a hostile position. The helicopter's speed makes transport dispersion at sea a matter of no disadvantage and introduces a time-space factor that will avoid presenting at any one time a remunerative atomic target. It should also be noted that transport helicopters offer a means for rapid evacuation of casualties, for the movement of supplies directly from ship to dump and for subsequent movement of troops and supplies in continuing operations ashore.[4]

He called for recommendations for helicopters to carry out these tasks, with the goal of quickly acquiring an experimental helicopter squadron.

On March 10, 1947, Lt. Col. Robert E. Hogaboom, who had been operations officer for the amphibious landings on Tinian and Saipan, submitted the report "Military Requirements for Ship-to-Shore Movement of Troops and Cargo." The report was prepared by the Marine Corps Schools' Committee of the Academic Board and stated that the Marine Corps should acquire initially an assault helicopter that could carry a 5,000-pound payload and would have a 200- to 300-nautical-mile range

(500 miles with an auxiliary fuel tank), 100-knot cruising speed, and 4,000-foot ceiling at which it could still maintain hovering flight. The now-famous Hogaboom report went into considerable and farsighted detail, also calling for self-sealing fuel tanks, an external hook and hoist, and dimensions that permitted it to operate off an aircraft carrier. Major General Hogaboom performed an even more farsighted service in another board proceeding in 1956.

It should be noted that while these requirements seem modest now, they were extremely demanding for their time, calling for about ten times the current capacity in payload and four times the maximum range. The desired cruising speed was high for the time and the service ceiling was a straightforward recognition of the limitations of the available engines.

The first Marine helicopter squadron (HMX-1) was established at the Marine Corps Air Station, Quantico, Virginia on December 1, 1947, with Col. Edward C. Dyer as its commanding officer. The squadron was intended to carry out General Vandergrift's goal of proving that the helicopter could provide the Marines with an amphibious assault capability in the atomic era.

The Marines went to work, using Sikorsky HO3S-1s to participate in Marine landing operations, and by November 1948 had developed the world's first manual on helicopter use in amphibious landings. Called "Amphibious Operations—Employment of Helicopters (Tentative)," the manual looked well into the future. It outlined operations that were far beyond the capability of contemporary helicopters but clearly about to become available in helicopters currently on the drawing boards. The manual was subsequently used as a basis for Army helicopter operations.

In contrast to that of both the Army and the Marines, the U.S. Navy's attitude toward the helicopter can only be called serene. It did not see it as a threat to any established order but rather as a new tool to be evaluated on its own merit. In the Navy, the helicopter's value as a "plane guard" rescue craft onboard aircraft carriers was recognized immediately. It also began to supplant scout planes for the traditional observation work. As with its service counterparts, the Navy's first helicopters were built by Sikorsky.

The United States military has too often been at the mercy of utter incompetents in the role of secretary of defense, many of whom regarded the office as a stepping stone to greater things. Outstanding among these was Louis A. Johnson, an ambitious if not acutely intelligent West Virginian who thought that his way to the White House lay through ruthless cuts in defense spending, without any regard for the implications for America's military capability. The resultant draw-down of American power in the Pacific virtually invited the North Korean government to launch its invasion into South Korea on June 25, 1950. The North Koreans acted with the full approval of both the Soviet Union and China, whose governments concluded that the United States (a) would be unable to defend South Korea and (b), despite its nuclear capability, would not elect to start World War III over an "incident" that the North Koreans would be able to conclude successfully in short order.

In another of the major decisions that later determined the prestige of his presidency, Truman elected to defend South Korea, calling upon the United Nations for support even as he put the weak American forces in dire danger of being totally evicted from the Korean Peninsula.

There was just sufficient airpower in the ragtag elements of the Far Eastern Air Force to stabilize the situation at the besieged Pusan Perimeter and then help reverse the course of the war at Inchon. When the Chinese intervened in December 1950, the war was converted to a conventional one in which the helicopter could shine in multiple roles.

Fortunately for the thousands of men it rescued during the Korean War, the helicopter had been backed by two men in crucial positions. One was the second Air Force chief of staff, Gen. Hoyt Vandenberg, who was a staunch supporter of SAR operations. Under his leadership, the Air Transport Command (ATC) was given responsibility for the newly established Air Rescue Service, commanded by Col. Richard Kight.

The new commander was initially uncertain about the future of SAR, given the ragtag collection of aircraft he had at his disposal, the inadequate manning of his unit, and ATC's indifference to the mission. A lesser man might have folded operations, but Kight saw that even the still-primitive Sikorsky H-5 helicopters were well suited for their intended role. His efforts made it possible for the 2nd and 3rd Air Rescue Squadrons (ARS), despite severe shortages of personnel and equipment, to be available in the Pacific theater when the Korean War broke out.

The four flights of the 3rd ARS were stationed in Japan, and in addition to a variety of fixed-wing aircraft (Boeing SB-17s, Douglas SC-47s, and Stinson L-5s), it had no fewer than nine H-5s on strength.[5] These were sufficient to launch a legendary career of service to humanity. (Contrary to many reports, the 3rd ARS had no Boeing SB-29s or Grumman SA-16s until after the war began.)

A few H-5s were dispatched to Taegu, South Korea on July 22, 1950. By August, all nine were operating, beginning a saga that extends to this day. The few 3rd ARS helicopters were immediately drafted into MEDEVAC duties and were soon used almost exclusively in that role. By the end of 1950, the squadron's strength had grown to include fourteen H-5s.

Field studies confirmed that the helicopters' speed saved lives. The 3rd ARS had evacuated 32 front-line patients by August 6, 1950, only fourteen days after the first H-5 had reached Korea. By New Year's Day 1951, the number had reached 618. (During the same period, the 3rd's fixed-wing L-5s had also evacuated 56 more wounded soldiers.)[6] By June 1951, the Army could reveal that only 2 percent of wounded soldiers died of their wounds in Korea, compared to 4 percent during World War II. The difference was attributed to helicopter evacuation.

These figures are all the more important when the actual performance capability of the Sikorsky H-5 is considered. Driven by a 450-hp Pratt & Whitney R-985 radial engine, the fully loaded H-5 weighed less than five thousand pounds. It had a nominal high speed of 106 mph, a range of 360 miles—stretching it—and a service ceiling of 14,400 feet. Performance fell off rapidly as altitude increased, always a critical factor in helicopters, and especially so in those powered by reciprocating engines.

The helicopter pilots were generally unaware of how primitive their new aircraft were, having nothing with which to compare them. The Sikorsky helicopters of the time were basically unstable, and a pilot was kept busy with both hands and both feet on the controls. Also, the battery frequently had to be moved to ensure that the helicopter remained within center-of-gravity limits.

Despite the pressure to use it in the MEDEVAC role, the Third was able to add to its missions, including that of rescuing downed pilots from behind enemy lines. On August 1, 1950, a Navy pilot had crash-landed 10 miles southeast of the North Korean capital of Pyongyang. A Third ARS helicopter flew 125 miles under heavy enemy fire to rescue him. The 3rd's resources were rapidly used on other tasks, including guiding 600 South Korean troops to safety from where they were trapped by North Korean forces near Pohang.[7]

The U.S. Army managed to put three helicopter detachments in Korea as soon as possible. Each was equipped with four helicopters, with four pilots and four mechanics assigned. Two of the units had the Bell H-13D by 1951, while the third used the Hiller H-23. The helicopters each had one pilot and were equipped with baskets for litter-borne patients. The familiar H-13 Sioux was etched into America's consciousness by the popular, if blatantly antiwar, antimilitary television sitcom "M*A*S*H," an acronym for Mobile Army Surgical Hospital. While the show's scenes of helicopter operations were always done with dignity, "M*A*S*H" imparted a darkly humored message that its madcap doctors were clearly superior to anyone who was actually fighting the war in Korea. The series never paid significant tribute to the dedicated men flying and maintaining the H-13s and H-23s that evacuated about eighteen thousand United Nations casualties during the war.

The Bell H-13 was adapted from the Bell Model 47, which was designed by Arthur Young and featured one of his many contributions to the discipline, the introduction of a short, weighted gyro stabilizer that was connected beneath the main rotor at a ninety-degree angle. This steadied the aircraft and made it easier to fly.

The H-13 was dubbed the "Sioux," beginning the Army tradition of naming helicopters after Indian tribes. There were only fifty-six H-13s in the Army's inventory in June 1950, but many more were procured, reaching more than eight hundred by the time of the Vietnam War. Although the Sioux was superseded in many roles, its later versions were useful for observation and reconnaissance.

The first versions of the Sioux were very underpowered by their 175-hp Franklin engines, while the more heavily laden later ones were equally underpowered by 305-hp Lycoming engines. With a slightly smaller rotor, the H-13 was lighter than the H-5 and had a slightly superior performance.

Although lesser known than the H-13, the Hiller H-23 did valiant service

The first helicopter to be built in really large numbers, the H-13 served well in combat and as a trainer. *(Courtesy of U.S. Army Museum, Fort Rucker)*

in Korea. Stanley Hiller had formed the United Helicopter Company in 1946 and developed a series of designs that led to the Model 360, the basis for the UH-12, which received the Army designation of H-23. The H-23 Raven was used for liaison work as well as MEDEVAC. The most commonly used version, the H-23D, was driven by a 305-hp Lycoming engine and had a top speed of 95 mph. The H-23 could carry two external skid-mounted litters. The Raven was also used in the early years of the Vietnam War.

Marine helicopters entered the war early. On August 2, 1950, four Sikorsky HO3S-1s of Marine Observation Squadron 6 (VMO-6) flew from Japan to South Korea across the historic Tsushima Strait, just behind the hard-pressed lines of the Pusan Perimeter. (The HO3S-1 was the first Navy helicopter to replace a fixed-wing aircraft and was the naval version of the Sikorsky S-51.) On August 3, Brig. Gen. Edward B. Craig made a personal reconnaissance of the combat area in an HO3S-1, later calling the helicopter "the emergency weapon" of his brigade. He said:

> Marine helicopters have proven invaluable. They have been used for every conceivable type of mission. The Brigade utilized them for liaison, reconnaissance, evacuation of wounded, rescue of Marine flyers downed in enemy territory, observation, messenger service, guard mail at sea, posting and supplying of outguards on outlying terrain features and resupply of small units by air.[8]

On August 4, 1950, an HO3S-1 flew a Marine MEDEVAC flight, saving the first of 9,815 wounded whose lives would be saved by the use of a helicopter before the war's end.[9] Four days later, Capt. Victor "Vic" Armstrong conducted the first of more than one thousand night MEDEVACs the Marines would achieve during the war.

General Craig, touring the front, was on board an HO3S-1 helicopter piloted by 1st Lt. Gus Lueddeke. They saw a Marine Vought F4U Corsair piloted by 2nd Lt. Doyle Cole of VMF-323 ditching just offshore. Lueddeke immediately went to the rescue, with Craig operating the winch that hoisted Cole to safety. The story goes that Cole happily slapped the general on the back, saying, "Thanks, Mac" before he noticed the rank insignia.[10]

Marine helicopters distinguished themselves during the tough fighting of December 1950. After having surged north to the Chosin Reservoir, the Marines were forced to fall back because of the massive Chinese intervention. The helicopters helped maintain contact between widely separated U.S. units and were invaluable for carrying supplies in and wounded out. At least two helicopters were shot down during this process. The altitude and severe cold reduced performance, but for the most part the tough little Sikorskys were able to sustain minor battle damage and continue flying. The loads were sometimes reduced, but they brought supplies in and ferried the wounded out, flying 1,544 sorties.[11]

By the end of the first year of the Korean War, Marine helicopters had flown every sort of mission except the one for which they had been first conceived—vertical envelopment during an amphibious assault. Marine Transport Helicopter Squadron (HMR) 161 arrived at Pusan, Korea on

September 2, 1951, equipped with fifteen Sikorsky Model HRS-1 helicopters.

Capable of carrying ten passengers or six combat-equipped Marines, the HRS-1 went into combat on September 13 in Operation WINDMILL I (sometimes called Operation BUMBLEBEE). The HRS-1s made twenty-eight sorties, airlifting nine tons of cargo and evacuating 74 wounded soldiers. Just one week later, the HRS-1s executed the first helicopter-borne combat assault in Operation SUMMIT. Ignoring a dense fog, the helicopters landed 224 fully equipped Marines on Hill 884, then made another series of flights to land another nine tons of supplies. Many historians claim this to be the first significant use of helicopters in combat. Many of the actions executed in this operation derived from the far-seeing principles laid down by Col. Victor H. "Brute" Krulak. With further experience, these were codified into the formal doctrine of the Marines and later the U.S. Army.

Practice made perfect, and the helicopter became an invaluable tool. Operations reached a highlight during February 23-27, 1953, in Operation HAYLIFT II. Two complete regiments were resupplied by helicopters, which delivered 1.6 million pounds of cargo. Despite exposure to heavy fire, none was lost.

The U.S. Marines had thus successfully employed the long-touted concept of vertical envelopment using helicopters. The work would continue until the end of the war, with HMR 161 flying 18,607 flights, lifting 60,046 people, and transporting 7,554,336 pounds of cargo. It also evacuated 2,748 casualties, while the veteran VMO-6 evacuated 7,067.[12]

The Sikorsky Model S-55 Chickasaw, known variously as the H-19, HO4S (Navy), and HRS-3 (Marines), first flew in November 1949 and, with the Piasecki H-25A, might be considered the first of a new generation of large U.S. helicopters. With a larger, all-metal rotor and driven by engines in the 500-hp range, the S-55 was not only adaptable to more missions, it performed better in them. The S-55 had considerable commercial success and was used by many foreign air forces.

Korea thus set several courses for the helicopter in modern combat. For the United States Navy, helicopters were invaluable as "plane guards" for aircraft-carrier operations. Some were stationed on cruisers and battleships and registered gunfire for ships. Later in the war, they flew off decks improvised on LSTs and were useful for clearing mines from coastal waters, saving several minesweepers from destruction.

Air Force helicopters were dedicated to the air rescue and MEDEVAC roles, with no fewer than 9,898 personnel being evacuated by the end of the war. The primary Army use of helicopters was also in MEDEVAC, but by 1953, with the arrival of the Sikorsky H-19s, they began to be employed more and more for resupply efforts. Like the Marines, the Army brought the helicopter right onto the field of battle. In June 1953, the Army and the Marines teamed up to airlift more than eight hundred South Korean soldiers to safety, a triumph and a first in combined operations for the region. This cooperation proved invaluable during the tension-filled days when thousands of Allied prisoners of war were at last released from North Korean prisons and flown to safety in helicopters.[13]

Perhaps one of the most important conclusions on the helicopter in combat was drawn by Eighth Army commander Lt. Gen. Maxwell D. Taylor, who said, "The cargo helicopter, employed in mass, can extend the tactical mobility of the Army far beyond its normal capability. I hope that the United States Army will make ample provisions for the full exploitation of the helicopter in the future."[14] Taylor's ideas would have enormous effect upon the manner in which the Vietnam War would unfold less than two decades later.

Other Wars, Other Services, Other Uses

In the same spirit with which Great Britain had shared the technology of the jet engine with the United States, America shared the technology of the helicopter with the United Kingdom. This began with the first production version, the Sikorsky R-4. Of a total of 131 built (including the XR-4 prototype), 25 were supplied to the U.S. Navy as the HNS-1 and 52 to the Royal Air Force (RAF), where it was called the "Hoverfly."

The new Hoverfly became a direct replacement for the Cierva C.30A "Rota" helicopters being used by No. 529 Squadron. Although invaluable for training, the Hoverfly was soon replaced by the Westland Dragonfly, the British-built version of the Sikorsky S-51 (R-5). These early Sikorskys began a long relationship between the U.S. and British helicopter industries that continues to this day.

The Sikorsky Model 51 gained fame in Korea as the H-5. *(Courtesy of Zaur Eylanbekov [Foxbat])*

In the tight postwar British budgets, there was little room for expenditures on weapons, especially those still obviously in a formative stage, such as the helicopter. Yet the empire that Great Britain sought so tenaciously to maintain was continuing to unravel. The independence of India and Pakistan had been granted in 1947 in a relatively tidy fashion—not without rancor on the part of some but without combative opposition that demanded military countermeasures.

The opposite was the case in Malaya, where in 1948 the so-called Malayan Emergency erupted, which was much more like the later American conflict in Vietnam than the Korean War. In Malaya, the very forces that the British had nurtured to fight the Japanese formed the basis for an essentially Communist opposition known as the Malayan National Liberation Army (MNLA). The MNLA (which was also known by more inflammatory names such as the Malayan Races Liberation Army [MRLA] or Malayan People's Liberation Army [MPLA]) sought an independence that Great Britain was not yet willing to grant.

The MNLA attacked the principal British targets—the tin mines and rubber plantations—using the guerilla tactics that had been successful against the Japanese army. There ensued a bitter twelve-year war that the British and the later Malayan federal state ultimately won, thanks in great part to the helicopter.

The Chinese population in Malaya had been oppressed during the Japanese occupation. Despite the fact that most of the Chinese were native to Malaya, there were almost a half-million foreign-born Chinese there, and native Malayans often regarded these as a foreign ethnic community. The Chinese in general, but the foreign-born group in particular, provided the most support for the MNLA. The rise of Red China under Mao Tse Tung undoubtedly stimulated their desire for independence.

Although never having more than about eight thousand soldiers, the MNLA nonetheless tied down up to forty thousand British and Commonwealth troops. On a Kiplingesque note, the cornerstone of the British forces was built upon the Gurkha battalions that came from Nepal, noted for their ferocity and bravery.

One irony of the war was the British resorting to their Boer War tactic of using concentration camps to isolate the ethnic Chinese from the guerillas. Fortunately, these camps were run in a humane manner and were able ultimately to reach that elusive goal of large nations warring with small ones, "winning their hearts and minds." They did so by providing land, food, housing, and a generally improved lifestyle.

In direct contrast to the Americans in both the Korean and the Vietnam wars, the British did not assign an independent role to air power. The British quickly learned that massive firepower was not useful in suppressing the elusive MNLA guerilla forces and that the swift transport of troops by helicopters to specific locations where combat was either ongoing or imminent was far more successful.[15]

In Malaya, as elsewhere, the initial and most rewarding duty of the helicopters was evacuating wounded soldiers. The sapping jungle heat, and sometimes the height of the position above sea level, diminished the already limited power available to the helicopters. The Westland Whirlwind (Sikorsky S-55), which could lift ten people in Great Britain, sometimes struggled to lift two in Malaya. However, just as General Craig had learned in Korea, a helicopter was the best means for a commander to check with all his troops in contact prior to making decisions on where and when to commit forces. The British helicopters also anticipated Vietnam War-style tactics by dispensing chemicals that destroyed the crops sustaining the guerilla forces.

Ultimately, one Fleet Air Arm and four RAF helicopter units operated in Malaya. Over the twelve years of the war, they evacuated 4,579 casualties, flew in 127,425 troops, ferried 17,865 passengers, and carried 2,649,327 tons of equipment.[16] These numbers are all the more impressive because with the helicopters available at the time, troops were carried in loads of three to five and freight in five- to eight-hundred-pound loads.

The Federation of Malaya gained independence by 1957, and the guerilla war could then be portrayed as an insurrection against a sovereign native government rather than an anti-colonial movement against the British Empire. By 1960, the Malayan government was able to proclaim that the emergency was over. The Communists renewed the insurgency in 1967 and continued it until 1989, when a combination of exhaustion and a booming economy brought it to an end.

While it cannot be said that helicopters had the greatest influence on the outcome of the Malayan Emergency, it is undeniable that the world took note of their admirable performance and the heroism of their crews. Furthermore, that performance was achieved by helicopters that had been only marginally improved over the period. The war began with a handful of Hoverflys and ended with a few squadrons equipped with Westland Whirlwinds (license-built Sikorsky S-55s) and the indigenous Bristol Sycamores, designed by an early autogiro proponent, Raoul Hafner.

The Malayan Emergency, as it was euphemistically called to avoid complications in insurance claims by landholders, is often compared to the Vietnam War. The principal question asked is how the 40,000 British and Commonwealth troops could have succeeded in a land with similar geographic, cultural, and climatic conditions to Vietnam, where more than 500,000 American troops failed.

The primary answer to this is that Vietnam was not a military failure but an abject political surrender engendered by a population whose weariness of war was nurtured by a media hostile to American interests. The most notable example of this insidious media influence is Walter Cronkite's fatuous analysis that the Tet Offensive was a victory for the North Vietnamese. It was in fact a catastrophic defeat that virtually destroyed the Viet Cong as a movement and mauled the North Vietnamese regular forces, as General Giap subsequently acknowledged.

There were other significant differences, however, including the fact that the MNLA did not have direct external support from a sovereign nation (North Vietnam) nor indirect support of any dimension from China or the Soviet Union. Perhaps more important, the Malayan population did not have the visceral hatred for the British that the Vietnamese population (rightly) had for the French, who had cooperated with the Japanese. North Vietnamese propaganda ensured that this hatred was transferred to the Americans.[17]

The First Helicopter War

While helicopters had been used in significant numbers to great advantage in the Korean War and the Malayan Emergency, they came into genuine prominence during the bitter French conflict in Algeria from 1954 to 1962. The Algerian conflict convincingly demonstrated how geography, terrain, and even foliage affect guerilla warfare and how much this determines the relative use that will be made of helicopters.

All of the anti-colonial wars were sad in the way they pitted one group against another, but the Algerian situation was perhaps the saddest of all. Seized by France on a pretext in 1830, Algeria was a classic example of genocidal colonialism, as the French slaughtered millions of the native population to impose their will. Ultimately, however, Algeria received a special status. Officially not a colony at all, it was thought of as a politically integral, if geographically separated, part of France itself. Unfortunately, this sense of belonging was conferred solely upon the minority French and European population, the so-called "*pieds-noirs*" ("black feet"), the term deriving from the black sandals they characteristically wore. This minority constituted only 10 percent of the Algerian population and was primarily Catholic. The majority of the population was Muslim, poverty stricken, often barefoot, and usually disenfranchised.

Algeria's huge landmass of 2,400,000 square kilometers was almost eleven times that of North and South Korea combined and more than seven times that of Malaya. It was bordered on the north by the Mediterranean and on its other sides by primarily Muslim states also vying for independence. The distances, arid climate, and diffused guerilla opposition spurred the French to pursue new methods of warfare, and they seized upon the helicopter as a major element in this.

The war began in Algeria on November 1, 1954, with attacks by armed Muslims against French installations. Calling themselves the *Fronte de Libération Nationale* (FLN), the Muslim fighters quickly gathered strength, growing from an initial estimated three thousand to more than thirty thousand in just two years. The stated goal of the FLN was liberation from France and the establishment of an independent Algeria; its combatant arm was termed *Armée Libération Nationale* (ALN).

Although primarily defensive at first, the strong and bloody French reaction provoked an increased fervor among the rebels, the intensity of which was heightened by France's granting independence in 1956 to Morocco and Tunisia, on Algeria's eastern and western borders, respectively. These new borders became instant routes for reinforcing the FLN and constituted a problem that France ultimately had to solve.

Algeria's population of 10 million then was concentrated in the northern coastal area of the country, shielded from the southern Saharan region by two daunting chains of mountain ranges, the Tellian and the Saharan. The Tellian was often forest covered, providing cover for the rebels, while the Saharan was a rocky-ledged and cave-filled wilderness. Either area was perfect for the rebels to use as training camps, rest areas, or places to muster for an attack. Both areas provided extremes in temperature as the seasons varied, and in summer, the combination of altitude and heat sucked the performance from all aircraft, whether fixed wing or rotary wing.

French armed strength built up rapidly, soon reaching more than 400,000, but the nature of the climate and the terrain dictated that the only way to combat the rebels was by the use of the helicopter for transport and, to a lesser degree, firepower.

As with other nations, the expense of helicopter procurement and operation had impeded their acquisition, and when the war began, France was required to borrow helicopters from Italy, the United States, and Germany.[18]

However, by the spring of 1955, France had established two helicopter units in Algeria, employing eighteen Bell Model 47Gs and the same number of Sikorsky H-19s. The first combat use of helicopters in the Algerian War came on May 4, 1955, when some of the famous French Legionnaires were flown to a mountain outpost in twenty minutes, a trip that would have taken two days on foot.[19]

The initial French reaction was necessarily defensive and reactive, usually constituting punishment expeditions against FLN attacks. In April 1956, the French began the so-called *quadrillage* (squaring) tactics in which large numbers of troops were stationed in the major population centers, while fewer troops were positioned in the smaller towns. The arrival of additional helicopters, and a better understanding of their use, resulted in new tactics being adopted in 1958. Ultimately both the French Army and Air Force considered the ideal mission ratio to be one armed helicopter for every five transport helicopters.

Violence became endemic, as the FLN formally declared that all Europeans between the ages of eighteen and forty were targets for assassination. The election of Gen. Charles de Gaulle as president in December 1958 put a new complexion on the war. It was obviously de Gaulle's aim to obtain peace in Algeria at any price, including the grant of independence, despite all the consequences this would have for the one million *pieds-noirs* who considered themselves citizens as much as (or more than) de Gaulle. The general's policies were equally opposed by many in the French Army.

There ensued what seemed to be an anomaly but became a pattern in guerilla warfare; the rebels suffered decisive military losses even as they gained political ascendance. By proper application of airpower, particularly through the use of the helicopter, the French Army was able to destroy the greater part of the ALN. Despite this, the FLN grew enormously in strength, not only in Algeria but in metropolitan France and in world opinion. The result was a referendum held on July 1, 1962, in which the majority of Algerians voted for independence.

Despite this ultimate political loss, it is instructive to review how the effective use of helicopters aided the French in defeating their guerilla opposition militarily. At first the helicopters were used primarily for MEDEVAC, and in that role they helped improve morale throughout the war. But as more capable helicopters became available, new applications were found, and these made possible a change in French tactics from the relatively passive *quadrillage* system to an active attack mode.

Through 1958, the element of surprise rested with the ALN, which could select the time and place of its attacks and then disperse, its members disappearing into the general populace. The helicopter's swift reaction time changed this, getting troops to the scene in minutes rather than hours and finding and attacking the enemy before they could disappear. With helicopters spread out at bases throughout the country, the geographic disadvantages of Algeria's size were in great part overcome. With good communications, enemy attacks could be countered over very wide areas in short order. Helicopters also gave the French the advantage of surprise in attacks on enemy encampments. Further, the helicopter permitted a concentration of force that could rapidly overwhelm the guerilla detachments. (It should be noted that when the guerilla units had built up reasonable defenses, it was always necessary to use conventional fixed-wing airpower prior to bringing in the helicopter-borne troops. This is a lesson frequently forgotten in later years, always at a cost.)

By 1959, two events occurred that permitted France to use helicopters so effectively that the guerilla forces were reduced to a marginal status. The first of these was the arrival of adequate numbers, including 98 light, 115 medium, and 44 heavy helicopters. They were used more effectively by a decentralized controls system that placed the decision level for how and why to use helicopters much farther down the chain of command. (This problem of command psychology has recurred over the years, most recently in the war in Afghanistan.) Perhaps more important, Gen. Maurice Challe of the *Armée de l'Air* was made commander in chief of all French forces in Algeria. Challe formed a 20,000-man tactical reserve composed of Foreign Legionnaires and parachutists. He used helicopters to place these troops in quick reaction strikes that decimated the ANL forces.[20] (Challe, unfortunately, became one of the four generals who took part in the ill-fated Algiers putsch of 1961. Sentenced to jail for fifteen years, he was ultimately pardoned by the man he had sought to depose, Charles de Gaulle.)

The successful prosecution of the war by the French has to be considered in light of the equipment available to them and how they employed it. As noted, the war began with a handful of Bell Model 47s (equivalent to an H-13) and Sikorsky Model S-55 (H-19). These were soon supplemented by Sikorsky Model S-58s (H-34) and Vertol (Piasecki) H-21s, which had top speeds of about 100 mph and could transport a maximum of twelve and seventeen troops, respectively. The first indigenous French helicopter used was the Sud-Ouest

The revolutionary rotor placement of the Piasecki H-21 proved itself over the years, and it may still be seen in combat today. *(Courtesy of Zaur Eylanbekov [Foxbat])*

Djinn. A light utility two-seat helicopter, the Djinn was powered by a Turbomecca-Palouste turbo-compressor, which ducted air through the blades to their tips.

Entirely new ground was broken with the revolutionary SNCASE Alouette II, the world's first jet-powered helicopter to enter volume production. First flown by Jean Boulet on March 12, 1955, the Alouette II would see the beginning of a new phase in helicopter history. It was eventually widely used in a variety of roles but was especially helpful in Algeria as an airborne command post and in liaison work.

The employment of French helicopters was greatly expanded when operations began to include one armed helicopter for every five transport helicopters. The armed helicopters could provide fire support for the transport helicopters prior to their arrival at the landing zone (LZ), although fixed-wing aircraft were preferred for this task. Once the transport and resupply helicopters were in the LZ, the armed helicopters provided effective assistance.

As would be the case with the U.S. Army, arming French helicopters was done on a sub-rosa basis initially. Led by Col. Felix Brunet, a series of ad hoc armament trials were conducted. Improvisation was the key, as always in warfare, and the French plopped machine gunners in the stretcher panniers on their Bell Model 47 MEDEVAC helicopters. As crude—and daring—as the approach was, it worked and was especially useful in combating enemy forces dug in on the hillsides. The French are to be credited with combat testing the first missile-firing helicopters when they mounted the Nord AS 11 wire-guided missiles on Alouette II and III aircraft. Used primarily for training and for operations against fortified caves and bunkers, this system presaged later heliborne anti-armor systems. Adopted by the United States Army as the AGM-22A, it was deployed on UH-1B Huey helicopters, eventually reaching combat in October 1965.

The trial-and-error experiments soon gave way to the well-conceived installation of heavy armament on a Sikorsky H-34. This included a 20-mm cannon in the cabin door and light machine guns installed at the windows. This successful combination was soon succeeded by a veritable flying fortress, an H-34 with one forward-firing and one side-mounted 20-mm cannon, multiple rocket-launching platforms, and a variety of machine guns. Weight and ammunition considerations finally tailored the configuration to include a single flexibly mounted 20-mm cannon at the cabin door, with two 12.7-mm machine guns mounted on each side.[21]

As new and more powerful helicopters were introduced, the French adopted new operational techniques to obtain the maximum from them. Perhaps the most important of these was recognizing how specialized helicopter warfare was and allowing the decisions on their use to be made much farther down the chain of command than was typical in the French Army. As early as May 1957, it was decided that every helicopter operation should have a designated commander to supervise its planning and execution. The helicopter operations officer had two men reporting to him. The first selected the LZ and conducted the aerial and landing operations. The second commanded the troops on the ground in combat. The helicopter operations commander supervised the operations, often from a helicopter over the scene, until the helicopter troops joined up with the ground forces in contact with the enemy.

As helicopter advocates always promised, the French found that helicopters provided both speed and flexibility in answering a demand for their services. The troops they carried arrived on the scene ready to fight, rather than being exhausted by a trek across the hostile desert. Most important, the troops could be landed as a cohesive unit, capable of mutual support rather than being strung out across a drop area.

The importance of both the helicopter and the terrain may be seen in a brief comparison of the French experience in Indo-China and in Algeria. In Indo-China, the French had to rely on primitive means of transport to move and resupply their troops. There were never more than one hundred helicopters available to them at any time, and these were of limited capability. By contrast, in Algeria they ultimately had, in addition to a superior local transportation system, more than six hundred modern helicopters to give a decisive military advantage. As would happen again in the Vietnam War, the military advantage was not of final consequence, as the outcome of the war was decided politically. The FLN won in diplomacy and politics what they could not win on the battlefield.[22]

By the conclusion of the Algerian War, helicopter development had proceeded to the edge of its limits while using the traditional reciprocating engine. Then, just as World War II fighters had been made obsolete by the arrival of postwar jet fighters, so did the turbine engine expand the horizons of helicopter performance.

Chapter Three

Helicopter Development

Helicopter development lurched through the first half of the twentieth century succored by enthusiastic and inventive proponents who worked hard to solve the many difficult problems that physics and funding imposed upon the type. There is perhaps some irony in the fact that each solution seemed to present new problems, each more esoteric than the last. Nonetheless, a series of major developments during this time set the stage for an explosion in helicopter technology.

The century opened with improvements already being made to the reciprocating piston internal combustion engine that had first been developed by Nicolas Otto in 1876. This provided a marginal engine for helicopters, one that would be improved over the years but that was never able to provide the power that rotary-wing aircraft required. Helicopters did indeed benefit from the improvements in piston engines in aircraft, but in the crucial rotary-wing flight envelope there were two critical areas that even the most powerful of the piston engines were unable to overcome. The first was their weight, which grew commensurately with their power and thus always affected the lifting capacity of the helicopter. The second was their characteristic power loss as available oxygen-laden air declined with altitude, increased temperature, or humidity. This sharply diminished their performance and added a third dimension to the demands of geography—the local density altitude.

A second defining improvement was the relatively efficient thrust-generating rotor as defined by Louis Bréguet in 1907. Bréguet used a lot of rotor blades (thirty-four, in sets of four) to obtain his thrust, but obtain it he did, rotating at 78 rpm and lifting about 1,300 pounds of gyrating mechanism for almost a minute. Over the course of the next few decades, there would come further improvements in blade airfoils and in the mechanisms that supplied power to them.

Lifting was not enough for a helicopter; it also needed to be able to hover, that delicate balance of flight in which the helicopter maintains a specified distance above the ground without any forward, aft, or lateral movement.

One of the difficulties encountered was the phenomenon of "ground effect." As aircraft approach within a wingspan of the surface of the ground, they create a cushion of air on the ground that results in a reduction in drag. Helicopters also experience this, within the length of one rotor blade, when attempting to take off or land. The pioneers found that "breaking the ground-effect barrier" was difficult to do and especially so when attempting to hover. In addition, flying out of ground effect usually introduced stability and control problems. Beginning helicopter pilots still find the same thing to be true.

The Petroczy-Karman-Zurovec PKZ 2 helicopter of 1918 managed to demonstrate hovering, although it was always tethered. This attempt, using counter-rotating propellers of about eighteen feet in length, demonstrated hovering at relatively low altitudes. Intended as a complement to observation balloons, the advanced thinking on the project included a ballistic parachute to save the observer if circumstances required.[1]

In 1924, the Argentine, Marquis Raul Pateras Pescara, developed cyclic and collective pitch. Cyclic control was obtained by changing the pitch angle of the blades, while the collective moved the rotors to allow forward movement. His system allowed the pilot to introduce changes in the flight controls that were transmitted to the rotor. To move forward or backward, or to roll to the left or the right, the angle of attack of the main rotor blades was altered during rotation to create different amounts of lift at different points. To increase or decrease the total lift, these changes were made at one time (collectively) to provide for acceleration, deceleration, ascent, or descent.

Pescara's system was refined over time, but a typical modern helicopter obtains the results he sought through three separate control inputs. These include the cyclic stick, the collective lever, and the anti-torque pedals, which control yaw. Their use is complicated by a lag in each of their effects that must be anticipated.

Pescara was also among the first to investigate whether or not a helicopter could autorotate, a problem that continued to puzzle some inventors through the first half of the century. He set a world record by flying eight-tenths of a kilometer at a height of six feet and a blinding speed of 8 mph.[2]

The next major step forward in the helicopter was made possible by the invention of the autogiro, a machine that also uses a rotary wing but in a completely different fashion. It was invented by Juan de la Cierva y Coroniú of Spain, who was inspired by the sad sight of the crash of an aircraft of his own design. The fatal accident made him determined to create an aircraft that would (as Pescara hoped) autorotate and thus perhaps be able to avoid disastrous mishaps.[3]

He named his invention the "autogyro," later, as noted, altered to the generic term "autogiro." In the course of his experimentation, Cierva discovered that the rotating blades produced unequal lift at different points of their rotation. The lift was not symmetrical, as the advancing blade generated more lift than the retreating blade. This caused the autogiro (as it would a helicopter) to tilt.

His solution was articulated hinges that allowed the blades to move around the hinge point. The retreating blade could flap downward as the advancing blade lifted up, balancing lift forces. He later added a drag hinge to the blade-mast junction. This allowed the blade to pivot forward or rearward slightly during rotation, relieving stress on the blade root. Cierva also fitted drag dampers to the hinges to avoid problems with ground resonance, creating the basis for the modern fully articulated rotor head of the helicopter. As with so many rotary-wing inventions, there were precedents for this, including efforts by Charles Renard in 1904.[4]

There is every possibility, even almost a certainty, that Cierva would have joined the ranks of successful helicopter pioneers but for the ironic tragedy of his death in a fixed-wing aircraft at age forty-one. Cierva perished in the crash of a Dutch Douglas DC-2 at London's famous Croydon airport, the very sort of accident that his goal of autorotation sought to avoid.

Just as Igor Sikorsky could never relinquish his dream of vertical flight, so did Louis Bréguet return to the field, establishing in 1932 a separate company, *Syndicat d'Etude du Gyroplane*. Three years of intense experimental work followed under the supervision of René Dorand, in which by adoption or reinvention they combined all of the development efforts listed above. The result was, as previously noted, the first successful flight of a helicopter on June 26, 1935—the Bréguet-Dorand *Gyroplane Laboratoire.*

Sadly, a combination of circumstances prevented the record-setting gyroplane from entering mass production. Yet it paved the way for an incredible generation of innovators who would bring the helicopter to a relatively refined state by the end of the 1950s, lacking only the great next step—the general introduction of the turbine engine. During this interval, the U.S. helicopter industry grew to become an important part of the transportation sector, exceeding $2.5 billion in sales by 1961, with more than seven thousand helicopters being produced. Helicopters were in production in many nations; the Soviet Union led with more than three thousand built.

The helicopter's role in changing modern war can be understood better by an examination of the state of the art of the industry producing the leading military helicopters prior to the introduction of the jet engine. Because there are far too many individual models to make a comprehensive survey, the following representative sampling will concentrate on those aircraft that had the greatest effect upon modern warfare, had large production runs, or possessed especially innovative characteristics. Doing so will reveal how rapidly the helicopter changed to meet a variety of needs, despite the inherent limits imposed by using a reciprocating engine as the power plant. It also allows us to avoid describing helicopters with performance that duplicates others in the field. The result is admittedly a greater focus on U.S.-built helicopters, but these are in fact the aircraft that had the greatest effect on modern warfare.

The United States: Igor Sikorsky and Frank Piasecki

The military services of the United States were blessed by a helicopter industry filled with innovative, risk-taking entrepreneurs who were far more focused on advancing the state of the art than on protecting the bottom line. Some of these leaders were astute businessmen operating independently. Some worked under the umbrella of a functioning aircraft

Widely recognized as the principal proponent of helicopters in the United States, Igor Sikorsky was beloved for his genius, persistence, and gentle personality. *(Courtesy of U.S. Army Museum, Fort Rucker)*

company's management. Some exposed themselves to more risk than a conservative board of directors might have wished but managed to persevere. Sadly, there were many other innovators who made excellent

contributions to the art but who lacked the business acumen or the necessary stroke of luck to stay in business.

Igor Ivanovich Sikorsky (1889-1972) embraced the helicopter as his first
aviation love in 1909 but in his experiments quickly recognized the daunting problems implicit in the discipline. He turned to the design of fixed-wing
aircraft with great success, designing, building, and test flying the first four-
engine aircraft in the world. This was followed by the large-scale production
of a capable four-engine bomber, also a first. In the post-Russian Revolution
years, he spent some time in France, then came to the United States, where
he founded the Sikorsky Aero Engineering Company. His aircraft were aeronautical, if not financial, successes and his firm became a subsidiary of United Aircraft and Transport Corporation (later United Aircraft) in 1929. There
he led the team that built a series of flying boats that were efficient from the
start and refined over time into also being beautiful.

Despite the difficult financial situation all aircraft companies found themselves in during the Great Depression, United Aircraft recognized Sikorsky's
genius and backed his abiding interest in vertical flight. He had remained *au
courant* with the rapid development of helicopter technology in the 1930s,
much of it thanks to Cierva's work with the autogiro. Sikorsky led a small
team that integrated his ideas and those developments into his third helicopter project, the VS-300 (Vought Sikorsky-300, the number deriving from
this being Sikorsky's third helicopter). This was the world's first successful
single-rotor, anti-torque, tail-rotor aircraft. Its precedent-shattering performance had been obtained by an endless process of refinement and modification that saw its configuration change, sometimes drastically, before it
matured into a workmanlike prototype. The task of rapidly changing the
aircraft was made easier by its simple steel-tube construction.

The VS-300 began a continuing stream of Sikorsky designs that became mainstays of many of the air forces of the world and created what
is perhaps the world's largest and best-known producer of helicopters.

His next development, the VS-316A, led directly to the mass production of the R-4, whose early exploits have been noted. Although following
the basic VS-300 layout, the R-4's 185-hp engine gave it a top speed of 74
mph and a range of 130 miles.

The next aircraft in the series was the Sikorsky R-5, which was given the factory designation of S-51. While it followed the basic R-4 formula, it was a cleaner design, larger and more powerful, with a 450-hp engine. This provided a 106-mph top speed and a range of 360 miles. Perhaps more important, the S-51/R-5 was designed to accomplish a far greater number of missions. It was also designed with more consideration for both production and maintenance concerns. In line with current systems of designation, the S-51 was known first as the R-5 and then the H-5 in the Air Force. The Navy called it the HO2S-1. (The inherent confusion of different United States military service designations for basically similar aircraft was resolved on September 18, 1962, when the Department of Defense announced a unified aircraft designation system. Originally based on USAF practice, the system has been revised, most recently in 1997.)

The S-51 was also built by Great Britain's Westland Aircraft Limited. This firm, which had produced some outstanding aircraft designs in the past, including the Lysander and Whirlwind, opted to discontinue fixed-wing production and concentrate on the helicopter. It charted a new course in British aeronautics by making a licensing agreement with Sikorsky to build the S-51 as the Dragonfly.

The combination of production experience and service demands next led Sikorsky to the first of its large helicopters, the S-55. Known also as the H-19 Chickasaw, it was immediately successful and led to a production run of 1,281 aircraft in the United States and another 547 built under license. (The policy of naming Army aircraft after Indian tribes, chiefs, or commonly used terms originated spontaneously as an attempt to give the new craft an easily remembered identity. It was eventually established officially by Army Regulation 70-28 of April 4, 1969. The names are selected in a sensitive manner, with the Bureau of Indian Affairs providing the choices. They are intended to convey a dignified message suggesting an aggressive spirit and military capability.)

First flown in November 1949, the S-55's large forward fuselage enclosed a radial engine in the 550-700-hp range, depending upon the model. While top speed remained moderate (112 mph), the range of 360 miles and the roughly 2,600-pound payload made it the first helicopter troop transport. It served nobly in conflicts in Korea, Malaysia, Indo-China, Algeria, and even Vietnam. More than thirty variants were built, including

One of the most widely used helicopters of its era, the Sikorsky H-19 met the requirements of many Western armed services. *(Courtesy of Zaur Eylanbekov [Foxbat])*

those constructed under license by Westland (as the Whirlwind) and by Mitsubishi and SNCAN. Different models of the S-55 were used by more than forty air forces. (As an aside, the author's first helicopter flight was in an H-19, and it ended with a crash—O.K., a very hard landing!—after an attempted autorotation at an altitude of about 6,500 feet.)

Sikorsky pushed the envelope with its S-56/CH-37 Mojave, which used two of the esteemed Pratt & Whitney R-2800 radial engines of 2,100-hp each, but the next very large production version was the S-58/H-34 Choctaw. A total of 2,261 were produced, 440 of which were built under license.[5]

The Choctaw, first flown on March 8, 1954, was slightly more streamlined than the S-55, and its bull-nose concealed a Wright R-1820 cyclone engine of 1,300-hp driving a four-blade rotor through a new transmission system. Generally larger, it was necessary to incorporate both folding rotors and a folding tail section into the design. Auto-hovering, a revolutionary new design capability that would become increasingly important over time, was available in the Navy version, the HSS-1 Seabat.[6] The Choctaw's speed was a far from blistering 122 mph, and its range was

The twin engine H-37 Mojave was one of the first to meet the visionary specifications of Lt. Gen. Victor Krulak, for it carried twenty-three troops into combat. *(Courtesy of U.S. Army Museum, Fort Rucker)*

With two powerful, reliable Pratt & Whitney R-2800 radial engines, the Sikorsky Model S-56 was used by the U.S. Army and Marine Corps. *(Courtesy of U.S. Army Museum, Fort Rucker)*

only 250 miles. However, its forte was lifting capacity, which gave it the versatility needed for the many roles assigned to it. The Army used it to transport as many as eighteen troops, and the Navy found room in it for the bulky anti-submarine warfare equipment then in use. The Marines received 603 as HUS-1s.[7] Their use in the recovery of "splashed-down" astronauts gave the Choctaw far more publicity than any previous type had enjoyed. The television series "M*A*S*H" would not debut until 1972, when it made the Bell H-13 the world's best-known helicopter.

Igor Sikorsky was a soft-spoken aristocrat, whose gentle manners reflected his deep spirituality. His industrial colleague and chief competitor, Frank Nicholas Piasecki, had a totally different personality but was driven by the same innovative fire that sustained Sikorsky.

Of the two, Piasecki had a far more daring entrepreneurial spirit, one that blossomed under adversity and was sustained by his relentless dedication to his chosen discipline. That choice had come not so much by inspiration but by study of challenging new disciplines. Piasecki studied mechanical engineering at the University of Pennsylvania and then transferred to New York University, from which he received a bachelor of science degree in 1940. In that same year, he and Harold Venzie formed, with other friends from the University of Pennsylvania, the PV Engineering Forum, the "PV" reflecting their initials. The Forum's task was to do what today would be called "thinking outside the box." Their goal was to conceive and execute a worthwhile, achievable, and profitable project. They selected the helicopter as the project.

The group's first design was the too-ambitious PV-1, which featured a fan blowing air as the anti-torque system. But on April 11, 1943, Piasecki personally flew the PV-2, which featured the first dynamically balanced rotor blades and a rigid tail rotor with a tension-torsion pitch-change system, along with full cyclic and collective rotor-pitch control. He thus became the second American to fly a successful helicopter, despite the fact that his total previous flying experience was about fourteen hours in a fixed-wing aircraft. Powered by a 90-hp Franklin engine, the PV-2 demonstrated very precise flight characteristics and was capable of 100 mph.

At this period of the helicopter's history, all potential users demanded more payload than was available from the Sikorsky line. The U.S. Navy set its first requirements at 1,800 pounds, perhaps five times the amount an R-5 could carry. The PV Forum had now acquired a small but capable engineering team that included the remarkable Elliot Daland, of Huff-Daland and Keystone Aircraft fame.

To meet the seemingly unreachable Navy requirement, Piasecki proposed a tandem configuration, with large rotors at the front and rear of a much larger helicopter. In Belgium in 1929 and 1930. a Russian-born engineer, Nicholas Florine, had conducted successful experiments with this arrangement. Florine was unable to overcome the engineering problems implicit in the design, but Piasecki did.

The ebullient Piasecki could speak colorfully and persuasively as a salesman but was also able to articulate his engineering ideas succinctly. He described his new design as follows:

> Two rotors permitted a low disk loading, yet allowed the blade spars to be within available material length. The tandem design provided a significant increase in center of gravity travel, thus negating the need for shifting ballast, as was necessary in single rotor helicopters. Since a tail rotor was not needed to counter the main rotor torque, more weight could be lifted with a given engine. It carried 10 men and reached 95 miles per hour without its fuselage covering. Critics predicted that downwash from the front rotor in forward flight would cause severe rear rotor turbulence, spoiling its control capability. This never happened when the proper differential collective pitch was added to the longitudinal control. Eighteen-hundred pound external loads (world's first log lift) were lifted with two, then one load line. An autorotative test was made with the interconnecting shaft between the rotors disengaged, as well as disengaging the engine.[8]

The forty-one-foot diameter tandem rotors also conferred a unique "bent" shape to the fuselage that earned the craft the immediate nickname "Flying Banana." The rear rotor was mounted higher than the front rotor to allow some overlap of rotation without interference. And as he relished telling, with the tandem rotors, no power was lost driving an anti-torque rotor.

Frank Piasecki attempted to sell the tandem concept to a Navy procurement official and was rebuffed, the official dismissive of his claim that an 1,800-pound payload was possible. His son, John Piasecki, now president of Piasecki Aviation Incorporated, tells with great enthusiasm of his father going to the office of a Coast Guard official and seeing on the wall a poster of a vintage Coast Guard rescue vessel that had oars fore and aft. He says that his father pointed to the poster and said, "There it is. You've already used a tandem arrangement." He then proceeded to convince his listener that his proposal was valid and received a contract on January 1, 1944, for the XHRP-X (the PV-3 in company terms).

Fourteen months later, on March 7, 1945, Piasecki, still with only a relatively few hours of flying time, made the first flight of the XHRP-X, called in the aviation slang of the time the "Dog Ship." Gordon Townson was the copilot. A production order for twenty HRP-1s, then the largest helicopter in the world, established Frank Piasecki as a serious contender for government business and set the firm on its way to prominence in the industry. The PV Engineering Forum was renamed the Piasecki Helicopter Corporation in 1946.

The Navy flew the HRP-1 through 1953 primarily for experimental purposes, its large load capacity suiting it for testing the helicopter as an antisubmarine warfare platform and heavy transport. The Marines immediately began testing the theories being developed along the lines General Geiger had suggested, including developing vertical assault tactics operating from the light carrier USS *Saipan* and the escort carrier USS *Palau*. The Coast Guard found that the helicopter could put new meaning into its classic motto, *Semper Paratus*—Always Prepared. Three HRP-1s were stationed at the Coast Guard Air Station near Elizabeth City, North Carolina.

There the 1st Coast Guard Helicopter Detachment (also called the Rotary Wing Development Unit) was led by Lt. Comdr. Frank A. Erickson, who, as noted, had flown the very first helicopter life-saving mission. Erickson taught his colleagues just how rigorous the environment was in which the helicopter was intended to operate. Their motto was a reflection of this: "No compromise. No rationalization. No hesitation. Fly the mission. Now!"

Under Erickson's leadership, the 1st Detachment experimented with landing on shipboard and open water. They introduced new rescue techniques, employing new hoists and improvising to create rescue baskets and harnesses. In spite of the still-limited speed and range of the HRP-1, the unit ranged over the country, landing onboard the icebreaker USCGC *Mackinaw* in Buffalo, New York, and testing flood-relief methods in St. Louis, Missouri. On December 31, 1948, an HRP-1 carried a fourteen-month-old baby girl suffering from pneumonia from Cape Hatteras to a hospital in Elizabeth City.[9]

The HRP-1 thus established itself as a reliable weight lifter and proved that its unusual tandem rotor arrangement offered benefits not yet obtainable in single-rotor helicopters. The aircraft was moderately improved in the HRP-2, which featured a more conventional-style aircraft semi-monocoque construction. Frank Piasecki's innovative nature expressed itself in a new manufacturing technique, as stretch milling process produced thinner skin and stiffened sections to keep weight down.

The firm edged toward serious mass-production efforts with the delivery of 339 of the Navy's HUP-1/2/3/4 Retriever and Army H-25 Army Mule. The prototype XHJP-1 made its first flight in October 1948, with William C. Knapp as the pilot. The most significant difference in appearance in the new aircraft was the positioning of the two rotors so that they overlapped. This required the aft rotor to be mounted appreciably higher than previous Piasecki practice.

A six-place, single-engine helicopter, powered by a Continental R-975 engine of 450 hp, the new aircraft had a top speed (108 mph) and range (360 miles) similar to its predecessors. Where it differed was its compact dimensions and degree of sophistication. Its size made it suitable for stowage on aircraft carriers without blade folding and on cruisers with blade folding. Among its more sophisticated features was the successful installation of an autopilot, which made instrument flight easier and hands-off hovering possible. It also featured a sling and hoist arrangement that permitted a live rescue without crew assistance.

The H-25 type had a twenty-year career, serving also with the Royal Canadian and French navies. It led directly to the famous H-21, the workhorse helicopter of its time.

Frank Piasecki had established a strong relationship with the Army, Navy, and Coast Guard. In 1949, the USAF ordered eighteen YH-21 aircraft to meet its requirement for a heavy-duty helicopter for the Military Air Transport Command's Rescue Service.

The H-21's first flight took place on April 11, 1952, leading to a total production quantity of 568. Its reliable Wright R-1820 engine (used by so many aircraft, including the Boeing B-17 and Douglas C-47) was de-rated to 1,425 hp. The H-21 had a maximum speed of 131 mph and service ceiling of 9,450 feet. It received the official USAF name of Workhorse, but the Army called it the Shawnee. The Army's version began production in 1953, with deliveries continuing through 1959.

Important corporate changes began during this same period. In 1956, Frank Piasecki resigned from the company he founded, which was renamed the Vertol Aircraft Corporation. He then founded the Piasecki Aircraft Corporation, which is today headed by his son, John. In 1960, Boeing acquired Vertol to form Boeing Vertol and in 1987 renamed the firm Boeing Helicopters.

Frank Piasecki's dynamic, forceful, and visionary character thus led directly to the formation of four important helicopter companies—Piasecki Helicopter Corporation, Vertol, Boeing Vertol, and Piasecki Aircraft Corporation.

In doing so, Piasecki set the stage for bringing reciprocating engine-powered heavy helicopters to aviation prominence, as his basic H-21 set world aviation records, became the first to cross the United States non-stop, and saw service in more than fifteen air forces around the world. The valiant H-21, including armed versions, fought in Algeria and Vietnam and led directly to the CH-46 and CH-47 turbine-powered aircraft that would serve well far into the future.

Frank Piasecki went with an entirely new series of innovative designs in a creative process that continued for the rest of his life. His son, John, speaks poignantly of how his father called only three days before his death to ask him to come over and discuss a new project he was developing for the Army.

Like Sikorsky, Piasecki was filled with enthusiasm for the challenge of vertical flight and never let the tedious requirements of ordinary business dim his vision.

Larry Bell's Arthur Young

It is hard to imagine two men with such different backgrounds, approaches to business, and even taste as Lawrence "Larry" D. Bell and Arthur Middleton

Young. Bell lacked an engineering degree, having earned his spurs the hard way, working first as a mechanic with early flyers on the exhibition circuit. These included his brother Grover and Lincoln Beachy, both of whom were killed in accidents. Bell learned his aircraft manufacturing skills under the tutelage of the often difficult Glenn L. Martin. Bell left when things with Martin did not work out as he wished, taking jobs that honed his salesman's skills until joining Reuben Fleet at Consolidated in 1928. His unique combination of pragmatic managerial skills, organizational genius, and empathetic personal manner that was developed over the previous fifteen years paid off, and Bell was soon a vice president and general manager.

When Buffalo's difficult weather convinced Fleet to move Consolidated to San Diego, Bell decided (as so many men who had worked for Martin did) to start his own aircraft company in 1935. It was the heart of the Depression, and European war clouds were only beginning to form, but Fleet was kind enough to sustain the new firm with contracts for parts. His salesman's instincts told Bell that, to break into the fighter business currently dominated by Curtiss and Seversky, he needed to have a spectacular product that would provoke the interest of the press. His first aircraft, the Bell Airacuda, did just that, despite the fact that its design was inherently flawed by its configuration, weight, and lack of sufficiently powerful engines. Nonetheless, the Airacuda, a twin-engine heavy fighter, excited the public and the Air Corps enough for his following design, the Bell P-39 Airacobra, to receive attention. The P-39 was also radical for the time, with a tricycle landing gear, car-type doors, and an engine mounted amidships, driving the propeller through a long driveshaft running between the pilot's legs. The Bell Aircraft Company would build thousands of P-39s and its successor, the P-63 Kingcobra, becoming well established in the industry.

Bell thus achieved success by gambling that his experience and contacts would allow him to break into a tough business. The P-39 also debuted at a time when the United States Army Air Corps was beginning to receive enough funds to experiment with new types.

In stark contrast, Arthur M. Young came from a patrician background. Born in France near Claude Monet's Giverny, where his father, Charles, was a distinguished artist and professor, Young grew up in an intellectual hothouse that encouraged his inquisitive mind.

There was sufficient wealth in the family for Arthur to graduate from Princeton in 1927, and then, instead of seeking employment, he launched a life in which he sought to combine philosophy and science in equal measure. He succeeded in this and later in life added a very healthy dose of mysticism as well.

The young graduate first assigned himself a too daunting task, devising a comprehensive theory of the universe, something that Larry Bell would not have puzzled over. Recognizing the implicit difficulty of this, he came to believe that in order to make a genuine contribution to philosophy, he would first have to demonstrate competence in a technical area. In 1928, he visited the U.S. Patent Office to determine what progress had been made in some areas of particular interest to him. From this he decided to tackle the creation of a practical helicopter.

Unlike most other investigators in the field, Young chose not to try to build a full-scale helicopter. Instead, he played to his strength as a modeler, building a long series of models to help him define and then solve many of the problems that discouraged or halted others in their pursuit of a full-size helicopter. He followed the field closely, attending symposiums in which such vertical-flight luminaries as Burke Wilford, Sikorsky, and others advanced their theories.

After more than a decade of building very precisely engineered models, he solved stability problems with a unique new system he patented. Young's design featured a two-blade rotor linked to a perpendicularly mounted stabilizer bar. Although simple in appearance, it was a very sophisticated concept, one that impels me, for accuracy's sake, to quote the expert Dr. J. Gordon Leishman directly. It was a "teetering rotor with a stabilizer bar," he says. "The bar had bob weights attached to each end and was directly linked to the rotor blades through the pitch control linkages. The idea was that if the rotor was disturbed in pitch or roll, the gyroscopic inertia of the bar could be used to introduce cyclic pitch into the main rotor system, increasing the effective damping and disturbance and giving stability to the rotor system."[11]

In 1941, Young, the model-making-philosopher-aristocrat, was introduced to Bell, the veteran aircraft maker, who was then embroiled in a vast expansion of his company at a time when war seemed imminent. It is to Bell's credit that he took time to listen to Young's ideas, witness his demonstration, and then look far enough into the future to recognize that it would behoove Bell Aircraft to have entrée into the civil commercial market after the war. If one excludes the manufacture of airliners, Bell was thus among the very few American aircraft companies to exploit both civilian and military markets successfully.

Bell supported Young with funding, scarce space in the factory, and the equally scarce engineering and mechanical support he needed. It was not always satisfactory to Young, who had expected that he would shortly be engaged in the full-scale production of helicopters. Instead, he continued his experiments on an adequate if not priority basis at Bell, building his first full-size helicopter, the Model 30, largely as he had built his models, using both theory and trial and error. The Model 30 was powered by a 165-hp Franklin engine, mounted vertically and driving both a thirty-two-foot rotor and a smaller anti-torque rotor at the end of the tail boom. The first flight was made on December 29, 1942. Two more prototypes were built, each incorporating the lessons learned from flight testing.

The Model 30 led directly to the stunningly successful Model 47, which made its first flight on December 8, 1945, and exactly four months later received the first ever Approved Type Certificate for a civilian helicopter. The Model 47 remained in continuous production at Bell until 1973. It was also manufactured by Agusta from 1954 to 1976. More than 5,600 were produced by Bell, Agusta, Kawasaki, and Westland. They were widely used for both civil and military purposes.

The Bell Helicopter Division was established in Dallas, Texas in 1951. Royal Little, a man with Larry Bell's energy and drive, founded a small textile firm in 1923, and under his leadership it became the giant conglomerate that purchased Bell Aerospace (which included Bell Helicopter) in 1960. The acquisition helped Bell remain in the forefront of the vertical-flight industry with a succession of excellent helicopters. It experimented for decades with the compound helicopter and now builds the world's only production tiltrotor aircraft, the V-22 Osprey.

After his success with the helicopter at Bell, Young returned to his joint philosophical-scientific pursuits and elaborated what some consider the first theory that unifies consciousness, physics, and the life sciences: the

Theory of Process. This is described in his two-volume work, *The Reflexive Universe* and *The Geometry of Meaning*. There were critics who felt that some of his pursuits, including his astrological interests, were so extreme as to undermine the intellectual standing of his work.

Larry Bell, unwell for many years, passed away in 1956, undoubtedly satisfied with his progress in aircraft and his choice of partners in pursuit of the helicopter. Young died in 1995, just four months short of his ninetieth birthday.

The two men—and the Model 47—firmly established Bell as a competitor in the helicopter business. The Model 47, an example of which was selected as an exhibit in the permanent collection of New York's Museum of Modern Art, would also be adaptable to the turbine engine and thus pave the way for Bell's entry into the jet age.

There were many other prominent contributors to the advancement of the helicopter in the United States, including outstanding individuals such as Stanley Hiller, Charles Kaman, and Frank Robinson and companies such as Hughes, McDonnell Douglas, and Boeing. However, for the purpose of this book, the most important contributions to the development of the piston-engine-powered helicopter, which effected the most significant changes in modern warfare, were made by the three giants named above.

The Soviet Union: Mikhail Leontyevich Mil and Nikolai Il'yich Kamov

As previously noted, the demand for the use of helicopters is greatly influenced by the nature of the terrain in which airlift is required. The vast extent of the Soviet Union (and its successor states) combined with the primitive nature of much of the country to create a genuine need for helicopters.

That same land also seems to nurture helicopter creativity, spawning not only Igor Sikorsky but many other pioneers, including Ivan P. Bratukhin, Nicholas K. Skrzhinsky, and two men who came to dominate their nation's helicopter industry—Mikhail Mil and Nikolai Kamov.

Unlike their American counterparts, both Mil and Kamov operated under a system where a surging entrepreneurial spirit was not the essential requirement for survival. In the Soviet Union, all weapon systems were assigned to design bureaus, and all major industries had specialized technological research institutes. At these institutions, a high degree of competence and a considerable amount of political finesse, rather than a quarterly bottom line, became the determining factors for an individual's success.

The design bureaus were designated by the names of men whose proven intellect, managerial skills, and finished product earned them that right. They included such giants as Andre Tupolev, Artem Mikoyan, Mikhail Gurevich, Sergei Ilyushin, and, in the field of helicopters, Mil and Kamov.

Although not faced with the starkly harsh competitive economic climate of the West, bureau chiefs were continually challenged to produce good products, and cost was always a consideration, if not necessarily the decisive factor. The design bureaus typically had a production capability to build and test prototypes. When a satisfactory prototype was developed, it could then be assigned to a state factory for mass production. The design bureau and the factory would cooperate on product improvement and the addition of new equipment. If national interests demanded it, the type could then be assigned to other factories (including those of satellite countries) for mass manufacture.

The system worked well for the Soviet Union, providing it with large numbers of first-class weapons, but it also had drawbacks that were increasingly important as weapons became both more sophisticated and more expensive. Inevitably cumbersome and bureaucratic, the system lacked the advantage a capitalist society had in spawning a host of small, experimental companies to advance technology at relatively low cost.

But for many decades, the design bureau system was a stellar performer, creating some of the world's best helicopters that were produced in great numbers.

Mikhail Leontyevich Mil was born in Siberia in 1909 and displayed an early interest in aviation. He was fortunate to be educated at the Siberian Technological Institute in Tomsk and the Don Polytechnical Institute in Novocherkassk. After graduating in 1931 he was employed at the famous TsAGI (Central Aero and Hydrodynamic Institute) in Moscow. Founded in 1918, it was the world's first institution to combine basic research in aero- and hydrodynamics with the design and testing of aircraft and the training of pilots.[12] By 1945 he had completed his doctorate and on December 12,

1947, was assigned to be head of the TsAGI Helicopter Lab, in effect the first Soviet helicopter-design bureau.

Mil had worked as an assistant to Nikolai Kamov at TsAGI, and there both men were involved in the development of the Soviet autogiro. During World War II, called by the Soviets the Great Patriotic War, Mil served as technical officer of an autogiro unit deployed as a part of the 163rd Fighter Regiment. Five A-7bis autogiros, designed by Kamov, were intended to drop propaganda leaflets and do reconnaissance on the Smolensk front. As in most military employments around the world, the autogiro did not prove to be very effective.[13]

Yet Mil's first helicopter drew heavily on Soviet experience with the autogiro. It was the first in the Soviet Union to go into mass production. The experimental versions were designated GM-1 (*Gelikopter* Mil) and suffered at least two fatal crashes during the test program. The Mi-1 prototype was first flown in September 1948, in the same single-rotor, anti-torque rotor configuration established by Sikorsky. In 1951, it debuted at the Tushino Air Display in Moscow, the traditional place for the public presentation of new Soviet hardware. As with so many "debuts" at Tushino, the Mi-1 was already in mass production and in use by many Soviet units.

The Mi-1 was very successful, being used by many nations in addition to those in the Soviet bloc. Thousands were produced in the U.S.S.R. until 1961 and Poland until 1965, when turbine jet engines began to enter wide use. Over their lifespan, the basic design was updated with new engines, rotors, and equipment, creating many Mi-1 variations to suit its many roles. These included training, rescue, observation, reconnaissance, liaison, postal services, and spraying crops. It received the NATO designation Hare. (The North Atlantic Treaty Organization created a system for naming aircraft and missiles of the Soviet Union and the People's Republic of China. Now called the Air Standardization Coordinating Committee, it designates aircraft with code names, the first letter of which indicates their type. Helicopters thus receive names beginning with H, without regard to the dignity of the aircraft or the feelings of the operator.)

Mil was successful in introducing helicopters powered by reciprocating engines. His next major success was the Mi-4, first flown in 1952 but not revealed to the public until a year later. Given the NATO name Hound-A, the Mi-4 was a larger helicopter, similar in size and shape to the Sikorsky S-55, with performance comparable to the S-58. It was very successful, being used in a wide variety of roles, and supplied not only to Soviet satellite countries but also many nonaligned nations. It was also produced in China, with a combined total of about 3,500 being built. Powered by Shvetsov ASh-82V two-row fourteen-cylinder air-cooled radial of 1,700 hp, the Mi-4 had a maximum speed of 127 mph, a range of 249 miles, and a relatively good absolute ceiling of almost 12,000 feet. It could carry up to fourteen armed troops or the equivalent in stores. Some versions were armed with machine guns and rockets.[14]

The Mi-1 was easily adapted to jet engines, leading to the Mi-2 and the pursuit of turbine power. Mil's onetime instructor and longtime rival, Nikolai Kamov, would stay with piston engines a bit longer.

Kamov was so much of an autogiro enthusiast that he flew in the backseat on the September 25, 1929, first flight of the KASKP-1 autogiro, which he co-designed with Nicholas K. Skrzhinsky. Born in 1902, he graduated in 1923 from the Tomsk Technological Institute, finding work at several Soviet aircraft factories. He worked at TsAGI from 1931 to 1948 and became interested in autogiros. When Soviet interest in autogiros declined, he made his first helicopter design, the Ka-8. This tiny aircraft was not practical, but it featured what became a signature trademark—the co-axial helicopter.[15]

More importantly, the Ka-8 caught the eye of one of the most influential leaders in the Soviet Union, the commander in chief of the Soviet Navy, Fleet Adm. Nikolai G. Kuznetsov. He saw value in the Ka-8 as a shipboard liaison helicopter and suggested that a design bureau be set up for Kamov with the special purpose of building it. This consolidated Kamov's standing and cemented a relationship with the Russian navy that continues to this day.

A series of small helicopters followed with the first major Kamov aircraft being the Ka-15, which was given the NATO designation Hen. Built in 1952, the two-seat Ka-15 served primarily agricultural purposes. It led to the Ka-18 Hog, a four-seater powered by an Ivchenko 255-hp radial engine.[16] First flown in 1955, about two hundred were built.

Like Mil, Kamov wished to use the turbine engine as a power plant. In the United States, Charles Kaman would be the first to fly a turbine-powered helicopter. As we will see in a following chapter, Kaman modified his successful K-225 helicopter with a Boeing 502 (YT-50) engine to create the world's first gas-turbine-powered helicopter, flying it on December 11, 1951. The Soviet helicopter-design bureaus would soon follow his lead.

In a manner that mirrored the comparative development of fighter aircraft, the United States and the Soviet Union each moved forward with helicopters, tailoring them to their differing doctrines, military needs, geographic considerations, and funding limitations. In both countries, the successful adaptation of the turbine jet engine to helicopters would open the door for more powerful, faster, and generally more sophisticated models that would profoundly shape not only modern warfare but, in some instances, national policies and politics. It transpired in the following manner.

The Introduction of the Turbine Engine to Helicopters

As has been noted previously, the first jet-powered helicopter was the *Weiner Neustadt Flugzeugwerke* WNF 342 using a conventional piston engine. Designed by a team led by the Austrian baron Friedrich von Doblhoff, the WNF 342 was impressive to see—and hear—in operation. Its 60-hp Walter Micron engine drove an Argus supercharger. The compressed air was injected with preheated fuel. This mixture of highly compressed air and fuel was routed through the three rotor blades. The tip of each rotor had a combustion chamber mounted, and the fuel-air mixture was ignited there. The resultant afterburner-like combustion expelled air and turned the rotors, generating lift.[17]

Time and the war ran out on the WNF 342, but in any case, its future was problematic because of the noise it generated and its high fuel consumption. In 1947, the McDonnell Aircraft Corporation built its XH-20 "Little Henry" helicopter on similar lines. The McDonnell aircraft had two ramjets mounted at each end of its two-bladed rotor and had a Garret Air Research gas turbine as power plant. The Little Henry, intended only as a demonstrator, was also hampered by noise and fuel-consumption problems.

The jet age came about largely through the visionary efforts of two giants in the industry, Sir Frank Whittle and Hans von Ohain. They had independently invented the jet engine for their respective countries, Great Britain and Germany. Ohain's engine was the first to fly. On August 27, 1939, the Heinkel He 178 took to the air with the great test pilot Erich Warsitz at the controls. Fortunately for the Allied nations, the potential of the jet engine was not immediately perceived by the Luftwaffe. While not entirely abandoned, jet-engine research languished while the Germans made their first easy conquests. The head of the Luftwaffe, *Reichsmarschall* Hermann Goering, became so confident of victory that in the spring of 1940 he ordered all projects that would not be ready for action within a year to be cancelled. If Goering had possessed even a shade of competence, he might have allocated relatively small funds to the pursuit of the metallurgy needed for the heat and stress of jet engines. Had he done so, Germany might well have had jet fighters in service by the fall of 1943, when their use might have been decisive in preventing or delaying the Allied invasion of Europe.

Whittle's long years of tenacious, farsighted effort were vindicated on May 15, 1941, with the flight of Great Britain's first jet, the Gloster E28/39, piloted by Flight Lt. Gerry Sayer. The inventor witnessed the flight and later spoke frequently of his intense satisfaction with his success after being treated so badly so often by the Air Ministry.

It just happened that the initial production jet engines in both countries produced power at about the levels of contemporary first-line piston engines. There were two great differences. First, jet engines were at the beginning of their development, while piston engines (and their propellers) had advanced to the point that any further improvements called for vastly increased complexity and cost. Second, jet engines were smaller dimensionally and weighed much less than piston engines of comparable power.

Aircraft manufacturers thus turned with alacrity to the possibilities of the jet engine, and they were not disappointed by the deluge of products from engine manufacturers. Jet engines rapidly improved in all ways, including power output, reliability, ease of maintenance, and fuel consumption. For fighter and bomber airframes to achieve their potential for higher performance, the jet engine became the only candidate.

The jet engine took longer to become suitable for other types, including passenger airliners, general aviation aircraft, and helicopters. The first jet-powered passenger plane to reach production, the de Havilland Comet, made its first flight on July 27, 1949. The Comet provided high-speed transportation, but catastrophic structural flaws in its fuselage design adversely affected its career. It remained for the landmark Boeing 367-80, which made its first flight on July 15, 1954, and was the prototype of the 707, to begin the new age of jet passenger planes.

Nowhere was the potential of and the need for turbine jet engines more obvious than in the helicopter industry. A Kaman K-225 modified with a Boeing 502 (YT-50) became the world's first gas-turbine-powered helicopter. The next Kaman design, the K-240 of 1950, was designated HTK-1 by the Navy. It was powered by two of the Boeing 502-2 gas turbines and used the signature Kaman two-bladed, contra-rotating, intermeshing rotors. It was the first twin-turbine-powered helicopter and led ultimately to the workhorse HH-43B Husky.[18]

The Boeing engine originated as part of a turbine-generator unit (a concept from the very earliest days of the turbine) that was used in Navy wooden-hull boats to furnish the enormous electrical power required for magnetic minesweeping. Almost inadvertently, Boeing found itself in the small turbine engine business, building some 2,500 before turning to other interests in 1968. A 1947 model of the 502 could put out 200 brake horsepower (bhp) on a continuous basis at a weight of 625 pounds. It could also use inexpensive fuel such as kerosene or "Jet-A."

The Boeing 502 was a free-turbine engine. Power was transmitted much as is done in the torque converter of a modern automobile's automatic transmission. The main part of the engine is the gas generator. It pushes air (rather than fluid as in an automobile transmission) to turn the output turbine and the output shaft.

In very general terms there are two divisions in the world of turboprop and turboshaft engines. One is the single-shaft engine and the other the two-shaft engine. (These are also called fixed-shaft and free-turbine engines.) The free turbine is more adaptable to the helicopter, responding readily to the changes in power demanded to drive the extraordinary rotating mass of the rotor through the transmission's reduction gearing. In turn, the fixed-shaft engine is more suitable to the airplane because of the different forces demanded by a turning propeller compared to a rotor.

As time progressed and more modern engines were introduced, such as the Canadian Pratt & Whitney PT-6, free-turbine engines were applied to helicopters with success.

Intensive research on both sides of the Atlantic soon led to the introduction of turbine-powered helicopters in earnest. In France, Sud-Ouest had the most success to date with tip-jet driven rotors. The third in a series, the Sud-Ouest S.O. 1100 Ariel III used a Turboméca Arrius turbine compressor unit and led to the very successful Sud-Ouest S.O. 1221 Djinn. Powered by a Turboméca Palouste IV turbo-compressor, 178 were built. It was used in several roles but was soon superseded by the vastly influential Sud-Ouest (Aerospatiale) Alouette (Lark) II.

The Alouette I had been powered by a conventional piston engine, but the Alouette II used a 530-shaft horsepower Turboméca Astazou IIA turboshaft engine and soon revolutionized the helicopter scene. First flown on March 12, 1955, the Alouette II was eventually used by 126 civil and military operators in forty-six countries, with more than 1,300 being built.[19] The famous French test pilot and author Jean Boulet set a series of new helicopter altitude records with the type, reaching higher than 36,000 feet on June 13, 1955.

The fame of the Alouette II thus spread swiftly, aided by the prototype's spectacular performance in July 1956. While testing it in the Vallot Mountain area of the Alps, its pilots learned that a mountain climber was dying from a heart attack suffered at an altitude of more than thirteen thousand feet. The Alouette II, operating at the extreme limits of its capability, rescued the man and swiftly transported him to a hospital, saving his life, the first of many in the Alouette's spectacular career.

In the United States, one of the great German pioneers in jet-engine history was paving the way for the conversion of Bell's wildly successful Model 47 into the even more promising turbine-jet-powered Model 204.

Born on January 20, 1900, in Schladming, Austria, Anselm Franz received his doctor of aeronautical engineering degree from the Technical University in Berlin. He joined the Junkers Engine Development Division in 1936 and in 1939 was assigned the task of developing the 109-004 turbojet engine. He created the first successful axial-flow turbojet engine, which developed a static thrust rating of 2,000 pounds and weighed

1,640 pounds. It was flown in the prototype Messerschmitt Me 262 jet fighter only thirty months after the design started. Some six thousand of the engines were built, and the Me 262 was the world's first operational jet fighter. In interviews later in life, Franz insisted that he had intended his 004 engine as a "breadboard model" from which to learn and was aghast when it was ordered into full-scale production. It also powered the world's first jet bomber, the Arado Ar 234, the forward-swept wing Junkers Ju 287 bomber, and the now much-celebrated Horton IX flying wing fighter. The Russians copied the design to get them started in the jet-engine business, building large numbers as the RD-10.

After the war, as a part of the famous Operation PAPERCLIP, Dr. Franz, a cheerful, even ebullient man, worked at Wright Patterson Air Force Base in Dayton, consulting for the Air Force with major engine manufacturers. He determined that there was a niche market for a gas turbine engine of medium power that would be suitable for a wide number of uses, including in helicopters and even tanks. With the approval of the Air Force in 1950, he proposed an engine of this type to the Lycoming Division of the Avco Corporation. Lycoming was well known for its piston engines, and Franz's engine suited their plan for entering the turbojet engine field. In 1952, Franz's T53 turboshaft engine won a competition that would have profound effects upon the helicopter.[20]

A 1955 U.S. Army requirement for a utility helicopter challenged Bell to modify its Model 47 to accept the smaller, more powerful Lycoming T53 turboshaft engine. The result was an outstanding helicopter that would form the basis for many Bell designs over the next forty years. The prototype, the Bell XH-40, first flew on October 20, 1956, ironically the very day Larry Bell passed away. The Army dubbed the production version the UH-1 Iroquois, with deliveries starting in 1959. (The UH-1 designation led inevitably to the cherished "Huey" nickname, even after the 1962 tri-service designation scheme forced a change to UH-1.)

Although initially intended to serve as an aerial ambulance, it was seen from the start that the new aircraft would have multiple uses. In its intended role, however, the extensive use of the Huey in MEDEVAC service showed how important immediate medical attention was to wounded soldiers. In the Vietnam War, the mortality rate was less than 1 per 100 casualties, whereas

The helicopter is a "maid of all work" and the Bell Huey did every possible job in combat that a rotary-wing aircraft could do. *(Courtesy of U.S. Army Museum, Fort Rucker)*

in Korea the rate was 2 per 100 and in World War II it was 4 per 100.

The combination of the Bell airframe and the jet turbine was wildly successful. It led to a series of variants, with an ultimate total of 8,983 of the type being built over the years, serving in every imaginable role.[21] The full sliding doors on each side of the fuselage and the large interior available because of the fuselage top-mounting of the small engine added to the outstanding performance. Franz's turboshaft engine made the jet helicopter eminently practical because of its reduced fuel consumption, lower maintenance and operating costs, and high power relative to its light weight. With a more powerful 1,400-shaft horsepower version of the Lycoming T53, a Bell Model 204B2 had a maximum speed of 127 mph, a hovering ceiling in ground effect of 15,200 feet, and a range of 238 miles.

The "stretch" in the basic Bell design is shown in the extraordinary number of models and variants that it engendered. The UH-1 came in two major versions, the Models 204 and 205. The Model 204 UH-1 sub-variants included the UH-1A, B, C, E, F, K, L, M, and P versions, each attuned to specific requirements. In a similar way, the Model 205 sub-variants included the UH-1D, H, U, V, and X. Further developments included the twin-engine Model 212 (UH-1N) and Model 412 (a 212 with four-bladed rotor) and the UH-1Y. The ultimate development to date of the series includes the Marine Corps Super Cobras, the AH-W, and the AH-1Z.

Perhaps even more important, the success of the Iroquois led to a series of improved designs that kept Bell firmly established in both combat and civil roles. As we will see, not least among these developments was the Bell Model 209 HueyCobra and Sea Cobra.

The jet engine was embraced with equal enthusiasm in the Soviet Union. Just as in the United States, development of the jet engine had benefited from both German and British efforts. The Klimov design bureau had long roots, extending back to 1912, when it was founded to repair Renault automobiles. The work was later expanded to include the repair of Sikorsky and other aircraft. It became a formal construction bureau in 1933 under Vladimir Klimov, with the task of manufacturing a version of the Hispano-Suiza 12Y engine. Klimov bureau engines were used in more than half of the Soviet aircraft produced during World War II.[22]

The bureau enjoyed a tremendous technical advance in 1946 when it received fifty-five Rolls-Royce Nene turbojet engines, courtesy of a British Labor government. Klimov's deputy, Sergei P. Isotov, led the design and construction of helicopter engines and gearboxes.

The Soviet Mil Mi-2 first flew in 1961 and was powered by two PZL GTD-350 turboshaft engines, each of 400-shaft horsepower. The Mi-2 was directly comparable to the Bell UH-1 in terms of influence and numbers built, as well as in general configuration, dimensions, and performance.

The Kamov design bureau also entered the jet arena in 1961 with the Ka-25 Hormone, using two Glushenkov GTD-3F turboshaft engines mounted above the cabin. Designed by Valentine Andrevevich Glushenkov, and produced at the Omsk Engine Design Bureau named for P. I. Baranov, the GTD-3F engine was first tested in 1960. Some 460 of the Ka-25s were built.

The turbine engine opened up the world for helicopter manufacture and the development of many different types specially adapted for warfare. It soon developed that, for perhaps the only time in the history of rotary-wing aircraft, the right helicopters became available for the right war and thus provided a perfect combat storm.

This change of pace would not occur at once, for the early days of the Vietnam War saw the United States, unprepared for war as usual, forced to rely on the piston-engine helicopters of the past.

Chapter Four

Early Days in Vietnam

While the finest measure of how the helicopter has changed modern warfare is its SAR efforts, the cruelest measure can be found in the staggering casualty figures its crews have suffered. In the Vietnam War, 11,827 helicopters were committed to action. Of these, no fewer than 5,086, a cruel 43 percent, were lost. A total of 4,906 persons participating in helicopter flight were killed, 2,202 of them pilots.[1]

In the plainest terms, this means that the United States found the services of the helicopter to be so valuable in fighting the war in Vietnam that it was willing to accept losses that would have been considered catastrophic in any previous war in any service. In the most intense periods of the World War II air war over Germany, such as the 1943 raids on Schweinfurt and Regensburg, loss rates approaching 20 percent were considered ruinous. They forced a change in strategy and doctrine from the idea that the unescorted bomber formation could always get through to the target to the demand for adequate fighter escorts. In Vietnam, there was no alternative to the helicopter, given the mission assigned by Washington and the infamous rules of engagement that were imposed upon the forces conducting the battles. It came down to this: use the helicopters, take the losses, and keep on fighting. Fortunately there was an unwritten corollary to this, for with the "keep on fighting," the troops who were involved kept on learning, coming up with new tactics to minimize casualties to the greatest extent possible.[2]

There was another telling sign that, however unpalatable it might have been, helicopters were indispensable in Vietnam. Helicopters were slower than available fixed-wing aircraft, much more vulnerable to damage, and far more difficult to maintain and operate—but it became indisputable they could do what was required. Only the longed-for dream of a "Sky Cavalry" could effectively engage the combined efforts of the regular North Vietnamese forces and their surrogates, the Viet Cong. Without any fixed combat lines and given the combination of terrain and vegetation, only the helicopter could land, provide the aerial firepower, resupply, reinforce, and, finally, evacuate the troops who did the fighting.

The grievous helicopter losses noted above would have been far worse had it not been for two factors, one from before the Vietnam War and one current with that war. The helicopter had received some minimal development funding prior to 1961, for it was seen as a possible counter to the Red Tide of Soviet tanks that were certain to be encountered in a war in Europe. Then, when the Vietnam War began to escalate, a fortunate and entirely unplanned confluence of new technology and massive funding suddenly became available.

It must be emphasized that this crisis in Vietnam was a self-inflicted political wound, engineered by articulate politicians led by Secretary of Defense Robert S. McNamara. Unfortunately, he and his so-called "bright young men" were not very bright. They had absolutely no concept of the psychology of the North Vietnamese nor of how determined, capable, and enduring they were. It was their absurd Pentagon and White House notion that this battle-hardened opponent, victors over the French and imbued with a stern ideology, could be "taught lessons" that would "win their hearts and minds" by the application of "graduated firepower." In other words, the White House group intended to apply American forces the way a careful gardener might water a flowerbed: gradually. In doing so, the United States would presumably not alarm the Republic of China, the Soviet Union, or the Vietnamese people. The North Vietnamese leaders were supposed to react to this gradual application of power by realizing that they could not defeat the United States militarily. Thus, in the McNamara scenario, this clique of tough, seasoned infighters would suddenly change their ways, forfeit their long-held goal of reunifying their nation, and surrender in the fight in which they had prevailed for decades. Only blind intellectual arrogance could have subscribed to the idea—but of that commodity there was plenty.

But undoubtedly the worst mistake of all the many made by these same bright young politicians was that they opted not to use airpower to its fullest extent and chose instead to fight a land war in Southeast Asia. This foolish strategy was bitterly opposed by almost every military advisor of the time with the exception of Gen. Maxwell D. Taylor (see *Dereliction of Duty,* by H. R. McMaster). The magnitude of McNamara's mistake was comparable to Hitler's decision to invade the Soviet Union in 1941.

In 1964, the Joint Chiefs of Staff prepared a list of high-value targets that could have removed the North Vietnamese capability to make war. There has been much confusion and no little balderdash written about the famed May 22, 1964, Joint Chiefs of Staff (JCS) 99-Target List. Most of it claims that the paper was based on a World War II psychology of destroying an industrial base—of which North Vietnam had little. Instead, the thirty highest priority targets included airfields to ensure air superiority, critically important command and control targets, and lines of communication. It was a means of swiftly taking out the small but tough and well-trained North Vietnamese military machine in a thoroughly professional manner. As the following table indicates, the list was thoughtfully chosen for the given circumstances:[3]

JCS Working Group 99-Target List for North Vietnam, May 22, 1964

Target Sets	Category A	Category B	Category C	Total
Airfields	5	3	-	8
Lines of Communication	4	1	-	5
Military Barracks	6	9	-	15
Ammunition Dumps	2	7	-	9
Military Headquarters	8	3	-	11
Supply Dumps	5	14	-	19

Military Training Center	-	1	-	1
Storage Areas	-	4	-	4
Ports	-	7	-	7
Storage Depot	-	1	-	1
Railroad/ Highway Bridges	-	9	-	9
Railroad Yard/ Shop Complexes	-	2	-	2
Chemical Plant	-	-	1	1
Iron/Steel Plant	-	-	1	1
Radio Broadcast Facilities	-	-	2	2
Thermal Power Plant	-	-	1	1
Machine Tool Factory	-	-	1	1
Industrial Plant (other)	-	-	2	2
TOTAL	30	61	8	99

The effectiveness of this list was proven in Operation LINEBACKER II of December 1972, when at last, long after the North Vietnamese had been able to build the most formidable integrated air defense system in history, that airpower was applied in full measure. When Operation LINEBACKER II was completed, its 729 B-52 sorties had reduced the North Vietnamese to a state of abject helplessness, as its leaders later confirmed.

Unfortunately, the lack of American insight into North Vietnamese psychology extended to that of the Republic of China and the Soviet Union. Both states were pleased to see the United States involved in a war that drained its attention and resources, but neither state held the People's Republic of Vietnam in high esteem. China indeed invaded North Vietnam in February 1979—and got a bloody nose for its efforts. In the following decade, China deployed as many as thirty-eight divisions along the border with Vietnam; thirty-two North Vietnamese divisions were stationed there to oppose them. The Soviets, preoccupied with their own problems of decline, were detached, happy to have the United States engaged but certainly unwilling to become directly involved themselves.

Having forfeited the proper application of airpower, the American decision to fight on land in Southeast Asia made it inevitable that the war would be long, which also meant that it would lose the support of the American public. This very long duration of the war also permitted the helicopter to effect its changes in the conduct of modern warfare in three stages. Helicopter operations began routinely, with training of South Vietnamese forces in late 1961 and then, in 1962, the ferrying of those forces to battle areas. Over time, as the war grew and more forces were committed, the helicopter as a major weapon was raised to a peak of lethal efficiency. This was done through necessity, invention, and the development of new techniques. Finally, the modern combat helicopter emerged, with new tactics, specialized versions (reconnaissance, transport, assault, and attack), and new weapons (missiles and mini-guns).

Despite the fact that this significant step forward in the rotary-wing revolution enabled the American military to dominate completely every battlefield in which it engaged, the role of the helicopter ultimately symbolized for too many the last, saddest scene of any war, anywhere. That scene was the evacuation by helicopter of personnel from a rooftop in

Saigon on April 29, 1975. After years of glorious victories in combat, the helicopter became the symbol of defeat.

Some facts were ignored. The first of these was that it was the largest helicopter evacuation in history. Two USMC squadrons, ten USAF helicopters, and other helicopters provided by Air America carried out 1,373 Americans and 5,595 foreign nationals. The second is that the symbolic photo was taken more than two years after Secretary of State Henry Kissinger threw our longtime ally South Vietnam under the unforgiving North Vietnamese bus at the 1973 Paris peace talks. The psychological effects of this symbol permeated Army thinking and, as we shall see, helped place a lower priority on the helicopter, particularly in funds allocated for R&D.

This dramatic fourteen-year arc of combat, from training to battlefield dominance to being the symbol of a lost cause, saw the helicopter provided with all the necessary constituents to change modern warfare. Everything came together, including the dreams of longtime proponents such as the Army's great Lt. Gen. James M. "Jumping Jim" Gavin. The necessary technology was available in the form of powerful new helicopters equipped with excellent weaponry. These helicopters were employed with newly developed tactics, based on sound, if hard–learned, doctrine, and manned by well-trained, skillful crews and maintenance personnel. To understand just how much was achieved, and by whom, it is useful to look back at some of the pioneers of airmobile warfare and analyze the growth of the concept during the Vietnam War. To place it in context, it must be noted that many of the lessons learned, and indeed, the very primacy of the helicopter itself, would be diluted by a change of focus after 1975. Then there was once again a preoccupation with the vision of thousands of Soviet tanks storming through Germany's Fulda Gap. And although the need for helicopters would be seen, that vision would not provide the same spur to helicopter development as had occurred prior to and during the Vietnam War.

The Army Pioneers

The soldiers who had combat experience with "vertical envelopment" using parachutes and gliders were, by the 1960s, in important positions in the U.S. Army. No one was more influential than the highly decorated

General Gavin (March 22, 1907-February 23, 1990), who endeared himself by personally leading his paratroopers into action. He also gained fame for his early support of desegregated service. And given our current submissive military climate, it is particularly noteworthy that he left the Army in 1958 to register his protest against the massive nuclear retaliation policy of John Foster Dulles. Gavin was also an outspoken opponent of the escalation of the war in Vietnam.

Gavin gave expression to the need for improved helicopter tactics in an article entitled "Cavalry and I Don't Mean Horses," in the April 1954 issue of *Harper's* magazine. In it, he decried the fact that the Army proponents of armor and other heavy vehicles had virtually eliminated the classic concept of cavalry as swift-moving, hard-hitting force as employed by Jeb Stuart in the Civil War. He cited the total lack of adequate U.S. Army cavalry as a principal reason for the early successes of the North Korean forces in their June 1950 invasion of South Korea. Further, he described how, when the time came for the breakout from the Pusan Perimeter, the U.S. forces were hampered by inadequate Army planning. The emphasis that had been placed on heavy armor resulted in a force limited by the speed in which a combined tank-truck column could operate on the few available roads. The United States had inexplicably chosen to fight an "Asiatic army on Asian terms."[4]

Gavin called for an integration of the armored forces with airborne forces to impart a much more mobile and aggressive character to our forces. He saw, as the Marine general Geiger had done, that any enemy in modern warfare would have to use a well-dispersed defensive system to guard against nuclear attacks. This meant that there was a great need to be able to concentrate U.S. forces rapidly in their attack and that the future was already at hand in the development of "assault transports, light utility planes, helicopters and convertiplanes."[5] (It should be noted that the current Bell Boeing V-22 Osprey fits the description of this last category.) These new, highly mobile vehicles were intended to airlift soldiers armed with automatic weapons, anti-tank weapons, and lightweight reconnaissance vehicles that also carried anti-tank weapons.

As is the case with all great generals, Gavin had an excellent eye for talent and selected then Col. but future Lt. Gen. John J. Tolson III as his director of doctrine and combat development. He also tasked Tolson to envision hypothetical cavalry organizations using the helicopter. This chapter owes much to Tolson's subsequent writing about his efforts.

Although it was not immediately perceived as such, a milestone event took place on September 1, 1954, when the Army Aviation Center and School was established at Fort Rucker, Alabama under the command of Brig. Gen. Carl I. Hutton. This coincided with the creation of the Aviation Staff Division in the Pentagon, headed by the influential Maj. Gen. Hamilton H. Howze. Both Hutton and Howze would have decisive effect upon helicopter employment in the future. One of the first senior officers to become an Army aviator, Howze graduated from West Point in 1930. He saw combat in World War II, commanded the 82d Airborne Division from January 2, 1958, to June 13, 1959, and was considered a "cavalry trooper" in all assignments.

The enormous superiority of the Soviet Union in manpower, artillery, and especially their excellent tanks presented the U.S. Army and its NATO allies with an almost insuperable problem. The most obvious solution was a counterforce of artillery and close-air support that could halt the tanks in their tracks. But there remained the long argument between the Army and the USAF on the type, degree, and amount of close-air support to be rendered. The Army was dissatisfied with the USAF's promises and—although it was less politic to say so—its performance. This relationship revolved around the definition or interpretation of a single word, as so many arguments do. That word was "support," which the Air Force felt it supplied but which the Army felt was neither "close" enough nor "immediate" enough. As existing Department of Defense agreements precluded the Army from employing capable fixed-wing aircraft for the task, it turned to helicopters to fill the gap.

As a way out of the definition dilemma, Fort Rucker's commander, General Hutton (called by many the "father of the armed helicopter"), took it upon himself to test the concept of the armed anti-tank helicopter at Fort Rucker.[6] He selected Col. Jay D. Vanderpool, who was not an aviator, to direct what was initially referred to as the Armed Helicopter Mobile Task Force.

Vanderpool chose a team of bright, enthusiastic crewmembers to assemble their own versions of an armed Bell H-13. They did so by salvaging parts from junkyards and begging for others from the manufacturers. The work had to be done in secrecy in order to avoid an Air Force assertion that it was in violation of existing agreements on roles and missions.

The small team, working in a clandestine fashion, tested everything from the beloved .50-caliber machine gun to 80-mm rockets and demonstrated them to other Army units. The Air Force eventually found out and objected to the experiments. Surprisingly, there was dissent within the Army as well, where some considered the minute amount of funds being spent on the experiments wasteful and a diversion from other needs.

Fairness requires that something nice be said about Secretary McNamara here. With Pres. John F. Kennedy, he witnessed a demonstration by Vanderpool's team at Fort Benning, Georgia and was favorably impressed. Further, McNamara later directed the Army to rethink its concepts of aerial mobility, giving a real boost to the concept. On April 19, 1962, McNamara sent the secretary of the Army a memorandum stating that he felt the Army's program was far too conservative and demanding that airmobile systems be substituted for traditional ground systems in order to achieve a maximum mobility.

The field demonstrations and McNamara's encouragement caused enthusiasm for the armed helicopter to become widespread and to have assured backing at the top. The Army went on the warpath, beginning development of machine-gun installation kits for not only the Bell OH-13 Sioux but also the Piasecki (later Vertol) CH-21 Shawnee and Sikorsky CH-34 Choctaw.

One fortunate aspect of the admittedly limited and specialized support of the armed helicopter was that there were few bureaucratic obstacles. The principal leaders of the movement, Gen. Bruce C. Clarke, General Hutton, and others, recognized that the new weapon required specialized training and doctrine. The Army Aircraft Requirements Board was established under the direction of Lt. Gen. Gordon B. Rogers and included as a member General Howze. Both Rogers and Howze would have their boards named for them and both would have profound effect upon the future of the helicopter.

The eponymous Rogers Board, established January 15, 1960, made many important decisions, but two stand out—one for its engineering prescience and the other as a potential political bargaining chip. The board recommended the procurement of the turbine-powered Bell UH-1 helicopter. This was a giant step that resulted in the provision of the most numerous and most suitable helicopters in Army history. The board also recommended acquisition of a fixed-wing transport that later became known as the de Havilland (Canada) C-7A Caribou.

The Bell helicopter became the heart of the Army force, serving in quantity for decades to come. The Caribou was ultimately transferred to the Air Force (always mindful of the weight and role of Army fixed-wing aircraft) in exchange for a virtually unlimited development of the helicopter as a close-air support and assault weapon. It was a worthwhile trade, for while the Air Force had no problem in using the C-7A to support the Army with troops and supplies, it still had not adopted the Army's outlook on the issue of close-air support.

In October 1962, the Cuban Missile Crisis caused the Kennedy administration to prepare for both conventional and nuclear warfare. General Howze had proposed some innovative techniques in war-fighting to the Rogers Board, but these were considered outside that board's purview and shelved. Secretary McNamara was made aware of the ideas and ordered that another board be formed under Howze to consider his proposals, setting a September 1, 1962, deadline.

The resultant Army Tactical Mobility Requirements Board (the Howze Board) was intended to recommend the equipment and organization required for the Army for the next thirteen years, a formidable assignment but one that Howze was entirely ready for. As a totally unexpected side benefit, the board's findings were so compelling that the Air Force recognized that it must respond to the demand for meaningful (in Army terms) close-air support. It did so both formally, requesting additional fighter-bomber wings from Congress, and informally, listening more attentively to requests from Army colleagues.

The Howze Board emphasized the requirement for a tank-killing air-to-surface missile and, more importantly, the development of helicopters designed from the start for the assault and attack tasks. Heretofore all armor, arms, and equipment had been bolt-on additions, largely scavenged from salvage yards. The Howze Board articulated what was needed: a brand-new helicopter designed with the specific tasks in mind.

There were good reasons for this. An off-the-shelf helicopter such as the OH-13 could be fitted with a machine-gun installation that seemed to work well. However, though the additional stresses imposed by the armament on the airframe did not reveal themselves instantly, they resulted in accidents and extra maintenance over time.

The most important recommendation from the Howze Board was the creation of two new types of units—an airmobile division and an air transport brigade.[7] These were the "Sky Cavalry" that Gavin had called for so long before, and they were revolutionary.

Another great name in helicopter history came into play with the organization of the 11th Air Assault Division (Test) under Maj. Gen. Harry W. O. Kinnard, one of the many airborne veterans who saw the value of helicopters. Outside of the Army, he is most famous for a suggestion he made while a lieutenant colonel, fighting with the 101st Airborne Division in the Battle of the Bulge in 1944. Under a white flag of truce, the Germans had sent an invitation for the Americans to surrender or be destroyed by an artillery barrage. Upon receipt of the note, the 101st's acting commander, Brig. Gen. Anthony C. McAuliffe, had commented informally, "Us surrender? Aw nuts." McAuliffe considered the matter and then asked his staff what he should say in his formal reply. Kinnard declared, "That first remark of yours would be hard to beat." And so it was that the note went out as follows: "To the German Commander, Nuts! The American Commander." While it initially puzzled the Germans, it made history for McAuliffe and the 101st Airborne Division.

Inside the Army, however, Kinnard is most famous for conducting the test work of the 11th Air Assault Division (Test) so well that it was renamed the 1st Cavalry Division (Airmobile). Kinnard had his pick of personnel and gave them both the responsibility and the authority they needed.

The 1st Cav developed the techniques and tactics that were subsequently adopted throughout the Army. Many of these are used to this day, including the employment of night vision equipment, forward refueling systems, and, perhaps most important, the combined arms-helicopter team so essential for special forces operations.[8]

It thus transpired that a happy mix of outstanding personnel, adequate funding, and a forward-thinking helicopter industry became available in the early stages of the Vietnam War. This combination produced exceptional helicopters and crews and was successful in a long series of battles, even as both the military and political complexion of the Vietnam War changed over time. It is perhaps the only instance in which all of the stars in the helicopter galaxy were in alignment. It had not happened in the past and has not occurred since. We can only hope that it will occur again in the future.

The Vietnam War: The Helicopter Changes Modern Warfare

It should be noted here that two divisions, the 1st Cavalry Division (Airmobile) and later the 101st Airborne (Mobile), generally receive the most recognition from the media and even from historians. They have become so identified with the term "Sky Cavalry" that other elements of the Army's huge investment in helicopters, such as the 1st Aviation Brigade to which the two Air Cav units belonged, are often glossed over. It is true that the 1st Cav and the 101st sometimes had more specialized missions than other units, but in general terms the varied tasks of aerial assault, transport of troops, resupply of materials, and MEDEVAC were performed by all the units under almost all conditions. From the point of view of history, achievements of the 1st Cav and 101st represent the heights of the helicopter's effect on modern warfare. Another huge element—the very widespread use of helicopters by other Army units—represents the depth and breadth of that change.

In truth, the helicopter came of age in all the armed services during the Vietnam War. For the purposes of this book, emphasis will be placed on the U.S. Army's use of the helicopter. This is not intended as a slight to any of the tremendous accomplishments of the helicopter in the Marines, USAF, or Navy but to avoid repeating basically similar development scenarios. The same goes for foreign helicopters, which, while effective, did not of themselves affect the conduct of modern warfare.

The helicopter's influence on warfare in Vietnam is generally recognized as profound. However, time and distance have obscured how difficult this was for the helicopter to achieve, having to combat not only the enemy but the terrain, climate, service apathy, intra- and inter-service

A Huey retrieves a Cessna O-1 for repair, one of the many unusual jobs never envisaged by helicopter pioneers. *(Courtesy of U.S. Army Museum, Fort Rucker)*

rivalry, and perhaps worst of all, an appallingly short-sighted array of rules of engagement that stifled efforts. The following short review of the history of the Vietnam War will provide a greater understanding of just how extraordinary the helicopter's achievements in Vietnam were.

The "First Vietnam War" began with the seven-and-a-half-year-long conflict between France and the "League for the Independence of Vietnam," usually called the Viet Minh. The latter organization was headed by Hồ Chí Minh, a communist revolutionary who from 1941 had led the fight against both the Vichy French and the Japanese army of occupation. He proclaimed the existence of the Democratic Republic of Vietnam on September 2, 1945. While his proclamation was not recognized by any foreign government, it set the stage for the removal of France from its colonial empire in Indochina (Vietnam, Laos, and Cambodia). Vietnam became essentially a bargaining chip between France and Nationalist China. It eventually became a reluctant part of the

French Union, a faltering attempt by the French to convert their cruel and largely ineffective colonial system of governance to one modeled on the British Commonwealth.

Despite enormous aid from the United States, the disheartened French fought a long losing war with the North Vietnamese. The most dramatic event was France's great spring 1954 defeat at Dien Bien Phu, which underlined both the inadequate French planning and the tenacity of the North Vietnamese. The French had fortified a base deep in a valley in northwestern Vietnam, believing that they could thus cut the Viet Minh supply lines. Instead, Gen. Võ Nguyên Giáp, hardly believing that the French would concede the high ground to him, rapidly occupied the heights surrounding the encampment. With massive amounts of manual labor, he brought in the heavy artillery, which ultimately pounded the French to the point that they could be defeated in hand-to-hand combat. The valiant French attempts at aerial resupply were inadequate. Their desperate—indeed, humiliating—request for unilateral intervention by the United States (including the use of nuclear weapons if necessary) was refused by Pres. Dwight D. Eisenhower.

Attacking repeatedly over the next two months, the North Vietnamese overran the French camp on May 7. It was the first time in history that a guerilla movement had matured to the point that it could defeat a Western-style army in a conventional battle. (Such victories often have unintended consequences. Fourteen years later, the triumph at Dien Bien Phu would lead General Giáp to a gross error in judgment trying to achieve the same results at Khe Sanh.)

Hostilities terminated with the Geneva Agreement of July 21, 1954, which ended French rule in Indochina. Laos and Cambodia immediately became independent nations, but as with Korea, Vietnam was divided. Hồ Chí Minh became prime minister of a communist North Vietnam. South Vietnam was ruled initially by the former emperor Bao Dai, who was replaced by Ngo Dinh Diem in October 1955. (Diem, a passionate anti-communist, ruled as president until 1963. Then, sadly and ill advisedly, his assassination was sanctioned by the United States and carried out by his internal political enemies.)

Hồ Chí Minh always intended to unite Vietnam into a single nation, and to this end he fostered the growth of anti-government forces in the south. These forces, consisting of Vietnamese citizens sympathetic to his cause and trained regular soldiers, were infiltrated into the south. They often came via what the North Vietnamese designated the Truong Son Road, which the Americans later called the "Hồ Chí Minh Trail." This was a massive engineering project, built up over the years, consisting of roads, routes, rivers, and trails that led from North Vietnam to South Vietnam via Laos and Cambodia.[9]

This supply jugular vein was just one of the characteristics that distinguished the problems the French faced in Vietnam from their problems in Algeria. The existing infrastructure in the latter allowed the French to seal off Algeria from its neighbors, denying the FNL access to supplies from other countries. In Vietnam, the French, and later the Americans, were faced with the intractable problem of a never-ending stream of people from North Vietnam and supplies from China and the Soviet Union coursing down the Hồ Chí Minh Trail into South Vietnam.

There were significant geographic and environmental differences as well. Algeria is the eleventh largest country in area in the world, with roughly 920,000 square miles. All of Vietnam, North and South, had only about 128,000 square miles. And while Algeria's area was shaped over a roughly equidistant-sided pentagon, South Vietnam was a slender sliver of a nation about 620 miles long and only 120 miles across at its widest point.

The environments of each country were also vastly different. In Algeria, the heat, sandstorms, and higher elevations took their toll on the performance of the piston-engine-powered helicopters. In South Vietnam, the heat remained a problem along with high humidity (especially during the tough monsoon seasons), while the elevations ranged from the sea-level plains of the southern delta region to the almost mile-high mountains of the Central Highland area.

This then was the trifecta that challenged the helicopter's ability to change modern warfare: geography, environment, and the experienced guerilla tactics of the enemy. The challenge was met slowly over time. It was possible only through the combined efforts of the military using helicopters and the industry providing them.

The United States was concerned that if North Vietnam conquered

South Vietnam and established a single communist nation, other nations in the area, including Laos, Cambodia, and Thailand, would subsequently fall to communist rule (the "domino effect"). President Eisenhower supported training the South Vietnamese Army and supplying equipment. Future president but then-senator John F. Kennedy backed Eisenhower's position while adding Burma, India, Japan, and the Philippines to the list of at-risk nations.

The initial American helicopters arrived in Vietnam in March 1958, in the form of Sikorsky H-19s for the 1st Helicopter Squadron of the Vietnamese Air Force (VNAF). These supplemented a handful of Alouette III helicopters left behind by the French. The H-19s were later replaced by Sikorsky CH-34s. While both were useful, neither had major effect on the war.

As president, Kennedy offered further support to the South Vietnamese, including authorizing Operation FARM GATE. Originally intended to train the South Vietnamese to develop a counter-insurgency capability, it became a combat arm of its own. In October 1961, members of the USAF's 4400th Combat Crew Training Squadron (CCTS) were sent to train South Vietnamese aircrews to fly the North American T-28, Douglas C-47, and Douglas B-26 aircraft. The American crews were soon flying combat missions.

The rotary-wing war was still a backwater, even though other helicopters were introduced in small numbers over time, including the Air America Sikorsky UH-34Ds. However, the U.S. Army's Piasecki CH-21s were the leading edge of what became the air-mobility wedge, as they arrived at Tan Son Nhut Air Base near Saigon in December 1961. The first group consisted of only thirty-three CH-21 Shawnees, plus some Bell OH-13E Sioux, but it was the start of a monumental effort. For its part, the United States Air Force began combat aircrew recovery with the Kaman HH-43B, reinstituting, then vastly expanding, a great tradition of selfless service.[10] The growth in Army aircraft numbers would be astounding, rising from this paltry start to more than twelve thousand in 1970.[11]

The helicopter was a far more reliable instrument than it had been in Korea, but it was still for the most part not battle tested, especially in the more ambitious roles that the Army now demanded of it. The American helicopter industry responded nobly to each and all of the services.

The introduction of the turbine engine allowed industry to provide new types of helicopters to match not only the nation's needs but its learning processes. Bell played on its strengths, delivering a seemingly endless series of variations of the UH-1 as transports, cargo planes, and gunships. The modified UH-1 did so well in its gunship role that it was developed into the AH-1G "HueyCobra." Now made by Boeing Vertol, the CH-47A was also tried in many roles, including that of gunship, and became particularly useful for its ability to airlift artillery to the battlefield. It was supplemented by the Boeing CH-46 Sea Knight, which encountered a spate of maintenance- and modification-related accidents before becoming a Marine workhorse. Sikorsky expanded on its basic themes with its Model S-61 (H-3, HH-3E, etc.) and S-65 (H-53). It also built, in smaller numbers, the S-64 (H-54 Tarhe) flying crane.

Before these more modern aircraft arrived in quantity, the Army continued to rely on its standard piston-engine types to learn how to fight what today would be called a "low-intensity" conflict. (It certainly never seemed to be low intensity to those doing the fighting in the flaming jungle battlefronts.) The learning process was shared by friend and foe. It took place from 1961 through 1965, as the intensity of the conflict increased. The real acceleration began after the August 1964 "Gulf of Tonkin Incident," which led to Congress providing Pres. Lyndon B. Johnson the authority to use military force in the Southeast Asian war. In the process, everyone involved—U.S., South Vietnamese, and Allied forces, the North Vietnamese, and their Viet Cong surrogates—proved to be both good teachers and apt pupils.

As the war ratcheted forward, the amateur strategists in Washington were generally overmatched by battle-hardened pragmatists in Hanoi. One unintended result of this was that the helicopter assumed an ever-greater importance and had an ever-greater effect. The ongoing conflict was not then termed asymmetric warfare, but so it was, with the mobility advantage imparted by the helicopter the key factor in a continuing series of U.S. military successes.

Unfortunately for the United States and the people of South Vietnam, there was also asymmetry on the political side. The policies initiated during the Kennedy administration under the influence of Secretary

The use of jet engines for helicopters enabled giants such as this Sikorsky H-54 Tarhe to be built. *(Courtesy of U.S. Army Museum, Fort Rucker)*

McNamara were perpetuated during the Johnson administration. These and a hostile, misunderstanding media would present the successor Nixon administration with an incontrovertible fact. A new generation of Americans, vastly misinformed by a strangely myopic media, believed that the war was lost and clamored for peace, no matter how lacking in dignity and honor. In that era, the Congress tended to listen to the public's demands; it does not seem to do so anymore.

From the earliest days of the helicopter war, the highly professional North Vietnamese army leaders saw that even the limited initial deployment of U.S. helicopters in support of the South Vietnamese was a formidable threat. An enemy pamphlet captured around November 16, 1962, clearly laid out both the advantages and disadvantages of using helicopters. The pamphlet noted that, until then, the helicopters had inflicted heavier losses than they had suffered but that proper tactics could reverse this trend. It was evident that the conclusions grew from more than just observations, indicating input from Soviet advisors. The pamphlet stated that the helicopter possessed the inherent disadvantage of being flown low and slow, making it vulnerable to ground fire, and that it required a great deal of maintenance.[12]

The Piasecki-derived CH-21s had been fitted with light armament, but they proved to be extremely vulnerable to enemy fire. In mid-1962 the Army created the Utility Tactical Transport Helicopter Company, using Bell UH-1 helicopters to protect the CH-21s in their transport role. Equipped with two .30-caliber machine guns and sixteen 2.75 rocket launchers, the sturdier, swifter Iroquois helicopters became the object of a study by the Army Concept Team, headed by Brig. Gen. Edward L. Rowny. A veteran of the Howze Board, Rowny was tasked with examining not only helicopters but also fixed-wing aircraft, armor, logistics, and communications. It was no accident that these were all special constituents of air mobility.

The study revealed that escorting transport helicopters was relatively safe during the en route or "safe altitude" phase. Things became more difficult during the approach phase, for the helicopters descended to "nap-of-the-earth" heights to achieve surprise. However, it was in the deadly, dangerous LZ that the suppressive fire of the escorting armed Hueys was the most valuable.

Sadly, even in the midst of combat, the ugly specter of roles and missions inhibited progress. The Air Force attempted to limit armed helicopter escort to "one minute of fire before the transport helicopters landed and one minute after the last departed," a clearly unworkable, faintly ludicrous stipulation.[13]

Perhaps the most encouraging development during this period was that a close working relationship was established between the Utility Tactical Transport Helicopter Company and the Marine H-34s operating in the I Corps sector. The Marines came to regard the armed Hueys as essential for their operations, supplementing or replacing fixed-wing aircraft such as the modified North American T-28s on which they had initially relied.[14] The Marines would subsequently make good use of their own versions of armed helicopters.

The armed version of Bell's doughty UH-1Bs weighed so much that

In all air forces around the world, the glory gained by helicopter crews depends upon the quality of maintenance that the unsung ground personnel provides. *(Courtesy of U.S. Army Museum, Fort Rucker)*

they could no longer carry troops or cargo. Weight was not the only problem, as the armament increased drag and lowered its maximum speed to eighty knots, slower than the transports it was escorting. It was clear that improvements were needed, and Bell worked hard to provide them.

Diplomacy, limited numbers, and experience all dictated that, from December 1961 until mid-1965, airmobile efforts were primarily in support of the Army of the Republic of Vietnam (ARVN). The Viet Cong were quick to respond to these efforts, stimulating development of new techniques by the ARVN. It was quickly seen that no one method would serve for long without the Viet Cong finding a countermeasure. As experience was gathered, a standard "Eagle Flight" formation was developed to provide the necessary flexibility in tactics. In deference to South Vietnamese sensibilities, the command and control Huey carried both the U.S.

Army aviation commander and his ARVN troop-commander counterpart on board. Five armed Hueys provided fire support to eleven troop-carrying helicopters, with a single UH-1B designated for the MEDEVAC role. These early Eagle Flights, singly or in combination, were a forecast of the later large-scale airmobile assaults, with their mix of surprise, power, and flexibility. (The Marines also conducted Eagle Flight operations with the H-34s of HMM-362.)[15]

The rough schooling the ARVN and their U.S. Army advisors were receiving in Vietnam was corroborated by extensive studies undertaken in the United States during the same period. On January 7, 1963, an initial plan was issued for the organization, training, and testing of an air assault division and an air transport brigade at Fort Benning. Named the 11th Air Assault Division (Test), the unit ultimately had 3,023 personnel, including 191 officers and 187 warrant officers. However, it had only 154 aircraft, 25 of them fixed wing.

Establishment of the 1st Cavalry Division (Airmobile)

The combined results of these tests and the operations in Vietnam led to the establishment of the iconic 1st Cavalry Division (Airmobile), uniting the resources of the Second Infantry Division and the 11th Air Assault Division (Test). There was a mad scramble to obtain the necessary personnel and equipment, but an advance party arrived in the Republic of Vietnam on August 25, 1965. It immediately proceeded to An Khe, where it began a new tradition.[16]

The 1st Cavalry initially fielded four types of helicopters, the Bell OH-13S Sioux, Bell UH-1 Iroquois, as transport (UH-1D) and gunship (UH-1B), and Boeing Vertol CH-47 Chinook. Each was significantly improved over time, and each received many specialized modifications. They were supported by other Army helicopters, including several Sikorsky models.

While the innovation was continual, the new techniques were impressive, and the results of both in-country combat and state-side testing were congruent, the Army possessed pitifully few assets. Between December 1961 and early 1965, the U.S. Army had only 248 helicopters in Vietnam, clearly not enough to perform the duties demanded of them. Few of them

Few helicopters have seen form follow function so evidently as the Boeing CH-47 Chinook, with its boxlike fuselage and easy access. *(Courtesy of U.S. Army Museum, Fort Rucker)*

were yet of desired combat standard. This disgraceful situation was the direct result of failure in previous years to invest in the necessary research, development, and production called for by the visionaries of the helicopter movement. Virtually the same condition exists today. Incredibly, current production funding is almost exclusively devoted to tired designs from many years ago. Many advances in both U.S. and foreign helicopter design are being ignored in the name of economy. As a result, the richest country in the world, the United States, is fighting twenty-first-century wars with twentieth-century helicopters. Unless there are radical changes, it may well be doing so in the twenty-second century.

From 1961 to 1965, the North Vietnamese and Viet Cong were learning much from the American efforts to use helicopters to profitably employ South Vietnamese troops. A study group headed by Brig. Gen. John Norton found that the Viet Cong had already introduced heavier machine guns (12.7-mm) into South Vietnam and planned to employ 37-mm cannon. The Viet Cong had also begun locating their anti-aircraft weapons to control the most desirable LZs, which, in effect, forced ARVN troops to use LZs preferred by the Viet Cong. The Viet Cong were also mustering larger forces, to the degree that they were expected soon to be using division-size units. Air-mobile forces would find that their work was cut out for them.

Fighting for a Place from Which to Fight

While the massive logistic and training efforts involved in moving the 15,787 personnel, 1,600 vehicles, and 470 aircraft (including 435 helicopters) of the nascent 1st Cavalry Division (Airmobile) were under way, an adequate base for the division had to be secured in the An Khe area by the 1st Brigade, 101st Airborne Division.[17] It did so in Operation HIGHLAND, conducted over a forty-day period beginning on August 22, 1965, with no fewer than eight airmobile assaults combined with extensive ground operations. Movement along Route 19 to An Khe was hotly contested by the enemy, and helicopters would soon become the preferred mode of transport. The first elements of the 1st Cavalry Division, an advance party of about 1,000 men, arrived in An Khe on August 27. The month of September was spent in the housecleaning necessary to establish an operating base in an area where the vegetation sometimes reached jungle proportions. The clean new area, quite literally chopped into existence, was promptly given the sobriquet "Golf Course" and became the largest operation of its type in the world.

The North Vietnamese, while well aware of the arrival of the 1st Cav, were proceeding with plans of their own. The North Vietnamese government recognized that the intervention of the United States on behalf of South Vietnam was drastically altering the efforts of the Viet Cong. That intervention had in fact reversed a trend, and the Viet Cong were experiencing a decline in recruitment. The local populace was also less willing to provide supplies and intelligence material. This forced a weighty decision at the highest levels of the North Vietnamese government. In the past, the North Vietnamese Army had been carefully husbanded, being used only in situations in which it could prevail without much risk. To offset the decline in the value of the Viet Cong efforts, the North Vietnamese were forced to accept the risks implicit in regular warfare by planning a drive from Duc Co on the Cambodian border through Pleiku to Qui Nhon on the South China Sea.[18]

With their customary disregard for national boundaries, they assembled three regular North Vietnamese Army regiments—the 32d, 33d, and 66th—in Cambodia and in the western part of Pleiku Province. These units began a series of attacks on October 19, 1965, and the commander of Military Assistance Command, Vietnam (MACV), Gen. William C. Westmoreland, ordered Maj. Gen. H. W. O. Kinnard, commanding the 1st Cavalry, to "seek out and destroy" the enemy.[19] This became the first genuine test of air mobility against a capable enemy adept at disappearing into the hostile greenery of Vietnam and then suddenly reappearing in strength at another point.

Beginning on October 27, the 1st Cav proved itself in a thirty-five-day struggle that became known as the Battle of the Ia Drang Valley. A contact on November 1 resulted in the capture of a large enemy hospital site, with seventy-eight enemy being killed and fifty-seven captured. Five men were killed in the 1st Cav, with fifteen wounded. It was the start of an important facet of the long war of mutual attrition, one in which the mobility and firepower provided by helicopters was the only means by which American and ARVN forces could contest the actions of the North Vietnamese.

By November 26, this first bitter campaign was over. Rather than splitting South Vietnam in half, the enemy had withdrawn its forces into Cambodian sanctuaries for redeployment. The hard-fought battles resulted in the loss of 151 troopers from the 1st Cav, with four more missing in action. Almost two thousand enemy troops were known to be dead. Over the thirty-five days of the campaign, more than thirteen thousand tons of cargo was airlifted to the troops in the field. Entire infantry battalions and artillery batteries were flown to crucial hotspots, and some 2,700 refugees were moved to safety. The CH-47 Chinook distinguished itself in a style that made Frank Piasecki proud during these massive movements over otherwise impassable terrain.

A number of hard facts came immediately to light. The enemy was resourceful, and its "bear-hug" or "belt-buckle to belt-buckle" style of close combat was difficult to counter from the air. As well supplied as the 1st Cav was for this one campaign, it was painfully evident that there were far too few resources to conduct the war throughout Vietnam in the same way. Offsetting this was the general consensus that the helicopters were providing air mobility at a previously undreamed of level of skill. Very few deficiencies in air mobility were mentioned in after-action reports. Many of the reports fervently praised the Iroquois pilots and crews, who ignored intense enemy fire to land or pick up troops. Four helicopters were lost, but three were recovered, two of them flown out beneath CH-47 Chinooks. This was an encouraging if perhaps misleading portent for the future.

Lessons abounded. The vertical lift and descent capability of helicopters was foiled by the jungle canopy. The 1st Brigade, 101st Airborne developed techniques in which engineer LZ teams rappelled into the jungle, with their gear and armament following them down. The big chainsaws used to fell trees were often choked by the dense growth of vines. Clearing a landing pad was hard, backbreaking work. (Later, thermo-baric "Daisy Cutter" bombs were sometimes used for this purpose.) When the situation did not allow time to create a clearing, it was virtually impossible to evacuate wounded personnel. The available winch systems were inadequate for lifting stretchers, so new equipment had to be invented, produced, and installed.

The "chop-chop-chop" sound of an approaching helicopter is music to the ears of soldiers in need. *(Courtesy of U.S. Army Museum, Fort Rucker)*

As 1966 loomed, the faulty planning of the past became evident. There were too few helicopters available and too few pilots to fly them. As usual, the slack was taken up by the force in place and resulted in both crews and helicopters being vastly and unfairly overworked. This is exactly the same condition in which the armed forces of the United States have been since 2000, in which they find themselves today, and which they will experience for the next decade at a minimum.

Then, as now, the dearth of helicopters and crews meant that operations had to be structured around the forces that were available rather than the enemy threat. This meant not only more exposure to risk but, worse, forfeiting a sometimes irrecoverable initiative to the enemy.

While the 1st Cav had a just sufficient number of organic aircraft, a decision was made to divide and prorate the remaining available resources. This meant that the ARVN divisions, the single division from the Republic of Korea, the U.S. Army's 1st Division, the 173rd Airborne Brigade, and the

1st Brigade of the 101st Airborne Division were provided with only one assault helicopter company per brigade in the II, III, and IV Corps Tactical Zones. The Marines provided aviation support in the I Corps Tactical Zone. This paucity of equipment was exacerbated by the variety of terrain and vegetation that was encountered by individual army units. It was found, for example, that the CH-21s were better employed in the flat Mekong Delta region than in the highlands. Operations in these vastly different areas also resulted in marked differences in the command and control procedures that were being improvised as the war progressed. All of this pointed toward the dreaded concept of "centralization," which went against the desire to provide control at the lowest possible level of command. With centralization came the specter of a new "Army Air Corps," with all the complications this would bring within the Army itself and most certainly within the United States Air Force.[20]

Despite these misgivings, the 1st Aviation Brigade was formed on March 1, 1966, with 11,000 officers and men and 850 aircraft. It was the first aviation brigade in Army history and consisted of eight battalions in the 12th and 17th groups. The forty-three companies of the Brigade were located from Hue in the North to Soc Trang in the South.

A veteran of the 11th Air Assault Division (Test) planning and testing, Brig. Gen. George P. Seneff was named commander. He managed to finesse all of the inherent problems by seeing that his organization coordinated and trained the non-organic Army aviation elements while ensuring that the ground commander retained operational control of the available airpower. Under Seneff and his successors, the 1st Aviation Brigade would grow into the Army's largest aviation unit and would successfully engage the enemy all over South Vietnam. It would work in concert with the 1st Cav, and later the 101st Airborne Division (Mobile), for the rest of the war.

Seneff's mode of operation proved to be a brilliant solution to what might have been a crippling dilemma. It also set the stage for one of the most crucial agreements ever reached by the Army and the Air Force, one that would have a major impact on the helicopter's role in changing modern warfare.

This April 6, 1966, agreement, between USAF chief of staff Gen. John P. McConnell and Army chief of staff Gen. Harold K. Johnson, in effect eliminated the Army's interest in heavier fixed-wing aircraft but established its rights to develop a vastly expanded capability in rotary-wing aircraft. The Air Force agreed to relinquish all claims on rotary-wing aircraft designed for intra-theater movement, fire support, supply, and resupply of Army forces. This gave a virtual *carte blanche* for backers of Army vertical-lift capabilities. (The Air Force did retain its right to use helicopters in the critically important CSAR role.) The USAF agreed to supply the Army's needs for transport in fixed-wing aircraft such as the de Havilland Buffalo and Caribou and Fairchild C-123.

By the end of 1966, the Army had learned much from its many engagements. First of all, it was evident that a static defense, in the style of the French *quadrillage* efforts in Algeria, had no application in Vietnam. Even though American strength had risen to nearly four hundred thousand, there was no way to occupy the territory of South Vietnam. The development of helicopter air-assault methods provided the American forces with a successful means of making a surprise attack en masse. In some respects this was frustrating, for attacks had to be repeated in areas where the enemy had been defeated several times before, due to the fact that the helicopter troops did not occupy the battlefield after the battle. On the other hand, the initiative remained for the most part in the hands of the American and South Vietnamese forces.

Since World War I, American forces have always been known for their reliance on excellent artillery fire, delivered accurately and in volume. Helicopters soon provided a means of getting large-caliber (first 105-mm and then 155-mm) artillery pieces into positions in the field to support ground operations. These were supplemented by a totally unexpected development, the formation of aerial artillery battalions. These were made up of thirty-six Iroquois helicopters armed with 2.75-inch aerial rockets. The Hueys were much easier to keep supplied with ammunition—they could fly to base and pick up their own. The artillery in the field, however, was limited to the ammunition that could be flown in by helicopters.[21]

The Marine Experience

The experience of the U.S. Marines with helicopters in Vietnam generally paralleled that of the Army. The Marine Corps diligently continued its

The dependable Boeing CH-46E Sea Knight can carry up to twenty-five fully equipped troops. *(Courtesy U.S. Marine Corps History Office)*

enthusiastic adoption of the helicopter as a natural element of its power. Its viewpoint was far more single-minded than that of the Army, and although it too had austere budgets, it prepared better for the future, thanks once again to Robert E. Hogaboom. His board expanded on the concept of the helicopter as an element of amphibious operations by introducing the LPH, the helicopter carrier ship. One of the board's recommendations led to the conversion of four veteran aircraft carriers, the *Thetis Bay, Boxer, Princeton,* and *Valley Forge,* to accommodate helicopters. These were eventually equipped with the Bell UH-1E "Huey," the Vertol CH-46 Sea Knight, and the much larger Sikorsky CH-53A Sea Stallion. However, through 1962 the Marines possessed only 341 helicopters, most of them the veteran piston engine-powered Sikorsky CH-34 Choctaws.

This shortage of equipment forced the Marines to "ease into" the Vietnam War. One of its most important developments was its own version of the armed helicopter, the Bell UH-1E, armed with four M-60

More than two thousand Sikorsky H-34 Choctaws were built, and they served in air forces around the world. *(Courtesy of U.S. Army Museum, Fort Rucker)*

machine guns and 2.75-inch rocket pods. These arrived at Da Nang, South Vietnam, in May 1965.

Again as with the Army, the Marines were desperately short of helicopter pilots. A draconian order to switch 500 fixed-wing aviators to fly helicopters was of course obeyed, but with some initial misgivings on the part of the pilots. As is usually the case in combat situations, the misgivings gave way to enthusiasm as the potential for the helicopter was unveiled.[22] The Marines would make particularly effective use of the development of the Huey into the Cobra, creating their own twin-engine version, which set the pattern for future operations.

The changes in helicopter performance and utilization after 1967 were remarkable and perhaps mark the most significant effect that the helicopter has had on modern warfare.

Chapter Five

Vietnam, 1967:
Changes in Scale, Tactics, and Results

Three years after the Gulf of Tonkin resolution, American forces had reached new levels of professionalism. Adequate amounts of equipment were available, tactics had been developed and, with them, the necessary skills for combating an able enemy. Planners were taught to think not about distances in miles but in minutes of flight, a crucial difference.

The capabilities of the enemy had also increased, but it was now evident that the North Vietnamese could no longer expect to win a military victory over the Allied forces. "Without the helicopter, the United States would be subject to defeat just as the French had been earlier," General Howze, now retired, observed on a visit to South Vietnam. "The French succumbed to the 'tactics of ambush.'" The helicopter allowed the U.S. not only to avoid ambushes and resolve them when encountered but also to establish them. General Howze went on to predict that the developments in Vietnam would have applications for a European battlefield.[1]

The increase in American strength, and perhaps even more, the startling increase in its operational tempo, made it seem possible that the long succession of successful engagements using the strategy of attrition might be the key to the United States and its allies winning the war.

To this end, a series of more ambitious operations were executed, all designed to defeat the North Vietnamese in the field and to root out the considerable infrastructure created for the Viet Cong over the years. In just one year, the 1st Aviation Brigade had grown to more than two thousand aircraft. Its 25,000 personnel were located in four groups of sixteen battalions and three Air Cavalry Squadrons. It was thus able to deploy the greatest numbers of helicopters yet in Operation JUNCTION CITY.

The attack began on February 22, 1967, against enemy bases north of Tay Ninh City, near the Cambodian border.

The operation began with the first major use of paratroopers in Vietnam. The paratroopers of the 173rd Airborne Brigade were ordered to seize enough ground to make possible the landing of a much larger force from helicopters. The operation illustrated how well a combined operation could work, with the paratroopers of the 173rd Airborne Brigade joining a large mixed force composed of South Vietnamese units, the 1st and 25th Infantry Divisions, the 11th Armored Cavalry Regiment, the 196th Light Infantry Brigade, and elements of the 4th and 9th Infantry Divisions. Fifteen assault helicopter units provided almost 250 helicopters to fly more than 5,100 fully equipped troops into the combat zone, with gunships providing cover at eight different LZs. Surprise was achieved and the force build-up went on as planned. After the first two days, the North Vietnamese began to react with more vigor, and there was heavy fighting through mid-May, when the last of some 2,700 enemy were killed.

One outcome of this was the discovery that paratroop operations took too long. They were limited by the time lag their execution necessarily imposed. Airborne forces carried by helicopters could respond to most threats far more quickly than paratroops could.

Operation JUNCTION CITY confirmed a favorable shift in the Americans' initiative. Instead of concentrating on small-scale operations in support of the South Vietnamese, full-scale drives to the heart of enemy-controlled country could now be made. American forces had built up to about 390,000 by 1966; another 100,000 were added during 1967. Nonetheless, the rules of engagement, most particularly the stipulation that the United States could not conduct any offensive operations outside of South Vietnam's territorial limits, diminished the utility of both paratroop and airborne assaults. For the North Vietnamese, this meant that Laos and Cambodia were havens where they could retreat or assemble forces.[2]

The maturity of American efforts was underlined by the remarkable cooperation of Army, Marine, Navy, and Air Force units in Operation LEJEUNE, which began on April 7, 1967. Diplomatically named for the "Marines' Marine" Lt. Gen. John A. Lejeune, the joint operation saw organizational borders blurred as the 1st Cav was called on to assist the

Marines in the Duc Pho area of the Quang Ngai Province. The mobility of the 1st Cav was demonstrated on April 7, 1967. It sped a battalion to the relief of the Marines in twelve hours and built up to battalion strength a day later.

The 1st Cav was following a North Vietnamese enemy that it had pummeled in the past. The Quang Ngai Province, in which the enemy was now seeking refuge, had been a Viet Cong stronghold for more than a decade, with the South Vietnamese controlling less than 10 percent. The province had also long served as a base for regular North Vietnamese Army (NVA) regiments.

An airstrip to handle Air Force Caribou aircraft was quickly built, followed by another that could handle first C-123s and then C-130s. The improvised base was soon handling more than one thousand takeoffs and arrivals per day, despite adverse weather and the sandstorms generated by the helicopters. As the American strength built, it was necessary for the Navy to bring in supplies via small ships. Tactical air operations were conducted from the landing strips to the discomfort of an obviously bewildered enemy, one not used to fighting against an air-mobile outfit.

Similar operations, principally Operation PERSHING, were carried out during the remainder of 1967, each one made possible by a combination of the flexibility and striking power of the airmobile units with a far greater appreciation of their worth by ground commanders. The range and striking power of individual airmobile units were essentially "force multipliers" for ground units. Almost every major engagement began with the reconnaissance helicopters of the 1st Squadron, 9th Cavalry discovering the location, strength, and direction of movement of Viet Cong forces. As skilled as the Viet Cong forces were, they were tied by their equipment to ground and unable to escape the 1st Cav's vigilance. There was a growing consensus within the Army that every division should have Air Cavalry squadrons available to them.[3]

In late 1967, the Army's rotary-wing capability was vastly enhanced by the arrival of two new aircraft—the Bell AH-1G Cobra and the Hughes OH-6A Cayuse. The Cobra was a perfect example of industry's support of the war despite the Army's continued vacillation on its requirements. As early

Helicopter warfare was "up close and personal" with the Cayuse, for it was flown at treetop level to engage the enemy. *(Courtesy of U.S. Army Museum, Fort Rucker)*

as 1962, the Army had seen a need for an advanced attack helicopter. By 1964, the requirement had been formulated as the Advanced Aerial Fire Support System. Bell, Sikorsky, and a newcomer to the field, Lockheed, competed for the contract. Lockheed won the competition in 1965 with a design fathered by its eccentric maverick engineer, Irv Culver. His design team created a series of rigid-rotor compound helicopters, which led to the advanced AH-56 Cheyenne. The Cheyenne was later cancelled, in part for some technical development problems, but in fact more because it muddied the ongoing roles and missions argument with the Air Force.[4]

Bell was disappointed but not disheartened at losing the competition, for it was well aware of the hazards implicit in the design (and politics) of a totally new helicopter such as the Cheyenne. It proceeded with an alternate design of its own, heavily investing company funds to do

Designed as an "interim solution" to the need for a specially designed helicopter gunship, the HueyCobra proved to be an instant success. (*Courtesy of
Zaur Eylanbekov [Foxbat]*)

so. Bell designed a much sleeker fuselage to use the basic components
of its very successful UH-1C, combining its T53 turbo-shaft engine with
the standard transmission and rotor system and introducing a Stability
Control Augmentation System (SCAS). The new aircraft (then called the
UH-1H, but later designated AH-1G) first flew on September 7, 1965. The
Army initially ordered 110, but more than 1,700 would follow. Officially
named the "HueyCobra," it is generally called simply the "Cobra."

The AH-1 achieved greater streamlining by placing its two-man crew
in tandem, the gunner forward and the pilot aft, allowing a much nar-
rower fuselage and a visibility more suitable for the attack role. Two stub
wings provided room for a variety of armament packages to supplement
the "chin turret" under its nose. The HueyCobra was faster and more
maneuverable than its predecessors, with a 150-mph cruising speed.
One surprise disadvantage was the relative quiet of the enclosed cabin;
the crew could not as easily hear the sound of fire from the ground. The

Arming Army helicopters was done initially on a "bootleg" basis to avoid a roles and missions dispute with the Air Force. *(Courtesy of U.S. Army Museum, Fort Rucker)*

Marines later upped the ante with the AH-1J SuperCobra, which featured a coupled twin turbo-shaft engine rated at 1,800-shaft horsepower.[5]

The Hughes OH-6A Cayuse was considered a Light Observation Helicopter (LOH), which prompted its universal nickname, the "Loach."[6] The Loach was successful in a competition to replace the Bell H-13, Hiller H-23, and Cessna O-1 fixed-wing aircraft. The bargain-price Loach ($29,415 per airframe at the time) could accommodate up to four soldiers. Powered by a 317-shaft-hp Allison turbo-shaft engine, the OH-6A first flew on February 27, 1963. Despite its small size, the Loach was favored by its pilots for its agility and, surprisingly, its crash survivability. It was used with dashing success in armed reconnaissance. It excelled in down-and-dirty, face-to-face combat—but at a cost, for most Loaches did not survive long enough to require their first 300-hour scheduled maintenance.[7]

As valuable as the new equipment was, the 1st Air Cavalry Division was experiencing something far more important—a sense of combat capability that led to high morale. This in turn inspired exceptional acts of courage and the fullest exploitation of the capabilities of available equipment. This new combative spirit was not confined to the 1st Air Cav but extended to all the other helicopter units and the non-airmobile forces being supported in the field. They were appreciative of the on-time fire support of the armed helicopters and of the essential transfer of fuel, food, and ammunition to the troops by the transport helicopters.

The Army, by necessity, had generated a primitive "just-in-time" inventory system that increased effectiveness by anticipating requirements. The result was that airmobile soldiers were well supplied with everything they needed, including food, water, and ammunition. Perhaps more important than anything else, every soldier's fear of being wounded was mitigated by the knowledge that aircrews of every type of helicopter—not just those dedicated to MEDEVAC—would make heroic efforts to airlift him directly from the battlefield to the clearing station or even the hospital, without regard to any hazards involved.

During 1967, the growth in numbers and the reaction of the enemy combined to force the 1st Cavalry into fighting two simultaneous, complementary, but very different wars in Operation PERSHING. The Viet Cong had spent years diligently preparing a sophisticated infrastructure that consisted not only of the well-publicized tunnels but also permanent bases, well equipped and totally submerged in the fabric of South Vietnamese life. This was particularly true in the Binh Dinh Province.

It might be noted here that the intrusion of the North Vietnamese and their Viet Cong allies into South Vietnamese villages was not considered as onerous as an invasion by a foreign nation might have been, nor did it provoke as intense a reaction. The Viet Cong superimposed their own political and administrative organizations on the local community, with all that implies. But in many respects, the tempo and tenor of village life were not significantly changed, particularly in regions where combat was rare or even nonexistent. This did not mean that the South Vietnamese welcomed the intruders and their demands for support, but they could become resigned to it without the rancor that, for example, a Chinese presence might have caused.

During 1967, the 1st Cav provided the strong support that made it possible for the South Vietnamese National Police Force to destroy the Viet Cong infrastructure in Binh Dinh Province on South Vietnam's southeastern coast. It was a tedious process involving searching some 4,300 dwellings and identifying 340,000 individuals. Identifying and apprehending more than one thousand Viet Cong made free elections possible for the first time.

The Binh Dinh Province is large, and the 1st Cav was also engaged in continuous fighting with NVA unitsNVA. In these actions, the 1st Cav killed 5,715 of the enemy and captured a further 2,323.

As 1967 drew to a close, an analysis of helicopter operations was rewarding to its advocates. For the first time in the war, the initiative had clearly passed to the United States and its allies, and it was no longer considered feasible for the North Vietnamese to achieve their objectives in South Vietnam. The geographic features of South Vietnam, which had so favored the North Vietnamese and Viet Cong, no longer did so, thanks to the most significant manner yet in which the helicopter had changed the nature of warfare. There was no longer a requirement to reach out, seize, and hold territory. With the mobility and firepower implicit in heliborne operations, all of the many areas in South Vietnam still controlled by the North Vietnamese and/ or the Viet Cong could be attacked and suppressed at will. The helicopter had turned a massive disadvantage into a tremendous advantage, for the distances for the North Vietnamese remained long and difficult to traverse and they did not have the helicopters to remedy the situation.

Further, the initial apprehension that helicopter operations would be utterly disastrous as a result of accidents and enemy action proved not to be the case. Losses were indeed severe and would have been considered catastrophic under other circumstances. The U.S. Army now deployed some 2,600 helicopters in South Vietnam, and they were engaged in the most dangerous missions. Fortunately, new tactics and the very number of helicopters resulted in only one being lost per every 13,461 sorties—a far smaller rate than many earlier predictions. (This number trades on the fact that a "recovered" helicopter, one shot down but retrieved by American forces for reconstruction, was not considered lost.) Still, the enormous losses give an idea of the scale of operations and the number of sorties that were flown.[8]

1968: Year of Victory, Year of Betrayal

The success of rotary-wing operations has to be considered in the light of the overall military and political situation in Vietnam. The political/ military decision to build up ground forces to engage in a land war on the Asian continent implicitly called for a victory by attrition: the combined Allied forces were to kill so many North Vietnamese soldiers and Viet Cong that a military victory was won. A secondary strategy was also being applied toward the pacification of South Vietnam, as was done in Binh Dinh Province. There, a sufficient application of force permitted a sufficient application of civil control, so that a more-or-less normal life could be led. The author Robert Thompson gave a precise definition of pacification as "an offensive campaign designed to restore the South Vietnamese government's authority (i.e. the authority of the South Vietnamese government) by a sustained advance in accordance with national priority areas, and at the same time, to protect the individual against selective reprisal attack so that he can play a part in the community, in cooperation with the government, against the Viet Cong."[9]

By 1968, one mistake (fighting a land war in Asia) led to another (the Army fighting a war of attrition and also managing the pacification effort),[10] and this made a third major mistake inevitable. This was the failure to take into account what the faltering military situation might drive the hardy, well-experienced leaders in North Vietnam to do.

Two great battles would dominate 1968, and the entire American effort would be reconsidered. These battles were Khe Sanh and the Tet offensive. In both instances, the North Vietnamese would receive jarring defeats, and the operations of helicopter units would be remarkably successful. The effect of those operations, however, would be diminished by the political conclusions drawn in the United States when the Tet victory was falsely portrayed by the media as a military success for the North Vietnamese.

There is no little irony that this cruelly erroneous portrayal was given its greatest credibility by Walter Cronkite, a man subsequently called "the most trusted man in America." Cronkite led the American media in what amounted to traitorous false conclusions on the results of the Tet offensive. His formulations were directly contrary not only to the facts but to the considered opinions of the North Vietnamese leaders. These leaders, including General Giap, recognized that they were denied the victory in the field that they sought and have since acknowledged that they were grateful to have it handed to them by the American media. It was America's misfortune that its media were commercially attuned to the rising demographic tide of the boomer generation. The media found that flower-child politics was considered a more "hip" attitude than old-fashioned patriotism. In an amazing about-face from all previous practice, the media turned its back on objective reporting and played to this new, laidback, "make-love-not-war" sentimentality. It did so with irreparable harm to the country and with outrageous indignity to the men and women who fought for the United States in Vietnam.

Air Mobility Forces Gather Strength

Before summarizing three of the major battles of 1968, it is necessary to measure how the airmobile forces had grown with the increase in U.S. troop levels in the Vietnam War. The success of the 1st Cav had led to a decision to convert the 101st Airborne Division into the 101st Air Cavalry Division on July 1, 1968. (On August 26, someone sensitive to words and feelings within the Department of the Army changed both the 1st and 101st designations to 1st Cavalry Division [Airmobile] and 101st Airborne Division [Airmobile], in deference to tradition.)

To accommodate the new 101st organization, the 1st Aviation Brigade had to make new dispositions of its approximately two thousand aircraft. Compared to its resources in May 1966, the 1st had acquired and employed a formidable force, consisting of assault helicopter companies, assault-support helicopter companies, heavy helicopter companies, and nine air cavalry troops.

A further description of the strength of these companies will give an idea of how much force the brigade possessed. Each of the thirty-eight assault helicopter companies had two transport platoons, each with ten Bell UH-1D/H helicopters (termed "slicks" for their lack of protruding guns). It also had a gunship platoon of eight UH-1B/C or AH-1Gs. The company headquarters had three UH-1s.

The Chinook derives from the original basic concept of Frank Piasecki and is a testament to his vision. *(Courtesy of Zaur Eylanbekov [Foxbat])*

The eleven assault-support helicopter companies each had two platoons, using Vertol CH-47 Chinooks, with two Hughes OH-6A Cayuse helicopters for command and control, liaison, and so forth.

The two heavy helicopter companies had a few (they were "high-value high-demand assets" before the term came into common use) Sikorsky CH-54 Tarhe "Flying Cranes," which could lift the heaviest loads but were the most vulnerable to ground fire.

Each of the air cavalry troops had eleven UH-1B/C or AH-1G gunships, along with six UH-1D/H "slicks" and ten of the "Loaches," the OH-6As.

Thus the 1st Aviation Brigade could provide 814 transport helicopters (UH-1D/H), 403 gunships (UH-1B/C or AH-1G), 99 heavy transports (CH-47), and 92 light helicopters (OH-6As). The Army also operated hundreds of helicopters in other Army units, while the Marines had about 340, the Air Force about 60, the Navy 45 (in their own attack squadron), and the South Vietnamese Air Force as many as 600. The North Vietnamese also operated helicopters but almost exclusively in transport and liaison roles. All of these rotary-wing forces would increase in strength over time, as the ground forces continued their buildup. They of course declined when the political decision was ultimately made to reduce the American presence.[11]

The utility and versatility of the 1st Aviation Brigade is manifest in the statistics for 1967. During that hard-fought year, Maj. Gen. Robert G. Williams, the commanding general of the 1st Aviation Brigade, proudly announced:

> The brigade had airlifted more than five million troops—the equivalent of 313 infantry divisions—in more than 2.9 million sorties. In that year aircraft of the brigade flew more than 1.2 million hours—the equivalent of 137 years. The brigade was credited with killing 10,556 Viet Cong, sinking nearly 10,000 supply sampans, and destroying more than 10,400 enemy structures and fortifications.[12]

This was force multiplication on an epic scale. The monumental effort made manifest the fact that helicopters had changed modern warfare in Vietnam—and elsewhere. The ground war was now thoroughly dominated by the employment of helicopters and would remain so. The ultimate importance of this type of ground warfare would be underlined in red in 1975, when the North Vietnamese dropped all pretence about abiding by the January 1973 peace accord. Their multipronged assault quickly devastated the South Vietnamese armed forces. The latter, shorn of their American support, and, most particularly, the American style of heliborne warfare, simply could not cope with the North Vietnamese attack. Their defenses crumbled quickly, which led to total defeat.

Khe Sanh and Airborne Operations

The year 1968 would see heliborne warfare reach its peak in two critical trials by fire—the siege of Khe Sanh and the Tet offensive. In this combination of operations, the forces of the United States would experience an increase in the killed in action (KIA) rate that would rise above that experienced in Korea or even the Mediterranean and Pacific theaters of World War II.[13] The North Vietnamese and Viet Cong were defeated militarily and in both cases suffered far greater casualties than the

American and ARVN forces. They would nonetheless reap a providential propaganda victory.

The battles of Khe Sanh and the Tet offensive overlapped both in time and strategy. The Marine base at Khe Sanh in the northwest corner of South Vietnam had been built up from a single company in March 1967 to more than six thousand men, the equivalent of a reinforced regiment. There were also Army and Marine tank units. Unlike the French at Dien Bien Phu, the Marines took care to occupy the surrounding high ground, principally Hills 558, 861, 861 A, 881 North and South, and 950. The numbers indicated the height above sea level in feet.[14] The American intent was to challenge the Hồ Chí Minh Trail and provoke an open conflict with regular NVA forces. (American forces had fought regular NVA forces in the past. For example, the 196th Light Infantry Brigade engaged the 2nd NVA division in the Que Son Valley, west of Tam Ky.)

For his part, General Giap had been gradually pulling back his forces from South Vietnam to the demilitarized zone (DMZ) and southern North Vietnam, believing that the increasingly powerful Americans might be contemplating an invasion of his country. But he also knew that he had to defend the Hồ Chí Minh Trail. Giap also perceived it to be in his interest to draw larger numbers of American troops to Khe Sanh. There he was willing to risk up to three North Vietnamese regular divisions to repeat his 1954 victory at Dien Bien Phu, believing that doing so might completely reverse the current downward course of the conflict. In addition—and some sources insist that this was his primary rationale—Giap was desirous of reducing American strength in South Vietnam, where the North Vietnamese planned a huge national uprising.[15] It would be perpetrated primarily by the Viet Cong, strongly augmented by regular North Vietnamese troops, and was to extend throughout South Vietnam.

The Marines were not alone, for General Westmoreland placed the two Sky Cav divisions, the 1st Cav and the 101st Airborne, along with many other Army and ARVN units, in the area. As Giap intended, Westmoreland drew down heavily on resources lower in South Vietnam to overcome a major North Vietnamese strike against Khe Sanh. It must be noted that Westmoreland took this risk because he believed that it was important to defeat regular North Vietnamese forces in an open battle.

He also felt intuitively that Giap would indeed wish to repeat his victory at Dien Bien Phu. He was determined to prevent that from happening.

On January 17, 1968, there was clear evidence that Giap's and Westmoreland's strategies were to be put to the test. An enemy mortar and rocket attack achieved spectacular results, blowing up the main Marine artillery ammunition dump and doing widespread damage. By January 31 it seemed certain that the NVA would attempt to overrun the base.

There followed seventy-seven days of desperate fighting that saw huge Boeing B-52s employed in their Operation ARC LIGHT role to provide the closest possible air support. They also saw the magnificent use of helicopters to resupply the base and the outposts on the surrounding hills, evacuate the wounded, and, perhaps most importantly, play the key role in the ultimate relief of Khe Sanh.

However, on January 31, Giap's other shoe dropped, in what became a failed attempt to incite the South Vietnamese population against the war in the notorious Tet offensive. The Tet holiday is far more than an Asian version of the western New Year celebration. It generally falls between the last ten days of January and the first fifteen days of February. According to custom, it is a time of peace, harmony, and goodwill, with careful attention paid to family relationships and engendering a sense of renewal. The Tet offensive was of a somewhat different nature.

The size and nature of the event had been masked by heavy holiday radio and vehicular traffic induced by yet another of the inane ceasefires that the Allied nations had announced. NVA soldiers mixed in freely with ARVN soldiers as they made their way back home on leave, the latter for the celebrations, the former for mayhem.

The major actions were in Saigon and five other major cities in South Vietnam, along with no fewer than thirty-four provincial capitals and a host of smaller towns and villages. Most embarrassing of all, the enemy outburst reached even the U.S. Embassy in Saigon.

In many instances, American forces reacted with such vigor that the uprising was quelled on the spot. But in some areas where security was in the hands of local authorities, the North Vietnamese scored important (if temporary) successes. At Hue (the former imperial capital, about halfway between Da Nang and the DMZ), the North Vietnamese gained almost immediate control of most of the city, including the walled Citadel area. Although Hue was substantially recaptured by February 24, the fighting did not end until March 2. The victory resulted in more than 1,000 North Vietnamese dead, but the propaganda loss was irreversible. The combination of the incursion on the U.S. Embassy in Saigon and the long, bitter struggle in Hue allowed the media to portray the Tet offensive as an overpowering North Vietnamese victory. In military terms it was just the opposite. The Viet Cong were comparatively impotent subsequently, and the losses to the North Vietnamese forces were more than they could bear. Estimates indicated that 37,000 of the 68,000 troops employed were killed.[16]

The greatest loss to the North Vietnamese leadership does not customarily receive comment. It was the destruction of their idea that the South Vietnamese people were on the verge of revolt. Many of them expected that the South Vietnamese would join them in the Tet "revolution" the way people flocked to the Communist banners during the uprisings in Russia in 1917. It was not to be.

Yet the presses in the United States of America began their drum roll of doom, combining the Tet offensive, the capture of the U.S.S. *Pueblo* by the North Koreans on January 23, and the continuing siege of Khe Sanh to sound the death knell for American efforts in Asia. What the press overlooked was the enormous strength of American airpower, something that the French had not had and which the North Vietnamese did not yet appreciate fully.

Winning the Battle of Khe Sanh

The airpower contribution to prevailing at Khe Sanh was manifested in many ways. One was the heroic air-supply efforts by both fixed-wing and helicopter aircraft, operating under all conditions of weather and enemy fire at many battle sites, but most particularly at the Khe Sanh base itself. Lockheed C-130s and Fairchild C-123Ks made daring landings under fire to offload their volatile cargos. Other C-130s delivered essentials without landing by using the Low Altitude Parachute Extraction System (LAPES).

Helicopters flew in at night and in bad weather to do the same. The northern monsoon prevailed then, producing very low cloud ceilings and frequent rain. After the North Vietnamese increased their antiaircraft capability, the Marines resorted to "Super-Gaggle" tactics in which Douglas A-4 Skyhawk fighter-bombers would bomb enemy positions just before a helicopter delivery was to be made. This cut losses drastically.

The North Vietnamese were also dazed by the mind-numbing, body-shattering power applied by 400 tactical aircraft and sixty B-52s, day after day. The big Boeing bombers flew 2,598 sorties, dropping a total of 59,542 tons of bombs. While the B-52s were officially restricted from dropping closer to American lines than one kilometer, Marine confidence in their accuracy grew to the point that they would sometimes call in attacks as close as 500 meters. The other U.S. air forces involved flew 21,146 sorties and dropped another 39,189 tons of ordnance.[17] In total, the air effort during the siege of Khe Sanh killed as many as ten thousand North Vietnamese—about one-half of the total number Giap had sent into battle.

All during the siege, helicopters had done what might have saved the French—bringing food, ammunition, and supplies from outside the camp, and then relaying it to the outposts as required. But it was during Operation PEGASUS, the attack to relieve Khe Sanh, that helicopters really shone.

Operation PEGASUS was under the command of Major General Tolson, who commanded the 1st Cavalry Division (Airmobile). Tolson gave his command several tasks, the first of which was to reopen Route 9 to create a ground supply road into Khe Sanh. To achieve this, Tolson employed 300 helicopters, 148 pieces of heliborne artillery, and 19,000 troops. In addition, 10,000 Marines and three ARVN battalions would follow his Sky Cavalry in.

Tolson reversed the siege by sending in his heliborne forces to seize high ground and set up artillery positions surrounding the enemy. The besiegers suddenly became the besieged. The air was filled with slicks and gunships, followed by Chinooks carrying 105-mm howitzers and Sky Cranes hauling bulldozers.

The formidable rocket-firing helicopters softened up the North Vietnamese artillery positions, allowing the Marines to break out of their perimeter and attack. What followed was essentially a cleanup action, as the NVA troops faded away, aware that the siege was broken.

It might fairly be said that the relief of Khe Sanh epitomized the effect of the helicopter on modern warfare.

The Mekong Delta

Although the Khe Sanh siege and the Tet offensive occupied most of the world's attention during the first months of 1968, there was much more fighting to be done. In the northern region of the Mekong delta area, south of Saigon, the tempo of the war permitted a clinical test of the effectiveness of the helicopter.

The 9th Infantry Division was assigned the task of engaging the enemy in the Delta region from March through August 1968. Initially, the heavy demands for helicopters elsewhere meant that the 9th did much of its fighting the old-fashioned way in a very difficult environment. The swamps and rice paddies of the Mekong River delta greatly hampered American infantry operations. The infantry units could move forward at the rate of about one-fifth of a mile per hour, meaning that they could engage less frequently and less effectively. When helicopter units became available, results were much better.

A careful statistical study was made to allow the comparison to be as fair as possible, with the major variable being the use of assault helicopter and air cavalry units. When the results were analyzed, it showed that without those two types of units, the 9th Division averaged .021 significant enemy contacts per day. When the same 9th Division was supported by an air cavalry troop and an assault helicopter company, the number of significant enemy contacts more than doubled. When Viet Cong losses were analyzed, the difference was even more pronounced. Without the air-mobility assets, the Viet Cong lost 1.6 men per day. When those assets were available, the losses rose to 13.6 per day.[18]

The study concluded with an acknowledgment that outstanding results obtained by the addition of air-mobility units might be above average in the terrain of the Mekong delta. It also pointed out that the area was conducive to an unrestricted employment of Army aviation, which might well not be the case in other areas of Vietnam. However, the final conclusion was that while divisions deployed with airmobile units have their greatest advantage in the delta, they would probably improve their performance by perhaps 300 percent in other areas.

The A Shau Valley

The dearth of helicopters in the southern part of South Vietnam was due in part to the extensive operations in the A Shau Valley at the same time. Located on the western edge of South Vietnam, not ten miles from Laos, the A Shau Valley is bracketed by two steep mountain ranges that reach up to about three thousand feet. North Vietnamese forces had overrun an American Special Forces camp in the area in March 1966 and had since controlled the area. They used it as a major staging base to facilitate the passage of personnel and supplies from North Vietnam through Laos and then into South Vietnam.

Troops of the 1st Cavalry Division were not yet finished with the actions in Operation PEGASUS when they were ordered to prepare for Operation DELAWARE-LAMSON 216, a move intended to deprive the North Vietnamese of their logistics base and massive amounts of stockpiled supplies. Plans called for the 1st Cavalry Division to operate in concert with the 1st Brigade of the 101st Airborne Division and the ARVN Airborne Task Force. The latter two units were to attack east of the A Shau position.

Operations began on April 19, 1968, after heavy preparatory strikes by B-52s. Enemy resistance was heavy, as multiple 37-mm antiaircraft guns ringed the target areas. Operation DELAWARE had been accelerated to avoid the worst monsoon weather, but the thunderstorms, low cloud ceilings, and fog immediately called for heroic performances by both the helicopter crews and the supporting USAF C-130s. The flights were made under the clouds, with only good eyesight and good reflexes enabling the crews to miss the obscured mountainsides.

Bitter fighting raged on for the next twenty-one days, by which time the enemy had fled the valley, abandoning tons of supplies ranging from a Soviet built PT-76 tank to flamethrowers. Then, in the manner characteristic of the Sky Cavalry, evacuation by air began on May 10, with the mission accomplished. The operation was later described as one of the most audacious, skillfully executed, and successful combat undertakings of the Vietnam War. Many people believed that the moral value of the victory exceeded the advantages gained from capturing all of the equipment, for previously the A Shau Valley had been considered a safe haven by the North Vietnamese. Operation DELAWARE served notice that there was now no place where the NVA and the Viet Cong could hide that was out of the reach of American forces.

1969-73: Years of Action and Frustration

By the end of 1969, the demands of warfare, the insights of the military leadership, the hard experience gained in the field, and the responsiveness and inventiveness of the helicopter industry had effected enormous changes in modern warfare. By 1969, the Vietnam War had already brought helicopter technology into congruence with the demands of modern counter-insurgency warfare; over the next four years it would continue to do so, but at a more moderate rate.

The United States was tired of the long struggle and welcomed a movement toward what became widely known as "Vietnamization." This term, coined from political expediency, meant that the South Vietnamese armed forces should be so trained and equipped that they could withstand an assault from North Vietnam without the aid of American forces. Equipment and supplies would still be furnished, but instead of more than a half-million troops in-country, there would be a steady draw-down to a virtual handful. More significantly, the aid would not include massive American aerial firepower.

In many ways, "Vietnamization" was practiced from the very beginning of the American presence in the conflict. By 1969, the South Vietnamese were already in full charge of operations in many parts of the country and especially so in the vital Mekong delta region. As pressure grew to reduce its presence, the United States greatly increased training and equipment programs to enhance South Vietnamese air-mobility capability. The success of these programs would be marked in later operations in Cambodia and Laos.

These operations would reinforce what was already known—that airmobile operations could be very successful but required tactical air support in direct proportion to the strength of enemy resistance.

The principal U.S. and South Vietnamese incursion into Cambodia began on May 1, 1970. It was intended to deprive the North Vietnamese of the storage and rest area facilities they had enjoyed throughout the war. Although the political repercussions were stunning, it was a successful military operation. It destroyed so much enemy equipment and supplies that Cambodia was no longer a useful haven for the North Vietnamese.[19]

One astonishing result of the Cambodian campaign was the discovery that the productivity of the helicopter units of the 1st Cavalry Division was far higher than had been anticipated. The aerial rocket artillery ships (ARA) had proven to be extremely powerful tools at pickup zones and LZs, so much so that fewer gunships were required. The versatility of the "Loach" (the Hughes OH-6) was also greater than had expected. As a result, field commanders were far better equipped to handle operations covering a larger geographical area. They found that they were in fact operating units equivalent to the Air Cavalry Combat Brigade as originally recommended by the 1962 Howze Board. It thus took eight years for changing warfare and changing helicopters to finally match the vision of that famous board.

There had been extensive covert operations in Laos over the years, but in the late winter and early spring of 1971, Operation LAMSON 719 was launched. It would meet with very skillful and extensive resistance by the North Vietnamese army, which had received from its Soviet and Chinese benefactors sufficient equipment to establish an extensive and well-integrated mobile air defense system. Besides the usual radar and communication system, the North Vietnamese deployed heavy antiaircraft artillery that included 23-mm, 37-mm, 57-mm, and even some 122-mm artillery pieces.[20]

Despite this resistance, armed helicopters were vital to LAMSON 719, for they were able to attack enemy troops on the ground in proximity to friendly forces with speed and effect. The combination of armed helicopters and ARA could blanket an area with firepower and permit troops and supplies to be airlifted in and out. While they benefited from fixed-wing support when the weather was good, the armed helicopters continued to operate when weather was bad. Then, when low ceilings dictated, they added to their own punch by directing artillery fire.

The importance of the helicopter in LAMSON 719 was underscored by two factors. The first was that some 165,000 helicopter sorties were flown during the operation, an enormous number for the time period. The second was that the loss rate amounted to one-quarter of a percent of those sorties. The number sounds innocuous in relative terms, but in real terms the cost was high for the combined U.S. and ARVN effort, for 106 helicopters were destroyed and 618 were damaged. By far the worst statistic of all was the losses among the helicopter crews, with 68 killed, 42 missing, and 818 wounded in action.[21]

The only reason that helicopter losses were not greater was the aerial firepower delivered in support of their airmobile operations. More than 8,000 sorties were flown by tactical fixed-wing aircraft, dropping more than 20,000 tons of bombs and napalm. The ubiquitous B-52 delivered again, with 1,358 sorties and another 32,000 tons of ordnance. In marked contrast to the helicopter losses, only seven fixed-wing aircraft were lost, six from the USAF and one from the Navy.

By 1969, the infusion of American training, leadership, and resources had stiffened ARVN forces to a remarkable degree. In subsequent years, different units of the ARVN worked at varying degrees of capability. These were demonstrated in the ultimately successful military (but certainly not political) outcomes of later campaigns in Cambodia and Laos, but only because they were backed by massive U.S. support, especially in air power. This situation, so obvious in the many battles of 1972, had great effect upon the negotiations being conducted in Paris on the final outcome of the war. Some, such as the April 1972 battle at An Lôc, underlined the importance of the helicopter again, but more importantly underlined the decisive influence of close air support by Boeing B-52s and other fixed-wing aircraft. The long, bitter Easter offensive, which ran from March through October of the same year, also saw the helicopter retaining its invaluable role, but once again primarily demonstrated the efficacy of massive fixed-wing airpower.

Sadly, absent this reinforcement of massive air support, the South Vietnamese were unable to prevent an overwhelming North Vietnamese victory in 1975.

The revolutionary performance of the helicopter in Vietnam was made possible only by the timely introduction of the jet engine. The performance was augmented by the appearance of new and more effective weaponry, and both of these advances will be addressed subsequently. In the following chapter, we will examine the helicopter in its most important, most heartwarming role—that of an instrument of compassion.

Chapter Six

The Helicopter as an Instrument of Compassion

The helicopter, advanced so greatly by the introduction of the jet engine, found its greatest and most noble use as an instrument of compassion. For the first time in the history of warfare, troops in combat operated with a moral certainty that, if they were injured or wounded, everything possible would be done to evacuate them to safety via any helicopter that might be in the vicinity. More importantly, they knew that even if they were not operating directly with helicopters, those swift lifters would be dispatched to aid them as soon as they were called upon.

The "mercy" helicopters were used in different ways, depending upon the branch of service. The Navy continued to operate them as plane guards, occasionally employing them in rescue operations if the location and timing were suitable. The Marines did not designate specific helicopters for use in MEDEVAC. All Marine helicopters were dedicated to the operational task in hand, combating the enemy, but any Marine helicopter would quickly respond to a call for help. The tactic served them well, with operational considerations rarely overriding MEDEVAC considerations.

The 1st Cavalry Division operated most of its helicopters much in the manner of the Marines. But the unit also incorporated a specialized Air Ambulance Platoon of twelve UH-1Ds.

The U.S. Army developed an entirely new program, thanks to the inspired leadership of the first MEDEVAC teams to reach Vietnam. Battlefield evacuation reached new heights of heroism in what became known as the "DUSTOFF" operations. The growth of this operation, from its initial limited efforts to its becoming an inspiration to both U.S. and South Vietnamese soldiers, will be covered in some detail.

Another variation on the rescue theme was the development of combat

For many, the helicopter's mission of mercy is its most important duty and certainly its most rewarding. *(Courtesy of U.S. Army Museum, Fort Rucker)*

search and rescue (CSAR) efforts by the United States Air Force. These tactics, while controversial because of the drain on resources that was sometimes involved, were eminently successful and provided aircrew members far beyond enemy lines with hope. They knew that every effort would be made to rescue them, without regard to expense or other missions.

DUSTOFF and Medevac

Every constituent of the helicopter's effect on warfare was advanced in Vietnam, including troop infiltration and evacuation, providing supplies from water to artillery shells, airborne fire support, and the introduction of information garnered from space-based surveillance equipment. For the most part, these were not the result of laboratory experiments but of hard-learned lessons in the field. The greatest advances by far were made by young men, averaging twenty years of age, flying vulnerable helicopters into the heat of battle to rescue wounded soldiers. Most of the following material has been abstracted with the permission of author John L. Cook from his outstanding book *Rescue Under Fire: The Story of DUSTOFF in Vietnam*. This, the definitive work on the subject, should be read by anyone interested in the single most important effect that the helicopter has had upon warfare.[1]

There were many supportive advances in the use of helicopters for medical work. Helicopter crews became well integrated, with each member of the typically four-man crew capable of doing some or all of the tasks required on the aircraft. Equipment and stores began with the basic necessities found in the field, but over time more life-saving equipment was installed, ready for immediate use. And it was that very "immediacy" that gave the helicopter its greatest relevance to the troops, who knew that help was almost always on hand. The wounded counted on being evacuated to a clearing station within minutes, confident that they would receive life-saving treatment during that short flight. They were dropped off at a much better equipped aid station, given further life-sustaining treatment, and then taken within hours to a field hospital or surgical hospital where treatment equivalent to that they might have received in the United States was available.

While the wounded were unaware of the statistics at the time, they knew very well that they were viewed as important, individual human beings and were *not* just a commodity that the Army was willing to discard. This undoubtedly added to their ability to survive. More importantly, from the viewpoint of the mission, it made them able to fight more effectively.

There was also an important political psychology involved. The very fact that the United States was willing to make the tremendous investment required for its MEDEVAC work, particularly with DUSTOFF and CSAR, signaled to the world its basic humanitarian qualities. No other nation had ever allocated so many resources to the assistance of wounded or downed soldiers, and the triumphant results of the recoveries were often lead stories at home. The fact that the recoveries were conducted under the most intense fire imaginable, at risks unacceptable to any but the recovery aircraft crews themselves, added to the sense of purpose and drama.

"DUSTOFF": A Heroic Name for a Historic Endeavor

The United States has a long-established pattern, truly ingenuous for a great nation, of being unprepared for war. Once engaged in conflict, it expends tremendous resources to build up to war-winning levels in all areas, including medical and rescue services. When victory is won (or in recent years, when public opinion has soured and the war is somehow terminated), there is a swift demobilization and military budgets are cut. Inevitably, and irrationally, the medical and rescue services are always among the first to suffer. It was in this feeble, counterproductive, intuitively flawed manner that the United States entered the Vietnam War step by step, from the introduction of "training forces" in 1961 to its ultimate buildup of more than a half-million personnel by mid-1968. Shamefully, in the first years of that unhappy conflict, there was literally no dedicated air rescue service available to U.S. armed forces.

Only about eight thousand U.S. military advisors were operating in South Vietnam, stationed in small groups throughout the country, when the first dedicated medical helicopter team arrived on April 26, 1962. The history-making 57th Medical Detachment (Helicopter Ambulance) arrived unceremoniously at Nha Trang, with no quarters, no prepared facilities, and no expectations from the 8th Field Hospital to which it was assigned.

Fortunately, the 57th would be blessed by a succession of legendary commanders, the first of whom, Capt. John Temperelli, was tasked with finding a base and a mission for his twenty-nine men and five Bell UH-1A Huey helicopters. It was not easy, for there were overlapping levels of command and the thousands-of-miles-long logistics system was just creaking into existence.

Temperelli acted as a unit commander should act, without regard to the disparity in rank that he often encountered. He went to the right people, pounded on the right desks, and ultimately achieved the bare minimum of support he required. At the same time he was asking for assistance, he faced unrealistic demands for his services, such as spreading his tiny force out in penny-packet sections all over South Vietnam. He refused to comply with that request, for reasons of maintenance and fuel supply. At the time he had five helicopters at his disposal, and these, as would be the case for all the helicopters to come, required enormous amounts of maintenance to keep flying under normal circumstances.

Battle damage raised the relative percentage of down time from 80 to 90 percent. There were other pressures as well, for some elements of the Army headquarters in Saigon resented that the 57th had the modern Huey helicopters and considered their dedication to saving wounded soldiers a misuse of scarce resources. Headquarters would periodically win this battle, shutting the 57th down for weeks at a time. One especially effective method was requisitioning key spare parts for "operational" helicopters from Temperelli's aircraft, basically grounding them.

In Temperelli's repeated battles with the bureaucracy, he usually won by doing things his way despite his relative rank or official position. For example, the 57th discovered that its official Army communication links were so convoluted as to be worthless for emergency dispatch. Too many headquarters had to be contacted and too many permissions had to be granted, consuming so much time that the mission opportunity was lost.

In somewhat surprising contrast, the South Vietnamese communications system worked perfectly for the 57th's mission. Yet the 57th was officially forbidden from transporting wounded Vietnamese. Temperelli finessed the situation with a quiet agreement with the Vietnamese to use their radio system in exchange for transporting their wounded. The system worked perfectly and from that point on, the 57th and its successors carried wounded of all nationalities, including the enemy. (It should be noted here that the South Vietnamese never embraced the idea of the rescue helicopter with any enthusiasm and often could not be persuaded to enter "hot" LZs. Their failure to do so, with all that it implied about their commitment to battle, would be costly to them after January 1973.)

Temperelli had also to instill the importance of the mission into the minds of his men. Their task was to go into the guts of a hard-raging battle, flying by far the most vulnerable instrument of war in the area. They had to determine the proper place to land, estimate the degree of enemy fire, and then, almost without regard to the hazard involved, land in the middle of the hottest area. Their next task was to pull out the wounded combatants, often bleeding and in shock, and somehow manage to take off through the storm of steel that was directed at them. While they were in the battle zone, they had to calculate just how badly incoming fire had damaged them—whether it imperiled their return flight or if they could make one more run in to pick up casualties. U.S. pilots do not have a *kamikaze* mentality, yet it is difficult not to assign the term "suicidal" to repeatedly flying a very vulnerable helicopter into a battle zone where every one of hundreds of weapons, ranging from rifles to machine guns to cannons to (later) missiles, posed a lethal threat.

Recording the difficulties and dangers encountered by the DUSTOFF crews does not begin to do justice to them. Their efforts can be truly appreciated only by those who called on their services, waited anxiously for the "whop whop whop" sound of the approaching Hueys, and watched appreciatively as the DUSTOFF crewmembers, "protected" by a fragile Plexiglas windscreen, thin aluminum, and not much else, calmly hovered amidst the din of battle to on-load the wounded. Some of those who experienced this valiant effort coined a term for the DUSTOFF crews, calling them the "Lunatics of God."

Fire was always heavy in the hot LZs, and the Viet Cong and NVA units were experts at setting up "flak traps" designed especially to shoot down the MEDEVAC helicopters. They were prime targets; the enemy knew that (a) shooting one down was a great physical and moral victory and (b) the shot-down helicopter would attract additional targets. A well-defended LZ became a sort of perpetual shooting gallery, with one helicopter after another presenting itself as a target. Once out of the shock and shell of the LZ, it was the DUSTOFF crewmembers' task to keep the wounded alive, using what can only be described as primitive equipment on the flight back to the nearest medical assistance, usually a clearing station but often an evacuation hospital or surgical hospital.

Under the most adverse circumstances of equipment, doctrine, supply, and supervision, Temperelli sustained the 57th by the force of his personality and incessant hard work. He turned over command to Maj. Lloyd Spencer in February 1963. Spencer's position was enhanced by the arrival of five new UH-1Bs, a vastly improved version of the Huey. It fell to Spencer to garner the immortal call sign "DUSTOFF" for the 57th and subsequently all of the Army MEDEVAC choppers. Until Spencer's arrival, all requests for rescue helicopters had been via their tail numbers, which was often garbled in transit. Seeking a call sign for the unit that would be quickly identifiable Spencer selected DUSTOFF as the most appropriate, for every helicopter landing and takeoff was accompanied by considerable dust. (The dust, and the characteristic sound of the Huey's rotor blades, came to immortalize the operation.)

The call sign was intended originally to apply to the 57th only, and then only for the normal period before routine changes were made. But in that first year, DUSTOFF became so famous that it was adopted by the additional rescue teams that arrived and was maintained until the end of the war. In time, the term DUSTOFF became more meaningful and far more dramatic than its predecessor, Mobile Army Surgical Hospital (MASH), had been in Korea. There, the majority of MASH operations had been conducted when the opposing lines of combat were fairly static. In Vietnam, the helicopter carried the war deep into enemy territory, and the DUSTOFF helicopters carried the victims back to safety.

Under Spencer's leadership, DUSTOFF flew 1,485 missions, air evacuating 2,000 people, without suffering any losses. He was succeeded in March 1963 by Maj. Charles L. Kelly, who had fought as an infantryman in Europe in World War II and as a paratrooper in Korea. In his new position as a veteran helicopter pilot, he would shape the destiny of the 57th and DUSTOFF with the force of his personality, his dedication to duty, and his clear perception of the mission.

Kelly drove himself and his pilots hard. They were mostly new and untrained, the veterans having done their year of duty and rotated out. Kelly saw to it that they flew as many as 140 hours a month, far beyond the normal—or medically prescribed legal—amount. He also instituted night missions as a routine, every evening personally making an almost five-hundred-mile circular cross-country flight over South Vietnam, just trolling for business. These trips engendered confidence in DUSTOFF operations in the ground forces, provided invaluable training for his pilots, and saved hundreds of lives.

Like his predecessors, Kelly had to fight internal battles with headquarters, where there were the same demands that his resources—aircraft and personnel—be devoted to tactical units. He dissipated his anger with the brass by flying more and more missions, sometimes stepping out of his helicopter to fire a machine gun at the enemy as the wounded were being loaded. Kelly led by example, and, while not loquacious, he could speak forcefully. He laid down his operational rules to his crews in short but brutally descriptive phrases that left no room for misinterpretation.

Kelly's pilots, young men straight out of the accelerated Army helicopter flying school, had little choice but to adopthis standards. In doing so, they wrote a noble chapter in helicopter history.

Kelly was following his own rules on July 1, 1964, on a mission to a firefight near Vinh Long. When he got to the site, he was warned to back off, as the enemy fire was too heavy. He replied, "When I have your wounded," and flew directly into the fire smothering the LZ. Kelly was shot in the heart, the first DUSTOFF pilot to die in combat. He would not be the last. Perhaps more important, Kelly imbued all of his successors with his own zeal for combat.

Safeguarding the DUSTOFF Tradition

One of the most important successors to Kelly was Capt. Patrick H. Brady, who, after Kelly's death, commanded Detachment A of the 57th, conducting operations in the Delta area from Soc Trang throughout 1964. Three years later, in mid-1967, Brady returned to Vietnam for a second tour of duty, this time a major and commanding the 54th Medical Detachment. There he maintained Kelly's strict policies on mission acceptance, and in doing so would become the first DUSTOFF pilot to receive the Medal of Honor. He also introduced new techniques to the DUSTOFF inventory.

In the three years since Brady's first tour, DUSTOFF operations had grown immensely. In 1964, it supported 16,000 troops and flew 4,000 patients per year. By 1967 it was supporting almost 500,000 troops and flying as many as seventeen thousand missions per month. On January 6, 1968, in the heart of the monsoon season, Brady once again used Kelly's techniques for a series of missions for which he is justly famous. A patrol from an ARVN camp at Hau Duc, twenty-five miles west of Chu Lai, had suffered casualties. A Special Forces medic supporting the South Vietnamese unit called for DUSTOFF to lift out several wounded South Vietnamese soldiers.

Before detailing Brady's heroism, it is useful to outline the courageous, innovative flying technique he developed for operating in the cloud-shrouded mountains where the fighting was going on. The following is excerpted from an oral-history interview of Maj. Gen. Patrick H. Brady conducted on March 24, 1987, by the Army Medical Department Regiment, Fort Sam Houston, San Antonio, Texas. Brady's statements will perhaps be most meaningful to pilots, but they convey the depth of the weather and geography problems he faced and the dexterity of his solutions to them.

But one day we were called out to evacuate a soldier who had been snake-bit. And he was up on top of a mountain, and halfway down the mountain was in clouds. Which is IFR [instrument flight rules] conditions. You lose reference to the ground in IFR conditions. You can't tell of course whether you're right side up or not. So we went out, tried to get in to get this guy. We started to fly up the mountain, straight into the stuff. And of course we went IFR, we couldn't see where we were, or whether we were right side up. I knew we could always fall off in the valley and we'd break out. And really worried about how we're going to get in and get this kid. They called to say he was going into convulsions, and everything. One trip up the mountain I was turned sidewards. And I thought I was going down, I looked out the window just to find a spot to go in, and I could see the tip of my rotor blade, and the tip of the trees. Which was about 30 feet away, or less. And I was in the stuff. So that told me I had two reference points. Told me I was right side up. So I knew I had it made. So I turned the aircraft sidewards, and I went up the side of the mountain sidewards, watching the tip of the rotor blade and the tops of the trees. And I went in and got the guy. No problem. The same technique worked in the valley. Now you had to have, be able to make an IFR transition pretty quick, or whatever. But, in the morning in Vietnam in the mountains, up to about 500 feet, there was nothing but dense fog. Straight IFR conditions. Very, very tough flying conditions.

So anyhow, I used the technique many times. And I'd go to the edge of bank, find a trail that I could find on the map, and then I'd work my way through that stuff sidewards. Can't see straight, 'cause of the attitude of the aircraft. You got to use the side window. It's like driving down the highway in the weather, if you ever do it, sometime just open your side window and take a look out and see how much better the visibility than it is through the, through the windshield. So anyhow, the day of the, when all this happened, and you're going to ask me for things, you know . . . as I said many times, that day was not unlike many other days. It just happened that on this particular day there was a bunch of people that saw this thing that went on, and wrote it up. Otherwise, you know, nothing would have happened. And the same is true of many other DUSTOFF pilots who had days like this.[2]

Flying DUSTOFF 55 with a volunteer crew, Brady flew in fog so dense that it resembled "a 500-foot-thick snow bank." He elected to fly sideways, blowing away sufficient fog that he could follow the trail in the jungle-covered mountains below. Several other rescue attempts had aborted because of the bad weather, but Brady persisted, landing under sniper fire to on-load the wounded soldier. He then made an instrument takeoff to get them back to the 2nd Surgical Hospital at Chu Lai. It was the start of a busy day.

Immediately after his return, Brady volunteered to fly to the rescue of American forces heavily engaged on the floor of the Hiep Duc Valley, northwest of Chu Lai. There, six companies of the NVA 2nd Division were firing rockets and mortars at a company from the 196th Light Infantry Brigade of the 23rd Infantry Division (Americal). The NVA units had set up a flak trap of 12.7-mm machine guns, covering all avenues of helicopter approach to the valley floor. When Brady got the call to fly, two helicopters had already been shot down, and a third was nearly lost to the pilot's vertigo in the dense fog.

Knowing there were already dozens of casualties to be picked up, Brady took a volunteer medical team along in DUSTOFF 55. This time he found a hole in the fog to let down before repeating his tactics of flying sideways to reach the battle site. Flying sideways in the fog threw off the enemy fire for the twenty-minute flight. The fog was so dense that he had to be vectored to the battle site from the ground, where a soldier directed him by the sound of his engine and rotor blades. Brady's medical team performed triage of the wounded, got the worst cases on board, and Brady made another instrument takeoff to carry them back to medics at a fire support base of the 196th.

Brady now briefed three other DUSTOFF crews on the nature of the mission, and they initially followed him back into the fog-shrouded mountain pass but found the combination of dense weather and heavy enemy fire too intense. Only Brady in DUSTOFF 55 pressed on, using his sideways technique to keep oriented. Incredibly, he flew four more rescue missions into the same area under intolerable conditions, eventually flying thirty-nine men out of what would have been certain death for them. But his day was just starting.

Brady refueled and flew to the next LZ, which was under so heavy a fire that the soldier on the ground would not carry the wounded to the helicopter. Calmly ignoring that this was the same situation in which his predecessor, Maj. Chuck Kelly, had been killed, Brady took off to circle the area, his Huey receiving major hits. A frantic radio call from the ground summoned him back, promising to bring the wounded to him this time, and Brady, despite the damage to the controls of his chopper, went back in and picked up the wounded.

Brady switched helicopters and was soon in the air again. He flew to yet another battlefield, only eleven miles away, and amidst hot incoming fire landed in a minefield. He and his crew worked with soldiers on the ground, walking through the minefield to drag the wounded back to the Huey.

After three more missions, the long day drew to a close for Brady, whose three helicopters had suffered more than four hundred hits from enemy fire. He had evacuated fifty-one wounded soldiers and was recognized for his bravery with the Medal of Honor, the first awarded to a DUSTOFF crewmember.

The Army was at last awakening to the tremendous importance of DUSTOFF and readied additional medical detachments like the 57th for Vietnam. The esprit de corps that Kelly had inspired in the 57th was soon adopted as the norm by new units, and there began to be a competition to undertake the hottest mission assignments. The rivalry reached a point where one unit would "scarf up" another unit's mission if they happened to be closer to the scene of the action.

In an unusual deviation from the normally rigid radio-code protocol, the new units also assumed the DUSTOFF call sign. This provided a signal clarity for front-line operations. There was no ambiguity when the call went out for DUSTOFF assistance. It meant that the troops in contact were in trouble and needed immediate help.

The new DUSTOFF units were augmented by the arrival of the 1st

Cavalry, which had its own Air Ambulance Platoon of twelve UH-1Ds and operated under the call sign Medevac.

As the intensity of the war increased in Vietnam, and the American presence grew to 184,000, there was more fighting and more requirements for helicopters to fly missions of mercy. In 1965, 8,896 MEDEVAC missions were flown. Of the 12,456 patients carried, 7,364 were Americans. This meant that the South Vietnamese were getting a remarkable share of DUSTOFF help, making it perhaps the single greatest factor in solidifying relations between the South Vietnamese and American forces.

The belated recognition of DUSTOFF and Medevac operations was finally supplemented by a continuing stream of improvements to the helicopters. The helicopter manufacturers did a magnificent job in incorporating new ideas from the field, and onboard medical equipment was systematically improved. Among the great innovations was a lightweight but powerful hoist, which was introduced to combat in March 1966. It permitted the helicopter to hover over an unsuitable landing area. A paramedic would be lowered to the ground, where he would get the wounded soldier into a sling that could lift them both back up to the helicopter.

For heavily forested areas, a "Jungle Penetrator" was devised. The streamlined shape could be lowered through the trees easily. On the ground, three seats unfolded like petals from the main body of the penetrator, and the wounded could be strapped onto these for the lift up into the hovering helicopter.

DUSTOFF established a new warrior culture in which young men, averaging about twenty years old, would on a daily basis engage in heroic activities without thought of themselves. In eleven years, from 1962 to 1973, a total of 496,573 DUSTOFF missions were flown, and more than 900,000 patients were airlifted to safety. The average victim spent less than one hour between the time he was wounded and the time he was in a hospital, and less than 1 percent of those evacuated died.

This amazing work was accomplished by a fleet of helicopters that never numbered more than 140 at any one time. But the DUSTOFF mission was three times as dangerous as a regular helicopter mission. More than two hundred DUSTOFF helicopters were shot down. More than two hundred crewmen were killed in action, and many more were wounded. And one must never forget that many casualties were evacuated by non-specialist helicopters in routine wartime actions.

Each of the men flying the DUSTOFF and Medevac missions was a hero, and two more men were awarded the Medal of Honor for their outstanding efforts. These include CWO Michael Novosel and S.Sgt. Louis R. Rocco. Both men are true heroes, and just as with Patrick Brady, their stories are detailed in Colonel Cook's *Rescue Under Fire: The Story of DUSTOFF in Vietnam*. A brief discussion of Novosel's life, taken from his obituary, will give the reader an idea of the heroism implicit in their work and some insight into the warrior psychology of the men flying the DUSTOFF mission.

Michael J. Novosel died on April 2, 2006, at the age of eighty-three after an eventful life. At just under than five feet four inches tall, he was a determined man and entered flying training during World War II, serving as a captain and flying Boeing B-29 bombers against Japan. He was recalled to service during the Korean War, where he flew transports. He remained in the reserves and rose to the rank of lieutenant colonel while concurrently pursuing a career as a commercial airline pilot. In the 1960s, he was flying for Southern Airlines when he was diagnosed with glaucoma, a disease that would soon end his commercial career.

By then too old and of too high a rank to return to active flying in the USAF, Novosel enlisted in the U.S. Army. There, the need for pilots was so great that his experience offset the impending visual problems, and he received helicopter training. During his first tour in Vietnam, he flew DUSTOFF missions with the 283rd Medical Detachment. He returned on a second tour with the 82nd Medical Detachment, and in the course of his career flew 2,532 missions and removed almost six thousand wounded personnel. He had the unique experience of rescuing his son, Michael J. Novosel, Jr., and in the next week being rescued by that same son after he was in turn shot down.

His most famous flight occurred on October 2, 1969. At the age of forty-seven—roughly twice that of the average DUSTOFF crewmember—he flew into Kien Tuong Province to rescue a group of South Vietnamese soldiers who had stumbled into a heavily fortified North Vietnamese

The heroism of Michael Novosel was properly recognized with the award of the Medal of Honor. *(Courtesy of Zaur Eylanbekov [Foxbat])*

training camp. They were surrounded and under pulverizing artillery, machine gun, and rifle fire.

Without hesitation, Novosel flew directly into the heavy ground fire the North Vietnamese were bringing to bear on the South Vietnamese unit. Unlike most missions, he had no support from gunships or fixed-wing attack aircraft. Novosel made fifteen passes into the heavily defended area, each time picking up badly wounded South Vietnamese soldiers. He would quickly transport them to a nearby Special Forces camp, then return to the fray. On his last trip in, he had to hover near an enemy bunker to pick up a wounded soldier. An enemy sniper fired, wounding Novosel's right leg and hand. For a moment, Novosel lost control of the helicopter, but he quickly recovered and got the wounded soldier aboard. He then flew out of the torrent of fire, bleeding badly but still in control of the wounded Huey. His actions and the support of his gallant crew resulted in saving the lives of twenty-nine South Vietnamese soldiers. When his heroism was recognized with the Medal of Honor, Novosel pleaded that each of his crewmembers be awarded a Silver Star for their actions. It was a typical Mike Novosel gesture.

Novosel retired in 1985 after serving forty-two years as a military aviator. He was the last World War II military aviator in the U.S. to remain on active flying duty, having flown 12,400 hours, including 2,038 in combat. The main street at Fort Rucker, Alabama, the home of Army Aviation, is named in his honor.

Novosel would have been the first to say that all of the DUSTOFF crewmembers were heroes, but among those same veteran crewmembers, there is general agreement that he represented the peak of their profession.

Combat Search and Rescue (CSAR)

As previously noted, after every war, the United States reverts to a peacetime mentality and immediately slashes the military budget. Within the armed services, the reaction is immediate: preserve whatever can be preserved of its offensive and defensive capability within the new budget limitations. Inevitably, that preservation deprives many essential services of the resources required to maintain them. For this book, chief among those services was what is now called combat search and rescue (CSAR) but was for many years termed the Air Rescue Service.

Ironically, the savings from gutting the Air Rescue Service, despite its fine performance, were minimal. Sadly, resuscitating it and bringing it to a practical capability during the Vietnam War took far too long and cost far too much in lives and equipment. The need was recognized and the action was called for, but factors of bureaucracy and budget delayed the necessary measures for years.

It is worth briefly recapping the history and achievements of the Air Rescue Service, to indicate the periodic heights of capability it reached along with the inevitable periods of decline. Established in March 1946, the Air Rescue Service served brilliantly in the Korean War, with almost one thousand combat saves, while using a ragtag collection of equipment. Flying both fixed-wing and helicopter aircraft, the brave 2nd and 3rd Air Rescue Squadron crews were dedicated to the precept, "These things we do that others may live." They carried 9,680 military personnel to safety, 9,216 of these by helicopter. They were later supplemented by the famed Army medical helicopter teams that transported a further 19,946 patients from the battlefield to the famous Mobile Army Surgical Hospital (MASH) units.[3]

The value of the Air Rescue Service was extended in Korea by a new and daring technique of effecting rescue of downed airmen behind enemy lines. During the three years of active warfare in Korea, no fewer than 1,690 U.S. crewmembers were downed inside enemy territory. The Air Rescue Service, with its still inadequate equipment, managed to save 170 of these men, 102 by helicopter.[4]

The Navy was also deeply engaged in CSAR from the Korean War on, and it is interesting to note that the guidelines that were laid down in a Korean War operations report would hold true in the Vietnam War. Among them were the following dicta:

> 1. Helicopters should not be dispatched to pick up a pilot downed in enemy territory unless he is in sight or in radio contact with rescue planes. The rescue helicopter should not be used for search. [This was in part because of the critical state of fuel supply on the short-range helicopters of the era; later, when in-flight refueling became available, the rule was less applicable.]
>
> 2. Search results and an appraisal of the rescue possibilities should come from pilots not too closely associated with the downed pilot. To obtain impartial reports, the search and rescue should be flown by pilots from a squadron other than that of the downed pilot. [This recognizes the very human tendency of pilots to go to extremes to recover a squadron mate.]

3. Authentication of radio messages or identification of friendly rescue personnel on the ground can be accomplished by use of information known to the pilot but not likely to be carried on his person. [This became increasingly difficult during the Vietnam War thanks to the expertise of the opponents.][5]

Sadly, by 1961, budget battles had reduced the Air Rescue Service from fifty squadrons to only eleven and from 7,900 personnel to only 1,600. There was irony in this, as the responsibility of the Air Rescue Service had become worldwide, with a special detachment formed to rescue downed Strategic Air Command crewmembers from the Soviet Union should the need arise. (This special detachment had a Potemkin quality to it, for its mission was to fly specially equipped long-range Douglas C-47s deep into an atomic-bomb-ravaged Soviet Union. There they were to locate downed aircrews, land at an unprepared site, rescue the crews, and bring them back home. I was a member of a Strategic Air Command B-50 crew at the time and went through a simulated rescue during survival training at Stead Air Force Base, Nevada. Neither I nor any of my fellow crewmembers believed that the system had one chance in a million of working properly.)

Perhaps even sadder and more discouraging than the cut in the Air Rescue Service's strength was the unconscionable time required to bring it back to a capable level when war threatened in Southeast Asia. U.S. military activity began on a limited scale in 1961 but escalated each year. U.S. aircrews engaged in combat and were lost, without any rescue service available to them. For political reasons, a decision was made to provide a covert rescue capability by supplying the Central Intelligence Agency's proxy company, Air America, with sixteen Sikorsky H-34 Choctaw helicopters. These helicopters were intended primarily to carry personnel and cargo but could be diverted for air rescue work if required. Incredibly, it was not until March 1964 that six Kaman HH-43B helicopters were scraped up from various resources to be assigned as a dedicated rescue unit in Vietnam. Designed originally as a short-range emergency vehicle, the Kaman was significantly improved over time with additional armor and fuel and a more powerful engine. Nonetheless, it was simply too small to be useful for extended missions that might involve operating behind enemy lines.

Although originally designed to fight aircraft fires and rescue crews after a crash near an airbase, the Husky was also used for SAR in Vietnam. *(Courtesy of Zaur Eylanbekov [Foxbat])*

Despite the equipment limitations, the rigors of the Vietnam War demanded further action, and the practice of combining existing assets into a Search and Rescue Task Force evolved. The equipment could scarcely have been less compatible in terms of speed, range, and capability. Grumman HU-16 Albatross amphibians served as control aircraft for the short-range HH-43s and a collection of Korean War-vintage Douglas A-1 escort aircraft. The "command and control" facilities of the HU-16s were primitive, and crews operated in cold, wet, unpressurized discomfort. In 1966 they were supplanted briefly by Douglas SC-54s, operating from Thailand before the mission was effectively filled by the Lockheed HC-130 in 1967. As noted, the HH-43s lacked the necessary range, speed, and lift capability to be truly useful. The Douglas A-1s, called Skyraiders officially but popularly called "Spads," proved to be excellent for the task, with their long loiter time and heavy ordnance loads, and they served well until 1972. Theirs was a dangerous mission, and the A-1 had the highest loss rate of any airplane in Southeast Asia, reaching 6.2 losses per 1,000 sorties on missions to North Vietnam.

Forever famous as the "Jolly Green Giant," the Sikorsky CH-3 was continually developed over the years and given new designations. *(Courtesy of Zaur Eylanbekov [Foxbat])*

Even though there was inadequate equipment in the early days, the basic task force idea was sound and was built upon over the years to become a remarkable concept, often capable of dominating the area where an aircrew was waiting to be rescued by suppressing enemy resistance with massive, sustained firepower. By June 1965, still using the HH-43s, rescue operations were undertaken that would never have been possible before. And only one month later, on July 6, 1965, the first really adequate rescue helicopters arrived. These were two Sikorsky CH-3Cs, which arrived at Nakhon Phanom Royal Thai Air Base to introduce a welcome new level of capability.[6]

Given America's wealth, and the massive effort then being directed toward the Vietnam War, it seems incongruous that only these two aircraft, borrowed from the Tactical Warfare Center at Eglin Air Force Base, Florida were available for so important a task. Huge in comparison to the HH-43s, and painted in the typical green and brown camouflage colors of

There was no more welcome sight for an aircrew downed in hostile territory in Vietnam than the arrival of the "Jolly Green Giant," flown by brave and skillful crews. *(Courtesy of Zaur Eylanbekov [Foxbat])*

the time, they immediately became known as the "Jolly Green Giants," a name that stuck because it was both apt and agreeable.

An improved version of this aircraft, the Sikorsky HH-3E, incorporated the latest equipment designed for rescue, and by January 1966, six were available at Udorn Royal Thai Air Base. These were in every way superior to any previous rescue helicopter and would set the pattern for future operations. The HH-3E was larger than desired for some operations, but in the main it served well, for it was adaptable, all the more so when, in time, an in-flight refueling capability was developed for it.

In January 1966 the Air Rescue Service became the Aerospace Rescue and Recovery Service, an acknowledgment of its expanded role in rescuing downed crewmen behind enemy lines. Despite the service's rudimentary beginnings and long, agonizing development period, by the end of 1966 it had saved 647 lives. Of these, 222 were combat aircrew rescues.[7]

Over the next three years, experience and improved equipment would hone the talents and capabilities of those involved in CSAR. More effective rescue packages were created using the services of Forward Air Controllers (FACs); additional escorts, including Bell AH-1 Cobra helicopters; a protective Combat Air Patrol of any jet fighters that were available; and the HH-3 and HH-53 helicopters. Perhaps the most important development was that of in-flight refueling, which meant that the helicopters could now reach long distances into enemy territory and remain there on orbit, awaiting the arrival of the necessary rescue forces. Lockheed HC-130P Hercules turboprop transports provided both command and control and aerial refueling for the Jolly Greens.

While the arrival of new equipment was often delayed because of the inevitable requirements for testing and the shortage of assets, the capabilities of the aircrews improved continually with experience. Nowhere was this more important than in the crucial role of the pararescue men, the fabled PJs (parajumpers) of the Vietnam War. Their role grew almost by accident, soon becoming one of the most prestigious and admired of any career in any service. The PJs went from casual crewmember status to being the most important member of the team, for they faced all the dangers of the flights in- and outbound but were in addition tasked with descending into hostile territory to assist downed airmen. They provided essential medical assistance and were invaluable when the crewmember was incapacitated or, sadly, when the mission involved the recovery of a dead person. The pararescue men often engaged in combat on the ground even as they conducted their rescue, and of the twenty-two enlisted personnel who received the coveted Air Force Cross, twelve were pararescue men.

One man, A1C William H. Pitsenbarger, was awarded the Medal of Honor for his heroism on August 11, 1966. Under sustained fire, Pitsenbarger secured the rescue of nine aircrew members before being killed in action.

By the end of 1970, with the Vietnam War taking a new direction, the CSAR teams had saved an additional 2,039 lives.[8] By this point in the war the Aerospace Rescue and Recovery Service had adequate equipment, well-defined tactics, and a strong contingent of well-trained personnel. But as the process of Vietnamization reduced the USAF commitment, the Aerospace Rescue and Recovery Service began to draw down. As previously noted, the South Vietnamese did not have the inclination, discipline, or additional fixed-wing assets to conduct effective CSAR operations on their own, one of the fatal flaws of the concept of Vietnamization.

A Point of Departure

However, the success of the CSAR teams had revealed that they could be employed in a new way—as offensive weapons, a unique form of "special operations." This would have a profound effect upon both the use and the effect of the helicopter in subsequent conflicts.

One of the most famous first demonstrations of this new concept was the brave if ill-timed raid on Son Tay prison in late November 1970. It has become convenient for purposes of diplomacy and trade to forget just how evil the North Vietnamese prisoner of war camps were and to ignore the fact that our captured airmen and soldiers were treated with a savage brutality. By 1970, the United States was aware of the names of at least five hundred Americans held in North Vietnam. It also knew that the suffering of the prisoners was great and that many had died from torture and neglect. Despite every U.S. effort, the North Vietnamese refused to consider an exchange of prisoners.

The Son Tay prison was particularly notorious, located as it was only twenty-three miles west of Hanoi, the capital of North Vietnam. The prison's location put it well within the capability of Hanoi's integrated air defense system, by 1970 perhaps the most formidable in the world. Approval for the raid came from the very top, with Secretary of State Henry Kissinger, deeply involved in his almost clandestine negotiations with the North Vietnamese, at one point selecting the month when the raid could take place.

The raid received the full support of the military services and was conducted as a joint force composed of USAF Special Operations and CSAR personnel, along with U.S. Army Special Forces. The Navy contributed strong forces from its carriers. It was decided that to be successful, the raid would have to be conducted at night, under good conditions of weather and moonlight, for the rescue helicopters would require in-flight refueling. Secrecy was important, because the rescue could be accomplished only through shock and surprise. There was a regular NVA regiment of 12,000 men stationed in the area, along with the personnel associated with nearby schools, depots, and air defense units.

Time was pressing, and a decision was made to conduct the raid on the night of November 20, 1970, from Udorn Royal Thai Air Force Base, some four hundred miles from the target. The attack was supported by more than 160 aircraft, including McDonnell F-4s, Republic F-105s, Douglas A-1s, Lockheed EC-121s, Boeing RC-135s, and a variety of Navy aircraft. For the purposes of this book, however, the Son Tay raid is important for the way in which the main force combined a variety of helicopters with specialized Lockheed C-130 aircraft known as Combat Talon.

The heart of the force was to be fifty-six U.S. Army Special Forces Troopers (Green Berets) led by the famous Col. Arthur D. "Bull" Simons, who had led a rescue effort on a Japanese POW camp during World War II. The elite force was carried on two USAF HH-53s and one HH-3. The prison at Son Tay was so small that only one helicopter could land inside the seven-foot-high walls that surrounded it. A decision was made to crash-land one helicopter inside the walls to create the shock and surprise, while the troops from the other helicopters blasted their way through the walls. The idea was to remove the prisoners quickly from their cells, load them aboard the two surviving helicopters, and bring them back to safety. [9]

Unfortunately, the prisoners had been moved to a new camp at Dong Hoi, some seven miles away, back in July. The North Vietnamese maintained activity of other sorts at Son Tay, which gave the impression that it was still in use. The objective of the raid was not attained, but no lives were lost, and the raid made it clear to Hanoi that American power could still be projected deep within its heartland.

What was important for the future was the fact that helicopters had now moved to a new area of use in warfare. They were no longer the passive instruments of compassion, at their best on missions of safety and rescue. Instead, they now had the capacity, thanks to in-flight refueling and better night navigation equipment, to conduct stunning raids of precision and power. This new capability would be demonstrated around the world in the years to come, not always with complete success but with sufficient promise to dictate the conduct of the initial operations in the many struggles in the Middle East and the Balkans. And, as always in warfare, the changes in capability in helicopters were matched by changes in the nature of warfare, as opponents struggled to deal with the new threats.

Chapter Seven

Changes in Helicopters, Changes in Warfare

The helicopter demonstrated its prowess admirably well before the dismal end of the Vietnam War, carrying the early concepts of vertical envelopment and airmobile warfare to new heights. The startling growth in helicopter capability and equipment changed modern warfare by allowing the United States, South Vietnam, and their allies to wrest the initiative from the North Vietnamese and fight the war on their own terms. The helicopter enabled the U.S. and ARVN forces to reach out from secure fixed bases to any point in enemy-controlled territory and there establish an LZ using helicopter gunships and transports. The seized territory could be held and exploited as enemy forces were defeated and their supplies seized. Subsequently, the same mixed force of gunships and transports could evacuate the forces and bring them back to their own bases. For wounded or fallen soldiers, the helicopter meant a swift return to safety. The U.S. and ARVN forces could thus dominate almost every battle, without respect to distance, terrain, national borders, or weather.

Inevitably the changes the helicopter made in modern warfare extended beyond those enabling the airmobile forces to achieve their desired results, for the enemy made changes as well. These included improvements in weapons and tactics to counter the effect of the helicopter. The North Vietnamese responded with far heavier antiaircraft defenses, more sophisticated deployment of personnel and material, improved camouflage techniques, and better decisions on choosing the time and place of battle. Later in the war, the introduction of the Man Portable Air Defense System (MANPAD) made LZs even more dangerous than before.

The first successes of the most notorious Soviet MANPAD, the SA-7 Strela (NATO code name "Grail"), took place in Egypt in 1969. The Strela, as with so many Soviet missiles, was derived in large part from an American design, in this case the Redeye missile. Lightweight at about thirty pounds, and with a range of about a half-mile, the Strela carried a warhead weighing just over two pounds. In Vietnam, its first victim was a Cessna O-2A, the push-pull twin-engine Forward Air Control aircraft. When the helicopters arrived to evacuate the FAC pilot, the Strela was used to shoot down several of them. During the course of the war it is credited with more than two dozen victories, including at least ten of the less vulnerable AH-1 Cobras.

Heliborne forces continued to dominate the battlefield, despite the counter efforts, but only because they, in turn, relied increasingly on conventional fixed-wing airpower in the form of tactical air and B-52s. The fixed-wing forces dramatically improved their accuracy and delivery methods to complement the heliborne operations of both U.S. and ARVN forces. It became imperative to put as much firepower as possible on selected LZs to permit helicopter operations. Even with the preparatory fire, the landings continued to be highly dangerous but perhaps just removed from the suicidal level.

Unfortunately, as effective as the combination of fixed-wing and rotary-wing attack was, it became the implicit material deficiency in the policy of Vietnamization. There was no way for South Vietnam to acquire the fixed-wing assets on the scale that the United States could deploy them on short notice, as it did during the Easter offensive of 1972 or as in its ultimate assertion of airpower during Operation LINEBACKER II. As a result, South Vietnam, however able it might have become in airborne operations, was doomed by Vietnamization to the fate it received in 1975.

The changes in warfare wrought by the helicopter inevitably brought about new challenges to the helicopter's future. These would be met in part as they had been in the past, by improvements to the helicopter and the introduction of some new models. However, for the most part, new equipment would be added to existing models. In the past, while modifications to existing helicopters were continuous, there was always a new model in the process of being fielded, one that would combine the best of previous designs with modifications that introduced new capabilities. Gradually after the Vietnam War, the combination of other priorities, limited budgets, and the increasing cost of new helicopters reduced the number of new helicopter types being brought into production in the United States.

There were also changes in the nature of the helicopter industry. As we have seen, it started with the dedicated efforts of such giants as Igor Sikorsky, Frank Piasecki, and Arthur Young. While each of these men had help from other engineers and technicians, they personally led the way as their helicopters were built and conducted the test flying. But as their success generated contracts and the volume of production increased, the net effect of these pioneers, while still important, was gradually diluted.

The initial rate of increase in the number of helicopters procured was relatively slight, with larger orders calling for perhaps a hundred aircraft. But as the size of the orders grew, manufacturing considerations inevitably began to affect some of the procurement decisions. As delighted as their investors were, the inventors found this annoying, for all of them wished to see each of their new improvements incorporated immediately.

To achieve larger production numbers, the manufacturers had to invest in the necessary tooling, arrange for the subcontracting of parts, create inventories of spare parts, and do all of the things necessary to service the aircraft already in the field. This naturally led to a desire to standardize, establish controls on configuration, and simplify the logistics requirements of the services using their products. The net effect for a fleet of helicopters that was performing well was to render the status quo more and more attractive.

This process was exacerbated by the natural tendency of the armed services to call for a wide range of improvements in new helicopter designs, making them far more complex to address more missions. This in turn required more testing and far greater expense for an entirely new helicopter. And all too often it resulted ultimately in cancellation of the project.

Background to the Changes

There came about an inevitable change in the industry, from its spontaneous, dynamic early days to a more stable, profit-oriented, efficiency-geared operation in the Vietnam era and beyond. The combined result of these situations is that early models of helicopters powered by jet engines would have far longer serviced lives than their predecessors, with model variants (as with the Huey line) sometimes proceeding from A to Z.

The turbine engine in its many varieties was at the heart of this progress. Turbine engine nomenclature is tedious. A "jet engine" (and purists dislike this term) is one where the power output is almost entirely jet thrust through the tailpipe. The turbojet, turboprop, turbo-shaft, and gas turbine APU (auxiliary power units) are all basically "turbine" engines, just as convention radial and inline reciprocating engines are "piston" engines. The term "gas turbine" was used simply to distinguish the new invention from the older and more common hydraulic turbine used in hydro-power plants.

For fixed-wing airplanes, the turbine engine arrived at a time when piston engines had about reached their peak in power, with such giants as the Pratt & Whitney R-4360, the Curtiss-Wright R-3350, and others being prepared for production and still others, such as the Lycoming XR-7755, falling by the wayside. These tremendously complex engines were encumbered with massive intercoolers, superchargers, and so on, and all were inherently limited by the complex multi-bladed propellers they required. The turbine engines came in at about the same power of contemporary operational piston engines but were much lighter and so had a better power-to-weight ratio. They of course consumed more fuel but at a rate less than had been long predicted by turbine naysayers. A less obvious positive factor was that the new turbines could be developed and put into service far more rapidly than could large piston engines. Naturally enough, these new engines went to fighters, bombers, and reconnaissance planes before filtering down to other fixed-wing aircraft.

Helicopters began with relatively low powered piston engines, as in the 100-hp Franklin engine that Igor Sikorsky used in the VS-300 or the 90-hp Franklin engine used by Frank Piasecki in his PV-2. As helicopters grew in size, there were ample varieties of relatively small piston engines, many of them available as war surplus, to accommodate their needs. But when larger piston engines were fitted, their increased weight diminished the desired growth in the helicopter's load-carrying capability. Economics and the ready availability of reliable piston engines were the primary reasons for the relative delay in the introduction of the turbine engine to the helicopter.

Status Report, 1973

By the end of the Vietnam War, a number of helicopters had reached a new peak of efficiency thanks to the introduction of the jet engine. The reduction in weight, increase in power, and capability to operate at higher-density altitudes transformed the helicopter inventory of the United States' armed forces. From being a useful support item, helicopters became the means by which land combat was conducted.

It is useful to review the levels to which helicopter performance had risen by the end of the Vietnam War. That war began with piston-powered helicopters such as the Bell H-13 Sioux, Piasecki H-21 Shawnee, and Sikorsky H-19 Chickasaw and H-34 Choctaw. Navy and Marine counterparts to these aircraft were also in use, differing primarily in designation but with some changes in construction (e.g., aluminum used in lieu of magnesium) and equipment. The only jets on the scene were the few French Alouette IIs still in service with the South Vietnamese Air Force and the jet-powered Kaman HH-43B Husky employed by the USAF as a rescue aircraft.

Even with their limitations, the available piston-engine helicopters proved invaluable, and their success may even have facilitated the White House's decision to markedly increase the number of personnel assigned to Vietnam. Without helicopters, the buildup to more than a half-million personnel would have been pointless, for there is no way that even a far greater number of soldiers could have controlled all of South Vietnam.

When the turbine-powered helicopter began to arrive in Vietnam, it opened up entirely new possibilities. It not only performed far better than its piston-engine predecessors, it soon became available in vastly greater numbers. The rapidly gained experience in combat conferred a number of new missions upon it, many of them never previously envisioned. The principal turbine-powered helicopters, as we have seen,

The Apache is an effective weapon system that has been continually improved through the years. *(Courtesy of U.S. Army Museum, Fort Rucker)*

included the Bell UH-1 Iroquois and AH-1G HueyCobra, Boeing Vertol CH-46 Sea Knight and CH-47 Chinook, Hughes OH-6 Cayuse (Loach), Kaman HH-43B Husky, Sikorsky HH-3 Jolly Green Giant and its naval variants, the HH-53 Super Jolly, and its many Pave Low variants, the Sea Stallion and the HH-54 Tarhe. In the post-Vietnam War years, additional helicopters were introduced, including the Sikorsky UH-60 Black Hawk, HH-60G Pave Hawk, and the powerful Hughes/McDonnell Douglas/Boeing AH-64 Apache. Their specifications may be found in Appendix Two.

The helicopter prospered in Vietnam and in the subsequent years because of an inherent ability to expand its potential through successive development—the installation of new engines, rotors, and equipment—while still retaining the basic design elements. This required two very important efforts. The first came from the armed services, which had to translate their new requirements into attainable specifications. While it was easy to call earnestly for more speed, firepower, armor, and range (all desperately needed), it was difficult to balance these needs against reasonable schedules (the helicopters had to arrive before the war was over) and budgets. The second came from the manufacturers, who looked at precisely the same needs from their viewpoint. While in almost every instance they would provide options to give the military everything desired, they also adopted a coldly objective perspective on what they could and could not reasonably deliver.

The results, inevitably, were compromises, but it must be said that the industry's hard-eyed view of the possible optimized the real-world results. No one understood better than the manufacturers just what changes in horsepower, rotor-blade design, and additional equipment would mean to production, delivery, and performance. It is to their credit that the outstanding designs that emerged during the late Vietnam War period and later were so advanced and so suitable for their time and still remained within the budget and schedule requirements of the services.

The following pages will try to illustrate this process by showing how basic designs were adapted by the helicopter industry to create multiple lines of brilliant aircraft that met a wide variety of purposes. These include the often mentioned Bell UH-1 and the Sikorsky Model 61 and 65.

The Huey

The Bell UH-1 Iroquois is perhaps the best example of how the operators and the industry responded to the needs of the war with useful modifications. Other helicopters used in Vietnam were modified in a similar fashion for similar reasons—experience, change in mission requirements, opportunity, and, most urgent of all, necessity—but none did so many things so well, nor did they look so good doing it.

The reader will recall that Bell had blazed its own path in the industry, leading the way with Model 47 in 1954. Also designated XH-13F, the turbine-powered Model 47 became a breakthrough helicopter in both civil and military applications.

The Army wanted a helicopter for the vital MEDEVAC role, which would be conducted on a previously undreamed of scale in Vietnam, and Bell responded with the Model 204, initially called the XH-40. First flown on October 22, 1966, it was obvious that it would also be useful as a trainer and a liaison aircraft. The XH-40 was followed by two more prototypes and six developmental aircraft, the latter with the original cabin expanded by twelve inches.

This information is rather dense but is an attempt to describe succinctly how Bell modified the basic design to meet the demands of multiple operators. It is important to note that the UH-1 was produced in two major single-engine types, the Models 204 and 205. Later, twin-engine Models 212 and 412 appeared, all with the same basic lineage. The Model 204 sub-variants included the UH-1A, B, C, E, F, K, L, M, and P. The Model 205 sub-variants were the UH-1D, H, U, V, and X. The Model 212 became the UH-1N, the bird of choice of the 1st Special Operations Wing. The Model 412 was the 212 incorporating a four-bladed rotor. To confuse matters, a four-bladed UH-1 was developed as the UH-1Y. There were many additional sub-variants, to reflect the installation or test of special equipment. There is no wonder that mechanics, configuration control experts, logisticians, and planners had to be careful about their choice of suffixes when working with the Huey. In more recent times, the list has grown to include the AH-1W (Whiskey) and AH-1Z variations of the Cobra.

The first production version, the HU-1A Iroquois, was delivered on June 30, 1959, and was the first turbine-powered helicopter to be used by any U.S. armed service. Every helicopter unit in the Army clamored for the aircraft, but the first deliveries would go to the quick-response forces of the 101st and 82nd Airborne divisions and the MEDEVAC experts of the 57th Medical Detachment. (As with all the aircraft of all the American services, the designation was changed by mandate in 1962, with the HU-1A becoming the UH-1A. This formal change could not alter the affectionate designation "Huey," which the Iroquois had already received.)

Form followed function in the Huey, but it happened that functions would also follow the form, as the Model 204's layout was suitable for many missions. The basic design was simple, with a large cabin surmounted by the engine and rotor mast section, with a long boom where the tail rotor could be installed. Pilot and copilot sat forward (pilot on the right, copilot on the left), with the extensive glazing providing excellent visibility. Each side had big windows in large sliding doors not unlike those that would appear later on the ubiquitous Chrysler minivans.

A single Lycoming T53 turbo-shaft engine of 770-shaft horsepower (shp) was positioned overhead and aft of the crew cabin, driving the two-blade rotor (with the identifying Arthur Young-trademark stabilizing bar) mounted above it. The long tail boom had two horizontal stabilizing fins; at its end was a single vertical fin with a two-blade rotor system mounted on the left side. Two well-braced skids served for takeoffs and landings and as stairs for people embarking and disembarking as well. The simple beauty of the Huey design had a Museum of Modern Art quality to it, and it was that same simplicity that permitted so many basic variations, including the twin-engine Model 212.

Just a sampling of the dozens of model variations will be sufficient to demonstrate the basic capability with which the jet engine endowed Bell's basic design and also be illustrative of the changes made in all of the other types engaged in the war.

The first large Army contract was for the HU-1A (soon UH-1A), which started out life as a "slick" a transport, but was soon modified in the field to become a gunship, equipped with two .30-caliber machine guns and 2.75-inch rocket launchers. Both sides seeing the potential of the project, the Army and Bell agreed on the production of the HU-1B (UH-1B), equipped with the Lycoming T53-L-5 engine of 920 shp. A longer cabin was introduced to provide for seven passengers or four stretchers and a medical attendant. The first production UH-1B was delivered in March 1961.

At the time, the Marines were operating under an unwavering directive from the twenty-second commandant of the Marine Corps, Gen. David M.

Shoup, to obtain an assault-support helicopter (ASH) that would replace both the OH-43 helicopter and Cessna O-1 fixed-wing airplane. The Marines were aware of the U.S. Army's fervent interest in the Bell UH-1B and ultimately and somewhat reluctantly decided that, with changes, it could serve the Marines as the UH-1E. The most immediate of these modifications was the installation of rotor brakes, to permit the helicopter blades to be brought to a halt quickly after landing on an aircraft carrier, an absolute necessity for shipboard operations. A personnel hoist was installed. But the most important, a boon made possible because of the increased horsepower of the jet engines, was the switch in airframe materials. In the past, magnesium—expensive, difficult to work, vulnerable to fires, and quick to corrode—was widely used to reduce weight. Magnesium was clearly unacceptable for shipboard operation because of its fire risk and corrosion from the salty spray. Fortunately, the jet engines now made it possible to go to all-aluminum construction, an invaluable improvement in subsequent models. The first production Marine UH-1E was accepted on February 21, 1964, marking the introduction of a Marine mainstay for the next half-century. The U.S. Navy promptly jumped on board, adopting the Huey with a 1,400-shp engine as the HH-1K, for use in SAR.

Even as the Marines and Navy were aligning their needs, Bell was already working to improve the basic design with the UH-1C in 1960. The increased drag and weight of the armed versions of the UH-1B incurred a performance loss, so the UH-1C received a 1,100-shp T53 engine. To take advantage of the higher airspeeds that were available, a new rotor system was installed. Here, the age-old problem of retreating-blade speed was addressed once again, this time reducing the incidence of the retreating blade when accelerating in a dive. But, as always, one change led to another, and the increased power and new rotor required a lengthened tail boom and an alteration to the vertical fin.

The close interplay of Bell and military engineers on the project enabled some needed improvements to proceed quietly and without argument over cost. Among these was the installation of a dual hydraulic control system to give some redundancy in the event of battle damage. This proved to be of incredible value, for the Huey was soon the primary target of all enemy shooters and control redundancy was a

Helicopters are at their most vulnerable during rescue operations, because skillful enemies often hold their fire until the rescue chopper presents itself as the best target. *(Courtesy of U.S. Army Museum, Fort Rucker)*

life-saving grace. Surviving Army UH-1Bs were eventually brought up to UH-1C standards.

The next major changes came with the Bell Model 205 UH-1D. The Bell engineers lengthened the fuselage by forty-one inches and increased the carrying capacity to a total of fifteen, including the crew. Six stretchers could be carried, raising capacity by 50 percent. Large doors, easily removed for low-level flight in the hot tropics of Vietnam, provided visibility and a site for firepower.

Things move rapidly in wartime, and the first Model 205 took off on August 16, 1960. The production versions were designated UH-1D as this became the most used, most familiar of the type, along with the UH-1H, which was virtually identical except for its larger 1,400-shp engine.

Given the many changes in engine power, equipment, and mission, it is somewhat surprising that the general performance of the successive types remained within very similar parameters, with top speeds, range, and ceiling varying not more than 10 percent in any direction. This was a familiar situation with helicopters, as torque, drag, and rotor complexities delayed their development.

The inherent flexibility of the design was apparent in the Model 212, basically a UH-1 powered by two 1,290-shp Pratt & Whitney twin turbo-shaft engines, the PT6T "Twin-Pack." The new version originated with a Canadian requirement for fifty helicopters using an engine built in Canada. The ubiquitous Pratt & Whitney engines are capable of generating 1,800 shp but are derated to 1,250 shp for takeoff and 1,150 in flight to extend their service life.

The great success of the Huey gunships signaled the need for a specially designed, dedicated attack version of the helicopter to serve in the escort role. The Army sought to meet the need with a competition for the Advanced Aerial Fire Support System (AAFSS). As is almost inevitable in such competitions, the specified requirements forced the rival design firms to reach beyond the state of the art. The competition was won by the very advanced Lockheed AH-56 Cheyenne, a compound helicopter featuring a rigid rotor, a propeller in the rear for thrust and heavy armament. (The term "compound helicopter" can mean many things but normally encompasses the addition of wings for lift and armament installations.) Such an advanced design required intensive testing and development. It encountered engineering and fiscal problems—both of which could have been resolved—and was cancelled, to the regret of many to this day.

Bell had also seen the need for a specialized attack helicopter, but its first effort, the Model D-262, was rejected by the Army in 1965. Discouraged but not disheartened, Bell continued development of the type using its own funds, eventually creating the Model 209. The aircraft was essentially a streamlined version of the UH-1C, with the addition of a Stability Control Augmentation System (SCAS) and wide-blade rotors. The Model 209 easily won a competition over rivals from Boeing-Vertol, Kaman, Piasecki, and Sikorsky, receiving an initial order for 110 aircraft as the AH-1. It was often called the HueyCobra, the name evoking the Bell P-39 Airacobra fighter heritage.

The AH-1 Cobra

Knowing the Army's dilemma—the question of what it wanted versus what might be attainable in the near term—the Bell company used the basic Huey design to create the Model 209 as a specialized gunship, building upon what had been learned with the wildly successful Huey gunships in Vietnam. As a result, it flew its Model 209 in September 1965. For many it was a painful decision, for Army leaders were already preparing for what seemed inevitable—a land war in Europe against the formidable armored forces of the Soviet Union. In that future war, an aircraft far more capable than the Huey was needed to offset the enemy's enormous numerical preponderance.

Once again, as happened so often in the history of the helicopter, the personal beliefs and known integrity of an individual came to bear. The vice chief of staff of the Army, Gen. Creighton Abrams, and the director of Army Aviation, Col. George P. Seneff, were called in by the Army chief of staff, Gen. Harold K. Johnson. The problem presented to them was this: millions of dollars had been spent developing the AH-56; were those millions now to be wasted and a less capable aircraft procured simply because it was available?

Colonel Seneff made a soldier's reply, telling Generals Johnson and Abrams that soldiers were dying in Vietnam now, no matter what the future held. He wanted to procure the Cobra for them as the best, most immediate solution to the problem. After due consideration, General Johnson agreed.

Seneff had emphasized that the Cobra was hardly a half-measure. While it lacked the AH-56's ultimate sophistication and development potential, it was still a revolutionary rather than evolutionary step forward from the Huey. With its slim, snakelike fuselage, tandem cockpits, stub wings for rockets and guns, and chin turret, the Cobra's speed, maneuverability, and reduced target area offered immediate and obvious improvements that were desperately needed in the field.

After the long and disappointing experience in developing the Cheyenne, the Army welcomed the idea that the Cobra could be developed from the Huey quickly, efficiently, and with a very high degree of certainty. The Cobra was deployed to Vietnam in September 1967, with the primary mission of providing firepower for the Hueys that carried in the troops. The results were immediate: the Cobra provided an air superiority on the spot, relieving troops in contact from having to call in Air Force assets. As the Cobra's crews gained experience, the variety of missions expanded accordingly. Tests revealed that the Cobra could in fact fulfill some of the Cheyenne's potential in future conflicts, operating in the vital antitank role, especially when new map-of-the-earth techniques were combined with modern night-fighting equipment.[2]

In the production HueyCobra, the two-man crew was mounted in tandem, with the gunner forward and the pilot aft. The slim, streamlined fuselage helped boost top speed to about 140 mph, but the great gain was in armament. The AH-1G featured a turret under its nose with two 7.62 miniguns (or 40-mm grenade launchers) and with hardpoints on the stub wings that could accommodate a variety of munitions. These ranged from rocket launchers to minigun pods and made the HueyCobra a fearsome weapon. Further, it lent itself to the development of advanced electronic aiming equipment.

Twin engines were installed in the AH-1J to create the SeaCobra for Marine use. Like the HueyCobra, it featured heavy armament, and it too has been continuously modified over the years. It is worth noting that while the Marines followed the Army's development of the AH-64 Apache with great interest, they elected to stay with the SeaCobra for both budgetary and operational reasons.

The flexibility of the basic Bell design was possible only because of the turbine engine, and the same is true of the progress made with the other great helicopters of the Vietnam War. They all followed a similar process. An initial model was introduced into the field. There the demands made upon it called for modifications, sometimes executed in the field and then reproduced in the factory, sometimes created in the factory for use in the field. The changes were myriad and included adding armor and armament as required; increasing engine horsepower; changes in the number, span, width, or material of rotor blades; differing structural materials; and improving maintainability. Often these changes were retrofitted to existing aircraft in the field, while at the same time being introduced on the factory production line. The result was a long series of familiar-looking helicopters, each with a change in model number, and each with an improved or more specialized capability.

The Versatile Sikorskys

An aircraft that gained international attention, respect, and even affection as the Sikorsky HH-3E Jolly Green Giant began life in a traditional way, an outgrowth of the Sikorsky company's phenomenally successful Model S-58 Choctaw. The first in the new series, the Sikorsky S-61, was ordered by the U.S. Navy as the HSS-2 in September 1957. Powered by two General Electric T58 turbo-shaft engines driving a five-blade rotor, the HSS-2 was initially an anti-submarine-warfare aircraft, but its many qualities soon found it other duties in the air forces of several nations. The USAF purchased the basic design as the CH3, and this, with suitable modifications, became the HH-3E.

Although the HH-3E was a vast improvement over the HH-43, it did have some tactical deficiencies, including limited armor, insufficient firepower, and not enough engine power to maintain hover in certain conditions. Fortunately, the U.S. Marines had already contracted for the Sikorsky S-65, a heavy-lift helicopter, and it became the CH-53A. The USAF decided to modify the CH-53A for its own needs as a rescue helicopter, the HH-53B, taking its first delivery of the type in June 1967. It was called, naturally enough, the "Super Jolly."

Although similar in appearance, there was a vast difference in capability between the HH-53 and the HH-3. The definitive model, the HH-53C, at 36,000 pounds weighed twice as much as the HH-3E and had a useful load of 13,000 pounds, compared to only 3,000. Almost 8,000 hp was supplied by two T-64 General Electric turbo-shaft engines, providing a top speed of 190 knots, compared to the 143-knot capability of the HH-3E. Less obvious, but equally important, the new aircraft had much more extensive armor plate and carried a formidable armament consisting of three 7.62-mm miniguns. Unfortunately, the HH-53C still lacked an effective night recovery system while on duty in Vietnam, but it led to other significant American designs.

Among the most important improvements in the HH-53 series was the installation of a Doppler navigation radar and the provision of a retractable in-flight refueling probe on the right side of the nose. The Lockheed MC-130P Combat Shadow was used as a tanker, with the MC-130H Combat Talon supply combat support including navigation and communications. An improved rescue hoist was installed along with very heavy armament that included three General Electric GAU-2/A miniguns of 7.62 caliber. The five-man crew consisted of a pilot, copilot, crew chief, and two of the vital pararescue men, the very heart and soul of CSAR operations.

The first of eight HH-53Bs began CSAR operations in Vietnam by 1967; these were followed by forty-four HH-53Cs. No fewer than seventeen of these were lost in combat, while three more went down in accidents. In addition, the Air Force procured twenty of the similar if less sophisticated CH-53Cs for general transport work, as well as for special operations. Over time, additional improvements, including specialized night vision equipment, resulted in the HH-53s being redesignated as MH-53H. A total of thirty-one earlier aircraft were eventually updated with more powerful engines, increased armor, and new avionics. The latter included the APQ-158 terrain-following and terrain-avoidance radar, an advanced inertial navigation system, and, later, Global Positioning System equipment, to become MH-53Js. Inevitably, given the built-in limitations of the helicopter, top speeds of the MH-53 series remained relatively low, reaching only 165 knots. After forty-two years of USAF service under various designations, the brilliant Model 65 flew its last MH-53 Pave Low mission in September 2008, when the remaining six helicopters flew combat missions in support of special operations forces in southwest Asia.

While the Air Force was thus developing the S-65 into a long series of highly specialized aircraft, Sikorsky found other markets for the basic design. The U.S. Navy adopted it as the RH-53D multipurpose aircraft, using it for sweeping mines, personnel transport, and CSAR. The U.S. Marines employed it in the traditional assault transport role as well as for other duties.

This then is the process by which an effective helicopter capability has been maintained, despite the lack of a prudent, measured system of replacing old designs with new ones. It is possible only through the adaptability of the industry and the common-sense attitude of the military services to do the best they can with what is available to them.

Changes in Perception and a Failure to Invest

The perception of ultimate defeat, even after all the victories in battle, was a legacy from Vietnam that haunted the U.S. military and may well have driven its leaders to welcome the concept that the next major battlefield would inevitably be in Europe.

Accepting such a challenge is one thing; welcoming it amounted to denial, for there was an obvious massive discrepancy between the size of the forces of the Soviet Union and its Warsaw Pact allies and those of the United States and its NATO allies. The communist bloc forces in Europe disposed of far more men, tanks, and artillery than did the U.S. and its allies. As the Soviet Union's military doctrine always embraced the first-strike option, it was presumed that it would launch the fateful assault.

As far back as the 1950s, it was generally believed that some fifty NATO divisions, complemented by nuclear weapons, would be sufficient to contain Soviet ambitions.[1] NATO never achieved its fifty-division goal, but in those early years the comfortable U.S. strategic nuclear capability mitigated the threat. And the "unknown unknown" of the time was what the consequences of a strategic nuclear exchange would be. In time, the growing parity in U.S. and U.S.S.R. nuclear capability brought about a philosophy of "mutually assured destruction," with its apt acronym MAD. Under this philosophy, the leaders of both nations recognized that the result of a general nuclear exchange would be catastrophic for both countries and it was, initially at least, a price neither nation wished to pay.

However, ideology that had its roots in the time of the tsars carried tremendous weight in the Soviet Union, leading to changes in its planning during the early to mid-1960s. The United States became aware of this historic shift in Soviet military thinking, realizing that the leaders of the Soviet armed forces were beginning to believe that there was a good chance that their nation could not only survive but win a nuclear exchange and that mutual deterrence was a defeatist, dead-end policy. Mutual deterrence was, of course, totally foreign to both native Russian and Marxist-Leninist ideology.[2]

This new mindset came about via a substantial change within the Soviet Union in which the military asserted its independence of the Communist Party when it came to strategy and the use of military force of
any kind. At the same time, the Soviet Union increased its strength in
virtually every area but particularly in its ability to initiate or respond
to a nuclear attack. As we now know, the Soviet Union's belief that its
crippled and distorted economy could compete with that of the United
States was delusional and ultimately led to the utter bankruptcy and dissolution of the U.S.S.R. on December 25, 1991.

The new Soviet military-based strategy no longer sought merely to destroy the United States and its allies while limiting damage to the Soviet
Union. Instead, the idea became current that highly trained, well-equipped
military forces could achieve victory in Europe by traditional means—that
is, overwhelming superiority in numbers of men, tanks, artillery, and aircraft. Used with surprise and dash, these forces could smash through Germany to the Channel coast and at minimum cost. Once this victory was
accomplished, there was little the United States could do to alter the situation except resort to a suicidal nuclear exchange.

The basis for this strategy reached back to the heady last days of World
War II, when Soviet strength had reached an incredible peak and a "drive
to the Channel" through the lines of former allies might have seemed
easily attainable. The successful introduction of nuclear weapons by the
United States, and the fact that the Soviet Union was in fact very weary,
precluded the establishment of the Iron Curtain along the Atlantic coast
in 1945. Long before the conclusion of the Vietnam War, such a drive to
the sea seemed much more feasible to both Moscow and Washington.

By the 1980s, the Soviet Union began to believe that if it could mount
a massive independent air operation at the very beginning of its war in
Europe, targeting airfields, communications, and especially nuclear delivery systems, it might just be able to achieve victory without starting
a nuclear war in the European theater. It was estimated that as many as
2,000 aircraft would have to be employed in this initial attack.[3]

It was implicit that the Soviets could choose the timing and the place
of their advance. The assumption was that the U.S.S.R. and its Warsaw
Pact allies would deploy their massive forces through the famous Fulda

Gap, which extended from the East German border westward toward Frankfurt and was most suitable to accommodate the huge amount of armored units they would use. An attack through the Fulda Gap would quickly overrun central Germany, taking its capital, Bonn, and Frankfurt. A second route, equally important, was over the Northern German Plain straight toward the Netherlands and the North Sea. A third route involved an attack through the so-called Hof Corridor, toward Stuttgart and encompassing Munich. Provisions were made for all of these, but an attack through the Fulda Gap seemed to be the most logical, given the dispositions of the Soviet forces and the huge numbers of men and material they involved.

The disparity between the forces of NATO and the Soviet bloc would have been great on the first day of the battle, and would have grown in the following weeks, as the Soviet forces had far more reserves to draw upon. While the figures varied over the years, at any instant in time the Soviets had a great advantage in numbers, as the following table indicates:

	Warsaw Pact Forces	**NATO Forces**
Soldiers	950,000	750,000
Tanks	17,500	7,000
Artillery	7,500	2,700
Fixed-wing tactical aircraft	2,700	1,150[4]

It evolved over time that the perceived need to defeat a Soviet attack through the Fulda Gap required the development of new weaponry of every kind. The effect of the defeat in Vietnam was not the only factor in this analysis. It was seen that the best choice was the development of such a qualitative superiority in airpower, including both fixed- and rotary-wing tactical airpower, that the Soviet forces could be contained.

This need became particularly urgent by 1975, when a large buildup in Soviet forces began. Additional strengthened divisions were introduced, and there was a perceptible increase in the quality of Soviet weaponry. This included the new and formidable T-64 and T-72 tanks and extremely efficient armored infantry fighting vehicles, such as the BMP-1, which gave excellent service in the 1973 Arab/Israeli war. The BMP-1 was essentially an ideal combination of a light-armored personnel carrier and a tank and was intended to accelerate any Soviet advance.

Soviet airpower had also been improved significantly with the introduction of the MiG-23 and MiG-27 varieties of the Flogger swing-wing aircraft, the Sukhoi Su-24 Fencer, and even, in small numbers, the Tupolev Tu-22M Backfire bomber. The Soviet helicopter force was also improving as the Mil Mi-8 went through its development process and the Mi-14 and Mi-24 helicopters came into service. In sum, the growth in Soviet forces seemed so formidable that a NATO leader, Belgian general Robert Close, made a public statement that he believed the Soviet forces could, if they wished, cross the Rhine River within two days of opening hostilities.[5] His sentiments no doubt resonated within the Soviet system, and they certainly accelerated the sense of urgency for new non-nuclear weapons that could save Europe from this fate.

The United States had learned many lessons in Vietnam about both fixed-wing and rotary-wing tactical aircraft, and many new development paths were opened. However, it happened that within the fixed-wing component a new and far-sighted leader had emerged, one of the few who could operate with equal success as a field commander and within the halls of the Pentagon. This was Gen. Wilbur L. "Bill" Creech. General Creech would revolutionize the Tactical Air Command (TAC) and become the generally acknowledged architect of the American air-war fighting style that proved so successful in Operations DESERT SHIELD and DESERT STORM and subsequent warfare in the Middle East and the Balkans.

Bill Creech knew warfare, having flown 103 combat missions in Korea and an additional 177 in the Vietnam War. He had been sickened by the fact that the United States had elected to fight the Vietnam War on terms dictated by the enemy, terms that ensured heavy losses and minimum results. As he assumed greater and greater positions of responsibility, he vowed to change how the next air war would be fought.

Creech was determined to avoid losses by suppression of enemy air defenses, to use the night as an ally and a vehicle of American airpower, and to provide the very best in equipment. At the same time, as the TAC commander, he instituted new ideas and procedures that increased TAC productivity by 80 percent based on sortie rates and other measures.

There is no doubt that Bill Creech was a hard taskmaster but he was utterly fair, without favorites. He demanded that his subordinates, regardless of their rank, give as much of themselves as he was giving of himself, and this extended not only to hours worked and flown but to dress—neat crisp uniforms, tightly tied ties, shined shoes, and, in the summer, V-neck undershirts. He elected not to attempt to change Air Force doctrine. Instead he focused on the practical art of fighting the air war.[6]

To achieve the changes he sought, Creech worked closely with the U.S. Army in meeting its needs and embracing its concept of the AirLand Battle. To some, this was a deviation from Air Force interests. In fact, Creech's actions and leadership induced the Army to understand and work more closely with the Air Force's concept of employing airpower from the point of view of the theater commander.

Creech's effort centered upon suppressing enemy air defenses to eliminate the dangers presented by modern surface-to-air missiles and radar-controlled antiaircraft artillery. In addition, Creech, like so many others, deeply resented the policies that had resulted in the loss of so many aircraft in Vietnam (for example, the 397 F-105s lost in combat).[7] He was determined to see that future attacks against an enemy were launched with every conceivable advantage: after the enemy defenses had been suppressed, under the cover of darkness if possible, and fighting from a distance, at high altitudes, using precision-guided munitions (PGM). If a low-altitude attack was necessary, Creech wanted the antiaircraft fire totally suppressed.

As eminently practical as this seems, his ideas were not automatically adopted. There was resistance at many levels, particularly in the budget, because the equipment that he demanded be developed was expensive in the short run, no matter how comparatively inexpensive its inherent effectiveness would prove to be in the long run.

Creech's success was acknowledged by the air commanders during the many operations from the August 1990 Operation DESERT SHIELD to the present time. Among the many commanders who directly attributed the success of USAF air operations to the discipline and tactics fostered by Creech are former USAF Chief of Staff Gen. Merrill McPeak, DESERT STORM air commander Gen. Charles "Chuck" Horner, and Lt. Gen. Hal M. Hornburg.

A key element of Creech's success was the fact that he reversed the usual process of attempting to tailor tactics to existing equipment, instead pushing for the development of equipment that would permit the tactics he insisted upon being possible. He was able to do this through his influence in the Pentagon and his ability to obtain swift and adequate financial backing for programs that enabled his pilots to attack, if not in safety, at least in the most advantageous possible way. These included a wide range of PGM programs, with the reluctant acceptance by the "bean counters" that their apparent expense was more than offset by their effectiveness.

It must be remembered that the Soviet Union was providing itself and its allies with increasingly more effective integrated ground-defense systems that created an intense electromagnetic environment designed to disrupt U.S. attacks and take away the very advantages Creech sought to confer. Through a careful selection of programs and managers, Creech was able to bring about the Low Altitude Navigation and Targeting Infrared for Night (LANTIRN) system, which transformed the combat capability of fighters such as the McDonnell (now Boeing) F-15 and General Dynamic (now Lockheed Martin) F-16. The LANTIRN system permitted these new aircraft—which Creech had also backed—to strike from low altitude at night, in any weather, with PGM. Other advances, including the General Dynamics/Grumman EF-111, McDonnell F-4G Wild Weasel, AGM-88 High Speed Anti-Radiation Missile (HARM), Lockheed EC-130H, and revolutionary stealth fighter Lockheed Martin F-117A, amplified the arsenal developed under Creech's leadership.

Creech did far more than just improve the Air Force's fighting capability. He introduced changes in training, logistics, and the development of morale and discipline that transformed the TAC. What is critically important to note for the purpose of this book is that no similar figure with similar effect emerged in the helicopter community. There were many able leaders within that community, but none had the transformational touch of Bill Creech, whose force of personality and single-minded approach saw to it that a sufficient priority—with its concomitant funding—was placed upon the research, development, and production of new equipment and ideas that would increase effectiveness and reduce casualties of fixed-wing tactical aircraft.[8]

The reasons that no one equivalent to Creech emerged in the helicopter community lie at the very heart of the helicopter problem, already mentioned so often: conflicting needs within the Army and competing needs with other services. No one, no matter how effective or powerful their personality, was able to dominate the helicopter scene as Creech was able to dominate the fixed-wing element. As always with helicopters, there were simply too many alternative ideas, too many alternative applications for funds, and no single focal point.

Thus it was that in the decades following the Vietnam War, far more R&D money would be spent in addressing the lessons learned for fixed-wing aircraft than for helicopters. As a result, in the generation of wars that were to be fought in the Middle East and the Balkans, new types of fixed-wing tactical aircraft would be the beneficiary of weapons and operational characteristics that greatly reduced their combat losses. Furthermore, the many and substantial changes in enemy capabilities—improved radar, advanced surface-to-air missiles, much more lethal anti-aircraft-guns—were of a nature that could be met with suitable changes in tactics. The tactical fixed-wing aircraft was more and more removed from the battle site, thanks to its ability to fight accurately from a greater distance and often at higher altitudes. In vivid contrast, the helicopter, as always, was thrust into the very heart of the battle, becoming at times the unlikely tip of the offensive spear.

This contrast—an able, focused leader with an unstoppable agenda versus several equally patriotic, equally well intended leaders with different agendas and priorities—has led to the current situation. In it we find that a generational failure to fund adequately the research, development, and production of helicopters has left the United States with (a) an aging fleet of obsolescent types, (b) no readily apparent alternatives to introduce into production, and (c) worst of all, battle statistics that show that loss ratios are greater today than they were in Vietnam As a single example, the Marines continued to rely on the forty-six-year-old CH-46 Sea Knights.

Keeping the Old Machines Flying

Helicopters had improved, but the changes in warfare had for the most part been adverse to helicopter operations, which remained close to the battle site. These changes dictated the increased employment of special operations forces, and they in turn depended upon the helicopter. The bewildering sadness of this situation, one somehow tolerated not only by the public and Congress but also the responsible military leaders, can be described in starkly specific terms.

Since the Vietnam War, the investment in tactical fixed-wing aircraft R&D has been nine times that devoted to rotary-wing R&D. In constant-dollar terms, investment in rotary-wing science and technology declined from $251 million in 1984 to $115 million in 2004. During the same twenty-year period, rotary-wing R&D funding fell from $7.9 billion to $2.3 billion.

By default, the services have had to rely on remanufacturing existing helicopters to maintain the fleet size, incorporating such improvements as can be fitted into thirty-year-old designs. A single example will serve to illustrate this point. The eighth prototype of the Boeing/Vertol JCH-47A was built in 1960 and carried the serial number 60-3449. While serving in Vietnam it was converted to the more capable CH-47B status, and its serial number changed to 66-3449. Twelve years later, about to serve in Haiti, it was converted to a CH-47C and renumbered 78-3449. In 1992 it was converted to a CH-47D and served in Bosnia, renumbered as 92-03449. Seven years later it was serving in Afghanistan. It is programmed ultimately to serve until 2032, with additional upgrades, of course, before (perhaps) retiring after seventy-two years of front-line service.[9] (To judge this service, one might consider a 1918 SPAD fighter being used in combat in 1990 or a 1942 P-51 Mustang still fighting and flying in 2014.)[10] Thus it is with the helicopter fleet. Existing aircraft, tired and worn, are put through a remanufacture process that can update them but never modernize them as they should be.

This is all the more disheartening because the helicopter today faces many of the same threats it faced in Vietnam, only much improved by time and technology. These threats include the inevitable problems of "brown-out" while landing in dusty, sandy areas, the proliferation of improved MANPADS, plus the inevitable (and often unseen until too late) effects of wear and tear on forty-year-old equipment.[11] The helicopters, allied with their fixed-wing counterparts, had an easier time establishing and holding a desired LZ in Vietnam than they do under the conditions of the Near East.

Budgets have dictated another important factor. While tactical fixed-wing aircraft receive a relatively uniform outfitting with new equipment, the helicopter fleet is selectively modified. Only those selected to go to the forward edge of the battle area (FEBA), such as the Apache, CSAR aircraft, and special operations forces, are fully equipped with the latest equipment. Others are expected to depend upon escorts to suppress the enemy defenses but are nonetheless often pressed into front-line service, where they are lost because they are not adequately armed and armored. It developed that in the Middle East there were no front lines. It was more difficult to prepare LZs than it had been in Vietnam, and there were no longer sufficient gunships to serve as escorts. Every clump of bush, every dusty house, every dilapidated truck could and often does conceal a MANPAD gunner.

The same faithful warplanes that flew in Vietnam—the Boeing Chinook, Sikorsky CH-53D, Boeing CH-46, Bell UH-1, and Bell AH-1—soldiered on in Operation IRAQI FREEDOM and beyond. All of these helicopters

The Chinook and Huey, two classic helicopters, in a mode of operation never envisaged by the pioneers. *(Courtesy of U.S. Army Museum, Fort Rucker)*

demonstrated an inherent worth and the potential for expanded mission use, none more fully than the remarkable products of the veteran Sikorsky firm.

They were joined by a very few new types beginning in the 1980s, including the Sikorsky UH-60 Black Hawk, the assault-helicopter replacement for the UH-1 series. The UH-60 was developed over time into a range of specialized aircraft for CSAR and Special Forces. However, the most important and perhaps most controversial new helicopter was the Hughes/McDonnell Douglas/Boeing Apache.

The AH-64 Apache

Now the primary Army attack helicopter, the Apache was designed as a quick-reaction weapon to halt enemy armor deep within enemy territory, without regard to daylight or weather. Air transportable in the Lockheed Martin C-5 and Boeing C-17 aircraft, the Apache is designed to be flown to trouble spots around the world and go into action in short order. The crew of two sits in tandem, the pilot in the rear with a copilot gunner forward.

First flown in on October 1, 1975, the Hughes Model 77 attack helicopter was intended to replace the Bell AH-1 Cobra. It won the 1976 U.S. Army Advanced Attack Helicopter competition, beating out a YAH-63 entry from Bell. With twin General Electric GET-700 turbo-shaft engines and a four-blade rotor, the AH-64 Apache's principal armament is a 30-mm M230 chain gun under the nose, along with four hardpoints on the two stub wings that can carry a mixture of AGM-114 Hellfire and Hydra 70 rocket pods. The effectiveness of the armament was vastly improved with the introduction of the Integrated Helmet and Display Sighting System (IHADSS). This permits the gunner to aim his M230 chain gun with movements of his head, pointing it at the target he has acquired visually. An alternate control method is the Target Acquisition and Designation System used in combination with the independent Pilot Night Vision System (TADS/PNVS).

The TADS has a laser range finder and target designator and is stabilized by electro-optical sensors. Like the IHADSS, the system is slaved to the crewmember's head and points the weapons where he looks. The PNVS uses an infrared camera attached to the pilot's head, allowing him to see almost as well at night as he can in daylight.

A study of gunship losses in Vietnam resulted in the Apache having a much stronger structure, with redundant systems to minimize losses and enhance the chances for crew survival in a crash. This has done much to stem the criticism that has always surrounded this aircraft. The first production Apache was obtained by the Army in 1983. There followed a series of corporate changes that saw the Hughes design sold in 1984 to McDonnell Douglas, the latter firm being acquired by Boeing in 1997. In that interval, McDonnell Douglas introduced the AH-64D Apache Longbow. With its distinctive mast-mounted Longbow Fire Control Radar (FCR), the AH-64D presented a new and capable silhouette on the battlefield. The Apache Longbow is a remanufactured version of the original AH-64A, improved with the millimeter-wave FCR target acquisition system, more powerful GE T700 engines, improved Hellfire missiles, and a much more sophisticated cockpit.

The FCR enables the Apache to detect up to 128 targets, provide a list of the 16 most dangerous ones, disseminate this information to other aircraft in the formation, and begin a precision attack, all within thirty seconds.

Due to budgetary limitations, of the 501 AH-64A Apaches designated to be upgraded to the AH-64D configuration, only 227 were identified to be equipped with the FCR. They also did not receive the engine upgrades and some of the other improvements.[12]

Army testing revealed an almost unimaginable improvement in capability of the AH-64D over the AH-64A. The Apache Longbow was tested and found to be more than 400 percent more lethal than the AH-64A, while requiring one-third fewer maintenance hours per flight hour. Perhaps more important from the crewmembers' viewpoint, tests indicated that they would be more than seven times as survivable as in the AH-64A.

After its introduction into service in 1986, the Apache was used in a succession of conflicts around the globe, beginning with Operation JUST CAUSE, the invasion of Panama in 1989. This was followed by action in Operation DESERT STORM in 1991, in the Balkans in the mid-1990s, and in Operation ENDURING FREEDOM in Afghanistan and Operation IRAQI FREEDOM in Iraq.

As will be seen in subsequent chapters, the Apache enjoyed success in most of these conflicts but also experienced some setbacks that called into question the viability of the helicopter on today's battlefield. Some of this derives from the fact that the Apache is comparable in sophistication to a modern jet fighter but is not stationed at well-equipped airfields with adequate repair facilities. Instead it is thrust into forward operating bases. The issue first arose during the Soviet adventure into Afghanistan. As the next chapter indicates, there was a vast difference between the abilities of Soviet engineers to create excellent helicopters and the ability of the Soviet military to employ them in adequate numbers in appropriate ways in Afghanistan.

Chapter Eight

Helicopter Development
and Deployment in the U.S.S.R.

The United States was far from alone in appreciating the advantages the turbine engine imparted to the helicopter, and no nation was more zealous in its pursuit of these advantages than the Soviet Union. Some hold that the U.S.'s successful use of turbine-powered helicopters in Vietnam led the Soviet leaders to conclude that helicopters could provide them a similar advantage in Afghanistan. In this they were only partially correct, for the Soviet Union inexplicably failed to apply its usual philosophy of mass numbers to its helicopter force. And despite the evidence late in the Vietnam War, the Soviet leaders failed to grasp the full implications of the arrival of improved weapons such as the Stinger, the most notorious of the MANPAD handheld surface-to-air missile (SAM) types.

Turbine-Powered Helicopter Development in the Soviet Union

Before examining the Soviet misadventure in Afghanistan, it is necessary to look at the effect of the turbine engine on helicopter development in the U.S.S.R. While the design bureaus had pursued several possible turbine-powered projects, the first production turbine-powered helicopter was the Mil design bureau's Mi-6. Then and for the next decade the world's largest helicopter, the Mi-6 first flew on June 5, 1957, with Rafil Kaprelian as pilot. The huge craft had an all-metal, five-bladed main rotor system that was 114 feet 10 inches in diameter and featured two removable wings, spanning 50 feet, mounted at a high angle of incidence on the bulky fuselage. The quickly detachable wings could produce additional lift, offloading the rotor by some 20 percent in cruising flight. The wings were not attached when the Mi-6 was used primarily as a flying crane.

The heart of the Mi-6 lay in its two Soloviev D-25V turbine engines, each producing 5,500 hp and capable of propelling the Hook, as it was known in NATO, to a top speed of 186 mph. The Hook went on to garner fourteen speed and height-with-payload records before entering service in eighteen air forces around the world. Some eight hundred of the type were built.

There were twenty-five variants, as the immense lifting capability of the aircraft lent itself to many roles, including anti-submarine warfare, airborne command post, air-sea rescue, and ninety-passenger civil transport. The Mi-6 was further developed into the Mi-10 "Harke," configured like the Sikorsky Tarhe for the flying-crane role. With its tall, widespread landing gear, the Harke could carry more than 33,000 pounds slung beneath it.

The Mil bureau made an enormous leap in going from the relatively small, low-powered piston engine Mi-4 to the large, jet-powered Mi-6. It was at once a risky gamble and an expression of the bureau's confidence

The huge Harke could carry up to twenty-eight troops or lift more than 33,000 pounds of cargo, thanks to its powerful engines and almost 115-foot-diameter rotor. (*Courtesy of Zaur Eylanbekov [Foxbat]*)

in its capability, given the huge increase in power provided by the twin turbo-shaft engines.

While a prototype had flown earlier, what became the workhorse Mil Mi-8 "Hip" made its first flight with 1,500-shp Isotov engines on September 17, 1962. This began a career that extends to this day, with more than ten thousand built, more than any other helicopter type. Roughly comparable in size and performance to the Sikorsky S-65, the Hip is operated in civil and military versions by more than forty countries around the world. The basic soundness of the Mi-8 design allowed it to operate in virtually any role desired of a helicopter, including that of gunship. After twenty years of service, the basic design was upgraded to the Mi-17 "Hip-H" by the installation of 1,950-hp Isotov TV3-117MT turbo-shaft engines.

The Soviet Union had closely followed the development of the American gunships in the Vietnam War, beginning work on the Mil Mi-24 "Hind"

The Hind was built in large numbers by the Soviet Union and used by dozens of air forces around the world. *(Courtesy of Zaur Eylanbekov [Foxbat])*

in the mid-1960s. The Mi-24 is larger than its American counterparts, the HueyCobra and Apache. While it was designed as both an assault transport and gunship, the KGB insisted that the rear cabin be used for scout teams for securing the border. Imposing size has long been a characteristic of Russian aircraft, and the Mi-24 follows in that tradition.

Developed from the Mi-8, the Hind has a five-blade rotor and features two stub wings that provide up to 25 percent of its lift in forward flight. They also provide stations for its heavy armament. Two Isotov TV3 turbo-shaft engines of 2,200 shp power the Hind and provide a top speed of 208 mph.

These three Mil designs, especially the Mi-6 and Mi-8, became the backbone of the Soviet helicopter effort in Afghanistan. There, they too would have an effect upon warfare. Unfortunately for the Soviet Union, warfare would have a more decisive effect upon them.

Kamov, the helicopter design bureau rival of Mil, had similar success in the creation of its own line of helicopters, although these were produced in far smaller numbers. The most important of the Kamov series was the Ka-25 "Hormone," designed principally for use with the Soviet Navy. The Ka-25 featured the signature Kamov three-bladed counter-rotating rotors, mounted at a goodly distance above the other, and a somewhat portly fuselage and twin rudders. Two Glushenkov GTD-3F turbo-shaft engines supplied 900 shp each, giving the Hormone a top speed of 135 mph.

The Soviet Union's Turn in Afghanistan

In 1979, the Soviet Union was at the absolute height of its power. It deployed 1,400 ICBMS, 900 IRBMS, 1,300 SRBMs, and 1,319 sea-launched missiles, thus meeting or exceeding U.S. capability in every missile category. For much of the time, Soviet missiles were more accurate than their U.S. counterparts and also housed within shelters that were much more hardened. The U.S. Strategic Air Command did have a superior aerial nuclear-delivery capability, but the Soviets had a great numerical superiority in tactical aircraft.

The disparity was even more marked in manpower. The U.S.S.R. had 3,638,000 personnel under arms, while the United States had 2,069,000, with far fewer reserves available. In terms of personnel, armor, and artillery, the Soviet Union and the Warsaw Pact States were numerically far superior to the United States and its NATO allies.

The Soviet Union seemed more stable politically than it had in years. Pres. Leonid Brezhnev had consolidated his powers by becoming the first man to be both president of the Soviet Union and the general secretary of the Communist Party. He had articulated the Brezhnev Doctrine, supporting enemies of the United States throughout the world. Afghanistan, despite its long and troubled history, must have seemed to him to have been a minor, easily resolved problem.

Many Western observers believed that the Soviet Union would obtain its goals in Afghanistan in contrast to America's failure in Vietnam. For one thing, domestic public support would not be a problem because of the Soviets' ruthless control of the media. The Soviet leaders were imputed to have a greater constancy in their goals because they were not subject to the elections that American leaders faced. Lyndon Johnson as dictator would have been a different man from Lyndon Johnson as candidate for reelection. With the unmatched firepower of the Red Army unhampered by restrictive, politically induced rules of engagement, Afghanistan was not seen to be a major challenge.

In the beginning, the Soviets' typically skillful intrusion seemed to work. The regime was changed, the capital of Kabul was taken, and the principal means of transportation and communication were quickly under control, all within a matter of days. The Soviets had won a conventional war in the manner in which they excelled. What they had not done was prepare for an unconventional war, which was historically Afghanistan's response to invasion. How this could be overlooked can only be attributed to Soviet hubris. There had already been unconventional wars in the Caucasus and in the Central Asian "republics" of the U.S.S.R.

As things developed, the Soviet tactics played directly into the hands of the resistance fighters. The Soviets' superior firepower worked in devastating villages ("draining the pond to kill the fishes" was one term applied to the process), but this simply forced the population into sanctuary areas across the fluid borders, where refugees were easily transformed into Mujahedeen.

The Soviets next attempted to destroy Mujahedeen strongholds. In these efforts, the Soviets deliberately included troops of Asian origin, to make the invasion seem "less foreign" and, in the phrase that is a cliché in every war and every country, "win the hearts and minds" of the local population. The ruse backfired, as the Soviet Asian troops felt sympathy for the local inhabitants, a sympathy that was not reciprocated at any level.

As the war developed, other notes were sounded, some resembling those of the Vietnam War and others hauntingly similar to the current situation in Afghanistan. The Soviet Union tried to "Afghanistanize" the war much as the Americans tried to "Vietnamize" their own conflict. They attempted to build up a regular Afghan military to strengthen their new leaders and instill a sense of nationality that encompassed the traditional tribal allegiances. There was only moderate success in this, as the typical Afghan recruit, born and bred to tribal customs, had difficulty understanding a rigid military hierarchy, the requirement to serve at all times rather than when it was convenient, and the troublesome nature of taking orders from someone who had been a perfect target only weeks before.[1] The United States faces the same phenomenon today.

A Muslim state since the ninth century, Afghanistan began its formal dalliance with communism in April 1978, when the Soviet-sponsored leader, Nur Muhammad Taraki, led a revolution to establish the People's Democratic Republic of Afghanistan (PDRA). This government, centralized but rife with almost incestuous political rivalries, was no more popular with the traditionally tribal Afghani populace than any it had endured in the past. Matters worsened when the regime instituted Soviet-style reforms—their version of what is now called "nation building." These reforms worked against the financial, theological, and political interests of the existing centers of power. The reaction then was identical to Afghanistan's current reaction to American efforts: rebellion.

The first rebel attacks were against outlying garrisons, and the central government's reaction was draconian, with thousands of executions, many of them including local tribal leaders. The Soviet Union supplied the PDRA Army and Air Force with equipment, "advisors," and training, and the central government lashed out with barbaric cruelty against the insurgency. The general effect was that of throwing gasoline upon a fire: the rebellion spread, following a now-familiar pattern. First, outlying areas would come under the control of the rebels, then gradually, parts of cities and then whole cities.

The central government increased its efforts, viciously bombing villages into rubble and killing thousands. As the violence grew, so did desertions from the PDRA armed services. Ultimately some 50 percent left to fight for the Mujahedeen. There were a number of reasons for this, especially patriotism, but a principal one was that the Mujahedeen style of warfare was the customary mode for these tribal warriors. Even the admittedly ragged discipline of the Afghan army was too much for these untamed individuals to bear.

The PDRA called for increasing levels of Soviet support to counter the clandestine support being furnished to the rebels by the United States, India, and other countries sympathetic to their cause. Initially they had called for company-size efforts but were soon demanding effort requiring a division. The situation became so serious that Brezhnev felt compelled to intervene to preserve his satellite's government. There followed a not-so-subtly conducted invasion by the Fortieth Soviet Army on December 24, 1979. (Twelve years and one day later, the Soviet Union would cease to exist.)

Just as it had done in Hungary in 1956 and Czechoslovakia in 1968, the Soviet Union prepared its invasion quietly, beginning its mobilization in October. Airborne battalions began arriving at Bagram air base in December and these subsequently moved to cover the vital Salang Pass, through which the major Soviet invading force, the 360th and 375th Motor Rifle divisions, would proceed. A well-executed military airlift, using 280 aircraft, transported troops to Kabul. The troops were combat ready, although Soviet airborne troops were not all volunteers, as their U.S. counterparts always have been. The airlift aircraft were first rate and included Ilyushin Il-76s, Antonov An-22s, and An-12s. One Il-76 crashed into a mountain on its approach to Kabul, killing forty-four of its crew and passengers.

Twice the size of Vietnam, with about 30 percent of its population, Afghanistan presented the Soviet Union with an austere terrain even more hostile than Vietnam's verdant jungles. Some 65 percent of the country is mountainous, less than 25 percent is a non-fertile plateau, and only about 12 percent is arable. That 12 percent is more devoted to growing poppies than food. The temperature range is extreme and compounded by sandstorms.

The Soviet Union was thus presented with challenges in terms of geography, climate, and indigenous personnel exceeding those faced by both the French in Algeria and the Americans in Vietnam. Though the ARVN forces in South Vietnam might not always have been the most capable of allies, they were far more supportive of the American forces than the Afghan government forces were of the Soviet Union. The Soviet forces were able to control the larger cities, useful military bases, and critically important facilities. However, even when more than 100,000 troops were deployed, they were unable to control vast areas of the country. And as in the past when other foreign nations occupied Afghanistan, the Soviet presence unified the opposition, turning tribesmen from fighting with each other to fighting for the national cause. The tribal forces were often augmented by regular Afghan army units, who fought far better against the Soviet invader than when they were supposed to be suppressing their fellow tribesmen, who might have been enemies in the past but now became brothers-in-arms.

There was no contest when Soviets met the enemy in open combat, for their airpower and artillery was overwhelming. But the Mujahedeen quickly adopted guerilla tactics, which made such confrontations increasingly rare. The Soviets had to be content with occupying some 20 percent of the country, emphasizing their strength where political considerations dictated, near the borders of Iran and Pakistan, and virtually ignoring the rest of the country. In time, as the insurgency gathered strength and occupied key areas, the Soviets would respond with large-scale attacks involving several divisions with strong air forces. These would achieve their objective of driving the Mujahedeen away from the areas where they had seized control, but the larger forces could not remain in the field indefinitely, and when they withdrew, the insurgents would return.

It was thus inevitable that helicopters would become the principal means by which the Soviet Union would attempt to sustain itself in Afghanistan, protecting the cities and serving as armed guards for the transport of supplies to the desolate outposts. What is amazing is that for a nation that always employed massive numbers of troops, artillery, and armor, the Soviet Union allowed its helicopter strength to grow from an initial input of about 60 to no more than 280 by 1980. Unfortunately for the Soviets, as much in demand as helicopters were, that number did not increase significantly at any time during the war. Ultimately, some 650 were supplied during the conflict, and more than half of these were lost.

The Soviet forces received only a fraction of the helicopters supplied to American and ARVN forces in Vietnam. The paucity of helicopters not only limited the number of operations but constrained them as well. Unlike the American system, where the helicopters belonged to the air-assault unit, the Soviet airborne troops had to coordinate with the Red Air Force to use its helicopters. This is astounding considering the steps the Soviets had taken during World War II to ensure that Army and Air Force operations were coordinated. Further, the very limited number of transport helicopters meant that operations often had to be carried out in small numbers, carrying a single company of troops. Larger operations had to be flown in waves, with the transport helicopters flying several sorties per mission, protracting both the landing and withdrawal operations.

The situation defies logic, for in the agonizingly long nine years of the war, there was more than ample time to ramp up production and training. The Soviet Union could easily have responded to the challenge despite its increasingly straitened circumstances. Its failure to do so must be attributed, as so much else, to the Soviet leadership.

The shortage of helicopters was initially exacerbated by insufficient crew training, a shortage of specialized equipment, and the fact that many operations were conducted at high altitudes and temperatures. In time, crew proficiency improved and new equipment was introduced, but nothing could be done about the environment.

The Soviets relied on fewer types of helicopters than the Americans employed in Vietnam. During the initial years, some piston-engine-powered types were used, but as the Soviet helicopter fleet stabilized, it operated about 40 Mi-6 Hooks, 100 Mi-8 Hips, and 100 Mi-24 Hinds. The Mi-6 Hook became a workhorse comparable to the Vertol Ch-47 in Vietnam, carrying troops and supplies or evacuating the wounded. Its stable mate, the Mi-8 Hip, performed its dual transport and assault roles. In the early years, before the Mujahedeen acquired experience, this aircraft was effective in countering guerilla forces in mountainous areas. As the resistance intensified, the Mil-24 became the Soviet weapon of choice because of its greater speed, armor, and armament.

Larger than U.S. assault helicopters, the Hind can carry up to seven troops or stretchers if used for MEDEVAC. The Mil engineers deliberately traded maneuverability for speed and survivability in the Hind, which is less able to hover than other gunships. Its large wings provided both lift and space for rockets and missiles. Earlier models, equipped with 12.7-mm machineguns, were found to lack the necessary punch, so the Hind-F was fitted with twin 30-mm cannon.

As in every war in every service, the failure of leaders to provide sufficient numbers of adequate weapons was offset by taking it out of the hides of the front-line soldiers. Soviet helicopter crews were tasked with innumerable roles, from protecting convoys to mine laying to aerial assault. Somewhat surprisingly, the Hip and Hind were often used as level or dive bombers, dropping bombs weighing up to five hundred kilograms on lightly defended targets.

The Mi-8

The Mi-8 was especially well regarded by its pilots and mechanics and warrants some special commentary. Just as the United States produced its Major Bradys and Kellys, the Soviets produced notable pilots. One was Maj. Vyacheslav Gainutdinov, a commander of the 181 OVP (Otdelnyy Vertoletnyy Polk Boyeogo Upravleniya or Independent Combat Control Helicopter Regiment) and proud wearer of the Hero of the Soviet Union medal. This distinction was conferred for his saving a reconnaissance party by flying through a heavy sandstorm, locating them, and pulling them out from under heavy fire. Sadly, again like his American counterparts, Gainutdinov pressed his luck too hard and was shot down and killed on August 19, 1980, ironically the Soviet Air Forces Day.

The typical Soviet requirement for security kept wraps on the full extent of its CSAR capability in Afghanistan. However, early research by Lt. Col. Johnnie H. Hall, published in the May-June 1982 edition of *Air University Review,* indicated a firm commitment by the Soviet Air Force to the task. The author took as a benchmark the following entry on the subject from the *Soviet Military Encyclopedia:*

Aviatsionnaya Poiskova-Spasatel'Naya Sluzhba (air rescue service). A special service that organizes and conducts search and rescue of crews and passengers on piloted airborne platforms. Its missions are: to search, to render assistance, and to evacuate crews and passengers on airborne platforms in distress; to provide crews with emergency rescue equipment and equipment for self-aid and mutual aid; to train the flight crews how to act during a forced landing or abandonment of an airborne aircraft and to use emergency rescue equipment; to organize a notification system of airborne platforms in distress and the sequence for transmitting and receiving distress signals. Search and rescue operations are performed by airplanes, helicopters, ships, vessels, and ground facilities equipped with radar search apparatus and rescue equipment, by ground search teams, and by parachute landing groups. Search and evacuation of cosmonauts and descending spacecraft modules can also be entrusted to the air service. For example, the United States has an aerospace rescue service intended for search and evacuation of astronauts and spacecraft as well as for search, rescue, and evacuation of the crews and passengers of aircraft in distress.[2]

To appreciate the effort given to pilot survival, one has to note the primitive level of care and comfort that the Soviet leaders afforded the rest of their population. The U.S.S.R. was at the forefront of technology in missiles and space but was for the most part unable to provide an adequate food supply to its people, much less the essential commodities found in all the countries of the West at the time. The people of the Soviet Union thirsted for good soap, jeans, automobiles, and other comforts and were unable to get them. The care given by the Soviet Air Force to the creation of a personal survival kit for its pilots was a remarkable step forward.

The adventurous MiG-25 pilot Viktor Belenko has in his writing and talks described how deficient the Soviet Air Force was in this regard for many years. It thus is all the more remarkable that the survival kit should contain a radio and other signaling devices, including a flare gun and emergency beacon. In addition, the kit contained about a gallon of water and rations for three or four days. Perhaps more importantly, as an indication of the efforts being made, it also included a medical kit with medications and drugs, dye for a water landing, distillation kits, matches, fuel tablets, a compass, mosquito netting, canteen, and blade-saw knife—all items that were difficult to obtain in that economy and through normal military channels.

The Mil Mi-8 became the standard rescue helicopter, reflecting both its capability and availability. However, there was at the time an apparent lack of a companion aircraft to perform the high-altitude search and the command and control of rescue missions. In marked contrast to this lack, the descriptions of a helicopter rescue training mission indicate that the medical personnel onboard included an emergency surgery brigade with a neurosurgeon, anesthesiologist, and internist. This rather implausible crew would be a wonderful addition to any rescue mission, but no air force could afford to carry such specialist personnel on a routine basis.

In their early days in Afghanistan, the relatively untrained Soviet crews were worked hard, essentially doing on the job training, making five or six flights a day, and logging eight or more hours of flight time. There were many echoes of the U.S. difficulties in Vietnam, where combat efforts had been hamstrung by inane rules of engagement. And just as American pilots had experienced, the Soviets had to learn how to overcome the extraordinary emphasis that had been placed on flight safety. The rules that had applied in the Soviet Union were unworkable in Afghanistan. As a single example, the Mi-8 helicopter had been limited to turns of no more than 30 degrees and dives of no more than 15 degrees. Either restriction could lead to quick destruction in the mountain gorges of Afghanistan. To survive, it was absolutely necessary to perform officially prohibited maneuvers, such as banking at 90 degrees and making steep dives. In addition, to get the job done, the aircrews flew with loads far greater than were allowed.

The flight restrictions were never removed, and some pilots were admonished and threatened with relief from flying duties for violating them. There were, inevitably, crashes resulting from breaking the official rules, both in test and combat, but breaking them remained the only way to achieve the mission. Many Soviet helicopter pilots later said they really learned to fly in Afghanistan.

In some instances, Soviet maps of Afghanistan were primitive and often useless because of the monotonous nature of the terrain. The few landmarks—a distinctive village or rock formation—were not depicted. Some crews were reduced to using the travel notes of the botanist-geographer scholar Nicholas I. Vavilov, made almost fifty years before. Improved maps were introduced, and the Soviets did a new survey to rectify the situation.

The navigation difficulties were compounded by the long distances between airfields and targets. To offset this, the Mi-8 was fitted with a pair of 915-liter fuel tanks, which gave a range of about six hundred miles. The drawback was that these tanks took up more than 50 percent of the available cargo space and added greatly to takeoff weight.

The versatility of the workhorse Mi-8 allowed it to be used for attack missions as well as transport. The Mi-8TV (heavily armed) version carried a 12.7-mm machine gun, six UB-32-57 rocket pods, and four 9M17P Skorpion antitank guided rockets. The weight of this armament severely taxed performance, particularly at higher altitudes, and made them unpopular with the already wary pilots. The sense of marginal performance and the battle losses led to a psychology of shooting first and asking questions later.

By June 1980, it was recognized that all the Mi-8s needed to have additional firepower, and machine guns were added fore and aft. Some carried the "Plamya" 30-mm AGS-17 automatic grenade launcher, which was effective for almost half a mile against ground personnel. In time, concerted tactics were developed in which two or more Mi-8s would approach a target from the front, then quickly turn to fire a salvo from the side of the helicopter in the manner of a broadside from an old-fashioned ship of the line. The Plamya was a very unsophisticated weapon, however, without an integral targeting ability and little compensation for its recoil. Its accuracy depended, as with so many weapons, on the skill of the crew-chief/gunner assigned to fire it.

As the Afghan resistance introduced heavier arms, including 12.7-mm weapons, the S-5 unguided aerial rocket was brought into play. The S-5M high-explosive fragmentation series was especially effective against personnel, while the anti-armor S-5KO version had a HEAT warhead that turned the profusion of local rocks into prolific producers of shrapnel. Circumstances forced the Soviet crews to use the S-5s against the wide-area targets for which they were designed and against point targets such as mortar emplacements, machine gun nests, or a fortified area. They were usually fired in volleys of eight, sixteen, or thirty-two rockets, thus saturating enough area to take out a point target. Although they were effective from as far as three-quarters of a mile, experienced pilots would fly to almost point-blank distances to achieve the kill.

Surprisingly enough, ordinary bombs were found to be the best to use against concealed weapon sites. A "helicopter bomber" usually carried two to four bombs and would be flown in a group of standard attack helicopters for concealment and protection. When the attack helicopters had put down their rocket fire to cover the target, the bomber would proceed in and drop from level flight, usually using the time-tested method of marking their windscreens with lines and then sighting by eye.

The *"vertushka,"* or revolving-door tactic, recalled World War II Ilyushin Il-2 "Shturmovik" tactics. A flight of Mi-8s would make a diving attack, flying in a close circle so that each machine protected the other. Flying about three thousand feet apart, they laid down a shield of protective fire to keep the Afghanis' heads down.

The Afghanis resisted as always, and at low altitudes, the greatest danger came first from machine guns and the standard Lee-Enfield 7.62 rifle, inherited from the British a half-century before. The Mi-8 was rugged and could absorb a lot of ground fire, but the hazard of mass rifle fire from the ground could not be ignored. Instead of wearing the armored vests and helmets that were ultimately produced, the crews used them as armor, draping them across seats and over critical equipment. In the 130-degree ambient temperatures, each crewmember flew in the dangerous (because of the hazard from fire) uniform of a pair of trousers and a straw hat.

As in all wars and in all air forces, the bulk of the work fell upon the crew chief, who had to get up early, prepare and fuel the helicopter for flight, get the crew onboard and settled, get the aircraft started, make sure the load was properly distributed, then climb onboard himself. In flight, he was a flight engineer, helped out the pilot and navigator, fired the machine gun, and then directed the offloading of equipment and the loading of passengers or wounded. Then, when the aircraft returned to base, he was tasked with seeing that any battle damage or mechanical problems were solved.

Whatever the role, the wear and tear on the helicopters and crews was significant, and Soviet morale was markedly lower than in corresponding American units in the Vietnam War. There was never anything approaching the DUSTOFF or MEDEVAC qualities of daring and élan; the Soviet system simply did not engender such efforts. Somewhat ingloriously, the greatest number of Soviet soldiers evacuated for medical care were victims of diseases, such as typhoid, paratyphoid, infectious hepatitis, acute dysentery, and myriad combinations of these and other maladies.

Through about 1985 there was a significant difference in Soviet airmobile operations from those of the Americans in Vietnam. The allied airborne forces in Vietnam were proactive, being used to destroy enemy soldiers and supplies by quickly descending on a predetermined area, executing the destruction, then just as quickly evacuating the scene. For the first five years of the war, the Soviet airmobile forces were primarily reactive, attempting to counter the attacks of the Mujahedeen. However, the Soviets ultimately followed American practice in using fixed-wing airpower to provide a powerful counterweight to the airborne mobile attacks.[3]

From the first day to the last of the agonizingly long Soviet invasion of Afghanistan, helicopters were essential for everything from transport to resupply to air support to—far less frequent than would have been the American case—CSAR.

The helicopters began their work prior to the invasion, being part of the weapons shipped to Afghanistan in anticipation of their eventual use on behalf of the government supported by the Soviet Union. In mid-December 1979, helicopter units in Turkestan and elsewhere were deployed to border airfields. An elaborate cover story, complete with maps of Iran, was established to indicate that their purpose was to go to Iran to support the anti-shah movement.

By the beginning of 1980, there were 110 helicopters of the 34th SAK (*Smeshannyi Avia Korpus* or Composite Air Corps) on strength in Afghanistan. Of these, about 85 percent were Mi-8s, which would serve as the principal helicopter throughout the war. As might be expected, the transfer of these helicopters to a foreign base resulted in initial supply and maintenance problems.

Soviet Helicopters Enter Combat

The first major helicopter combat operation took place on January 2, 1980, when a large force of Mi-8s was used to seize Kandahar, Afghanistan's second largest city. This was part of the general plan to establish garrisons over a wider area in order to seize more territory. Only by doing so could the Soviets maintain control of communications and other vital installations. There was a backlash to the expansion, however; as each of the provincial centers was taken, the opposition increased.

There began a long series of attacks and counterattacks. In February, the "rebels," as they were termed, managed to cut a road on the outskirts of Kunduz, in the northern region. In response, the Soviets sent a *desant,* an airmobile company carried by Mi-8 helicopters. The troops seized the only bridge in the area, cutting off the rebels but suffering seven deaths, the first in a long series of helicopter-related losses in the war.

Ironically, given the long support that Father Winter had provided to Russia against foreign intruders, the Soviet invaders were caught short by the severity of the Afghan weather. Snow closed most of the roads, and helicopters became the only means of supply for everything, including such heavy necessities as firewood and water. The need was so great for everything from ammunition to construction material (wood, tarpaper, canvas) for huts that the helicopters were often overloaded, flying with lumber protruding from the doors. In some instances, only the overtaxed Mi-8s kept some settlements from starvation.

Despite the overt nature of the occupation, the Soviets had attempted to disguise their intrusion by painting Afghan insignia on their Mi-8s and even selecting personnel from regions where the inhabitants resembled the Afghans in appearance and language. This effort was undermined by the fact that Russian remained the common tongue of the force.

Spring came eventually, and the rebel activity increased. The Soviets quickly learned that the terrain, with its deep ravines and limited roads, made the traditional weaponry of tanks, armored personnel carriers, motorized artillery, and supply trucks useless. It became increasingly obvious that the helicopter was the weapon not only of choice but necessity.

The huge demand combined with the terrain imposed almost impossible tasks on the still limited number of Soviet helicopters. The Mi-8s were often forced to work in small units, sometimes only flights of two, flying from small rough fields where fuel was short. The obvious logistic solution of supplying rubber bladders for the fuel was augmented by storing it in any handy field cistern. In some instances, helicopters were dedicated to the fuel-service task, being filled with fuel to their operating limits and then sent out to the smaller field to serve as "cows." These aerial filling stations were soon being used to support combat operations.

Later, as more forces became available, helicopter regiments usually consisted of four squadrons of sixteen aircraft each. Throughout the war, the Mi-8 was used in a variety of ways, supplemented by Mi-24s and a few others such as the Mi-6 Hook. Only late in the war were there sufficient Mi-24s to form a squadron.

The failure of Soviet training discipline became evident in the operation of the assault helicopters. As usual, helicopter squadrons were attached to individual divisions. Unfortunately, many of these squadrons were not made up of homogenous crews, well-trained and used to operating together. The proficiency level was barely adequate for peacetime operations, and during assault operations, shortcomings were quickly revealed. Pilots proved unable to find the appropriate LZ, and navigators attached for the task were equally inept. If by chance they found the correct target area, their limited training often made their weapons almost useless.

Extraordinarily complex tactics were used to transport Soviet troops or supplies into guerilla territory. While some Hinds patrolled over the ground force, looking for possible ambush sites, other Hinds would land troops on a high point well ahead of the advancing ground unit. These troops would provide flank security until the ground unit had passed, being protected themselves by the Hinds that had carried them in. They would then be picked up and "leapfrogged" to the next key position. It was costly, but it made the guerillas' efforts far more difficult.[4]

As always in wartime, some extraordinary leaders emerged. Maj. Vladimir Kharitonov became famous for the manner in which he trained the new pilots, showing them what the helicopter could do and how best to use it in combat. He went an unusual step further, particularly for the Soviet system, by seeing that all crewmembers were able to perform the duties of the other crewmembers, to the point that pilots could repair the helicopters and mechanics could fly them.

This was far from the norm. When SAMs forced the Hinds to resort to "nap-of-the-earth" flying, there were many accidents. This was partly because the helicopters were not designed for this kind of flying but primarily because crews remained improperly trained. The new tactics also caused increased wear and tear due to foreign-object ingestion, reducing the number of aircraft available.

Characteristically, the Soviet bureaucracy refused to profit from the experience being gained, instead punishing pilots who damaged an aircraft by exceeding its limitations in combat. Before the invasion, the Soviet forces had been told that they were on a "high and noble mission to bring international assistance." It is not surprising that the first year's losses made them choose their own battle slogan, which became "shoot first and ask questions later."

When the much more capable Mi-24 was in short supply, the Mi-8 was used for assault missions, and crews became adept at modifying it for the role. A limited amount of armor was added in crucial spots and a variety of firepower was added, including heavy machine guns mounted fore and aft and automatic grenade launchers. These lacked adequate sighting equipment and were effective only to the degree that the crews could use Kentucky windage to hit their targets. Some specialized versions, such as the Mi-8TV (*Tyazheloe Vooruzenie* or heavily armed), carried a 12.7-mm machine gun, six UB-32-57 pods carrying S-5 57-mm rockets, and four 9M17P Skorpion antitank guided rockets (AT-2C Swatter-C). In the thin mountain air, however, the weight and drag of these weapons further degraded the Mi-8s' performance.

Protected targets were usually attacked with bombs, with the pilots generally using horizontal and angled lines painted on the canopy, just as their forbears in World War II had done. Mi-8s usually carried two bombs but sometimes staggered along with four. A typical tactic was to fire a volley of rockets at the target, then follow up with bombs. In time, more sophisticated tactics came into use, with several helicopters cooperating. The helicopters would fly in a circle, with one breaking off to dive to the attack while the others laid down protecting fire.

The Mujahedeen responded by firing everything they could shoot, from their Lee-Enfield rifles to machine guns and, once they obtained them, shoulder-fired SAMs. Even the 7.62-mm Lee-Enfield could inflict significant damage, but the Mi-8s were toughly built and often came home despite multiple hits. The rugged Hind was really vulnerable at only three points—the tail-rotor assembly, the turbine intakes, and an oil tank that was by chance located just behind the red-star insignia on the fuselage.

In 1986, the increasingly frustrated Soviet Union, already in the process of destabilization at home, adjusted its tactics and began to use its airmobile forces more proactively, striking against enemy strongholds. While this might have been a more successful strategy, it was countered by the widespread introduction of the handheld SAM. In the mountains of Afghanistan, the environment lent a helping hand to weaponry. A small number of British Shorts Blowpipe missiles were followed by an ever-increasing flood of Redeye and Stinger missiles, an American joint product of Hughes, General Dynamics, and Raytheon. Weighing less than thirty-five pounds, the Stinger could be employed in terrain where machine guns and cannons were too heavy to use. Their deadly supersonic efficiency was complemented by their relative ease of use. And the less sophisticated but ubiquitous rocket-propelled grenade was always a danger.

The Stinger, a distant relative of the WW II bazooka and *Panzerfaust,* consists of a "fire and forget" missile encased in a launch tube and fitted with a separate grip-stock assembly. The latter was sufficiently like a conventional rifle or machine gun to be of comfort to the Mujahedeen being initiated to its use. The Stinger employs a passive infrared seeker to home in on its target and was sensitive enough to be able to attack the Hinds on their inbound runs. Once the Stinger was fired, the operator was free to move to cover elsewhere.

The initial Stinger attacks came as a relative surprise to the Soviet crews flying the Hind, and it took time to develop defensive tactics. The Hind lacked adequate defensive measures, relying primarily on an ineffective flare system to decoy the missile away from its target. The changes in tactics were reminiscent of those of American tactical air forces in Vietnam. Those early tactics required flying at relatively high altitudes to escape small-arms and machine-gun fire. This moved them to an altitude where the SAMs were effective. The greater kill capacity of the SAMs made low-level tactics more attractive, even though the enemy forces, both in Vietnam and Afghanistan, took advantage of the situation by increasing the number and caliber of the machine guns.

In time the Hinds tended to fly at low altitudes, using terrain as cover. If they saw that a SAM had been fired at them, they would turn into it and descend if they could. Too often, however, the SAM arrived without warning and Hind losses soared. Some one hundred helicopters were lost to the Stinger by mid-1987.[5]

The losses were not the greatest effect of the Stinger, however. It became a part of the manner in which warfare produced changes in the helicopter. The major change was a loss in operational efficiency. The Soviet helicopter forces could not achieve in Afghanistan what the American and ARVN airmobile forces achieved in Vietnam—a relative operational impunity. There were far too few Soviet helicopters to match the American effort, and as a result, their effectiveness declined. That decline coincided with the general deterioration of the Soviet system, and a decision was made to begin withdrawing Soviet troops in 1988. The withdrawal was completed by February 15, 1989, to the general relief of all involved.

The helicopter had not proved to be as effective for the Soviet Union in Afghanistan as it had for the Americans in Vietnam, but it did not matter. In both situations, the spectacular failure of leadership and in political will by the respective national governments rendered the success or failure of the helicopter military capability moot. The Soviet mess in Afghanistan ended much as the American mess in Vietnam ended, with the foreign troops being pulled out ignominiously under the cloak of spurious claims of diplomatic successes and good wishes for the future.

A key element permitting the relatively new and progressive Soviet leader, Mikhail Gorbachev, to conduct a withdrawal from Afghanistan after the tremendous expense and horrendous casualties was the Geneva Accords. The format for these accords had been agreed upon in 1985. The accords were based on the premise that once the foreign threat to Afghanistan was ended, the Soviet Union could leave. It was not until April 14, 1988, that the crucial bilateral agreement between Afghanistan and Pakistan was signed. With Pakistan nominally no longer supporting the resistance, Gorbachev could claim that the Soviet Union's original goals had been fulfilled and could begin the withdrawal of forces.

It may be argued that the Afghan debacle had even more far reaching effects upon the Soviet Union than Vietnam had upon the United States, for the resulting social, economic, and military problems added to the probability of the U.S.S.R.'s collapse. Ironically, however, the failure of the Soviets and the harm done to Afghanistan and its people led directly to the later U.S. involvement in what was termed Operation ENDURING FREEDOM but actually evolved into what should be called "Operation ENDURING NIGHTMARE."[6]

Chapter Nine

Operations in the Near East

The success of the helicopter brought about changes in warfare in the Vietnam War, and the prospects, however fragile, of its containing the bold armed presence of the Soviet Union in Europe encouraged its advocates. Unfortunately there was a side effect to these events, a naive expectation on the part of many, particularly those who had never personally experienced its use in actual combat, that far more could be done with the helicopter than its performance warranted. Oddly enough, this expectation was most strongly held by those who had made the biggest budget cuts to military expenditures as a part of Pres. Jimmy Carter's administration. Under Carter, Special Operation Forces (SOF) were cut to 95 percent of the strength they had reached during the Vietnam War.[1]

In terms of hardware, most helicopters in the American inventory had reached their aerodynamic developmental peak, and further improvements would come only through the installation of more sophisticated equipment. The basic performance parameters of speed, altitude, and range remained roughly the same as those of a decade before. Notwithstanding this, the concerted effort necessary to develop new, more advanced helicopters was betrayed, as it had been so often in the past and would be in the future, by traditional budgeting and procurement processes. As we will see in a series of examples, these included the system of advocacy, the inevitable "hobby-shop" approach on requirements, and the hazards of securing congressional approval based on the benefits accruing to particular congressional districts. The hard unpalatable truth is that poor procurement practice combined with inadequate funding in both the science and technology and R&D sectors has resulted, for the most part, in a diminished fleet of aging helicopters.

Overexpectations

The most blatant example of overexpectation was the Iran hostage crisis, which began on November 4, 1979, and lasted for 444 days. Militant Islamist students, under the banner of a group with the catchy name of the "Muslim Student Followers of the Imam's Line," demonstrated on behalf of their new government by seizing the United States Embassy in Tehran. Sixty-six embassy personnel were taken hostage, and of these, fifty-two were sequestered for the entire time. Over the next five months, Pres. Jimmy Carter was hesitant in his response to the crisis, being outwitted by his Iranian opponents in each of his efforts to free the captives.

Humiliated by the Iranians, and faced with the prospect of defeat in the fall 1980 elections, President Carter at last decided upon using military force to rescue the hostages. The result was an overly elaborate rescue plan named Operation EAGLE CLAW involving U.S. intrusion into Iranian territory for two days. This intrusion was to be conducted with the close cooperation of a team of fixed-wing and rotary-wing aircraft flown by personnel from the Air Force, Army, Navy, and Marines. Sadly, not as a result of an oversight but of an excessive concern for security, these able, proficient airmen were not provided with an opportunity to train as a unit.

A distinguished team of planners was given the task of rescuing the hostages, but their efforts were hampered by continual interference from the White House and the inexplicable looseness of their organization, which lacked a clearly defined chain of command. With multiple commanders for the fixed-wing, rotary-wing, and SOF components, a genuine unity of command proved to be impossible. The band-aid solution showed an extraordinary degree of cooperation among the leaders, for the most part, but the plan's inherent inflexibility caused this to break down when unplanned contingencies arose. In the end, this left the exact chain of command confusing and even unknown to most of the mission's participants. Perhaps even worse, considering the scope of the project about to unfold, simply combining Air Force, Navy, Army, and Marine forces was difficult. The concept of joint operations, although always paid lip service, still had not jelled. And even more crucial for this mission than any other, the U.S. military was not yet prepared for missions demanding interoperability of personnel and equipment. For security purposes, each of the components trained in separate areas, and, as a final fatal mistake, there was never a full-scale rehearsal of the entire operation.

The incredibly optimistic planning fell into three phases. Phase I was the nighttime insertion of the SOF and the assembly and refueling of the helicopters. Phase II was the assault by ground forces on the embassy, where it was hoped the hostages would be found. Phase III was the extraction of the embassy personnel to safety and the return of the combatant forces to friendly stations.

Working with inadequate equipment and depending too much upon good fortune, Operation EAGLE CLAW was destined to fail from the start. The plans called for a rescue team of U.S. Army Delta Force personnel to be placed inside Iran at a site called Desert One, a long 265 miles south of Tehran, on the first night of the mission. This was a temporary airstrip carved out of the desert for use by three USAF Lockheed MC-130E Combat Talon I aircraft, which were to bring in the combat forces, and three Lockheed EC-130Es to provide ground refueling stations for the helicopter force. Aerial refueling was not an option with the selected equipment. Eight Navy RH-53D Sea Stallions (the ubiquitous Sikorsky S-65) were to launch from the USS *Nimitz,* flown by U.S. Marine Corps personnel. The Marine crews were not familiar with the selected mission aircraft and had only one opportunity to fly the RH-53Ds before the mission.[2]

The lack of experience of the mission planners was reflected in the number and the type of the helicopters they selected. They believed the RH-53D to have a mission capability of 74 percent, but this was the fleet-wide experience, not of the individual aircraft chosen for the mission. Further, the type was notorious for being difficult to start after exposure to cold. Failure to understand the nature of helicopter operations was exacerbated by the long 865-nautical-mile night flight required to get from the *Nimitz* to Desert One. At an air speed of 120 mph, reflecting the still primitive nature of helicopter performance but in fact higher than the heavily loaded CH-53s could initially attain, more than seven hours of precise navigation was required of the aircrews.

After landing at Desert One, the helicopters were to pick up the rescue team and fly it to a second destination within Iran, closer to Tehran and designated Desert Two. There the team was to hide out until the following evening, when the CIA was to supply trucks to transport them to the U.S. Embassy and rescue the hostages. (It should be noted that here, as at Son Tay in Korea, the exact location of the captives was not known with 100-percent certainty.) The SOF were to overcome all armed resistance at the embassy, and the newly rescued hostages were to be taken to a nearby soccer stadium. There, the helicopters were to fly in, pick them up, and fly them, not to freedom, but to yet another staging area. This was the Manzariyeh Air Base outside of Tehran, which was to be seized by a force of U.S. Army Rangers. Following the seizure of the field, USAF Lockheed C-141 transports were to fly in, pick up the hostages, and take them—at last—to freedom. Subsequently, the other members of the rescue force would find their respective ways back to the United States.

Most military planners would never have agreed to such a complex plan, one that depended not only upon skill and bravery but sustained good luck. It should have been apparent that it was not feasible to operate a significant military force undetected for two days within the territory of another sovereign country, even one with great isolated areas such as Iran. The possibility of discovery was simply too great. Further, the very small invading force was tasked with establishing a commanding presence inside a sovereign nation at five different locations—Desert One, Desert Two, the American embassy, the nearby soccer stadium and the Manzariyeh Air Base—all within a forty-eight-hour period. At face value, the whole operation was more akin to an action screenplay than a well-thought-out military plan.

The initial portion of Operation EAGLE CLAW went well enough, with the approximately 150 members of the U.S. Army Delta Force being delivered to Desert One by the MC-130 aircraft, one of which was slightly damaged in landing. The MC-130s departed after offloading the personnel and were followed in by EC-130s, which set up fueling stations in the form of 6,000-gallon collapsible bladders.

The helicopters ran into problems early on. Two of the eight RH-53D Sea Stallions were lost when, about 230 miles inbound from the USS *Nimitz,* they encountered a desert weather phenomenon that concentrated fine particles of sand in the air, shutting visibility down to less than a mile. The first of the helicopters, code named Bluebird 6, was abandoned in the desert, its crew being picked up by Bluebird 8. A second helicopter, Bluebird 5, became disoriented in the desert sandstorm and returned to the carrier. A third helicopter, Bluebird 2, encountered problems with its hydraulic system and had to be abandoned. All command coherence within the helicopter flight was lost. Each of the remaining helicopters flew in to Desert One on its own.

The force was now down to five helicopters, less than the minimum number required to carry off the operation. After much controversy among the on-scene personnel, President Carter issued an abort order on the recommendation of the 1st Special Forces Operational Detachment-Delta (1st SFOD-D) commander, Col. Charles Beckwith.

Sadly, there were more serious difficulties to come. The inevitable chance discovery of the mission occurred when an Iranian smuggling fuel in a tanker truck happened upon the site. His truck was fired upon and destroyed. Unfortunately, the resulting explosion and fire lit up the area for miles around. Shortly thereafter, a civilian Iranian bus with forty-four people onboard happened upon the landing site and had to be detained. Then, in the tragic way that untoward events compound themselves, Bluebird 3, moving in to be refueled, collided with one of the EC-130s, resulting in a catastrophic explosion and fire.

In the terrible aftermath, five USAF crewmembers onboard the EC-130 and the three U.S. Marines on the RH-53 died. Two crewmembers—the RH-53 pilot and copilot—survived but were badly burned. The five RH-53 helicopters on the scene were abandoned, and all personnel were flown to safety in the EC-130s.

The following morning, the White House was forced to announce that the rescue attempt had failed. The debacle was a moral tonic for the Iranians, who had the satisfaction of retaining the hostages and exploiting the scenes of the damaged and abandoned American equipment that included no fewer than seven helicopters and one EC-130. They refused to deal with President Carter over the hostages for the remainder of his term and added insult to injury by arranging to release the hostages immediately upon the inauguration of Pres. Ronald Reagan on January 20, 1980.

The loss of lives and the injuries incurred during Operation EAGLE CLAW were by far the worst part of the operation. Fortunately, analysis of the debacle, and it was surely that, came swiftly and ultimately brought about some good results that shaped the conduct of modern warfare by helicopter forces.

In May 1980, the former Chief of Naval Operations, Adm. James L. Holloway III, was tasked to form a board to analyze the results of Operation EAGLE CLAW. The results were carefully modulated to avoid too much criticism of the participants but still provide a means for operating better in the future. Thus it was that while the operation was officially considered "a feasible plan," it was noted that it was risky and complex. The Holloway Board imputed a 66 percent chance of success to the plan if all had gone well. However, it was noted that there were few measures for adapting to surprise developments and few options left for the mission planners to use if things changed from the original plan. In short, the plan was not flexible.

The Holloway Board also noted the failure to assess the reliability of the RH-53D helicopters correctly and the lack of preparation for unexpected weather conditions. The requirement for security and the compartmentalization of the various components—fixed-wing, rotary-wing, SOF—made joint planning impossible. In addition, the board found that there was insufficient intelligence provided to the force by the Defense Intelligence Agency, in part because of the extraordinary self-imposed security requirements. The rivalry between the Central Intelligence Agency and the Defense Intelligence Agency also caused problems.

Despite the evidence and the results, the Holloway Board decreed that the training for the mission was adequate except for the failure to have a full-scale dress rehearsal. The board did not emphasize that refueling training had been completely overlooked, despite the fact that refueling from ground-based bladders in the middle of the night in the Iranian desert was bound to be difficult.

A political desire to allow each service to participate resulted in the failure to make full use of Air Force SOF helicopters and pilots for the mission. The Air Force had both better equipment and better training than that selected for use and could probably have overcome the weather and navigation problems that were encountered. Though the Holloway Board does not—indeed, could not—say so, it is my belief that this sort of tweaking came from Carter's political advisors, such as Jody Powell and Hamilton Jordan, primarily because the tweaks smacked of politics and not military policy.

In a final moment of candor, the Holloway Board made two important statements. The first reemphasized the unnecessary amount of security that resulted in poor communications, poor training, and a poor understanding of the chain of command. It also cited the inadequate maintenance of the helicopters by the U.S. Navy onboard the carrier, not as a swipe at the *Nimitz* but as emphasis on analyzing the assets that were actually to be used rather than assigning a fleet-wide statistic to an individual helicopter.

The Other Side of the Coin

Operation EAGLE CLAW was not the only flawed operation in U.S. military history, but it may have been the one resulting in the most profound and timely changes. While many other factors were involved, Operation EAGLE CLAW helped spur the military reforms implicit in the Goldwater-Nichols Department of Defense Reorganization Act of 1986. It also clearly established the need for the long-discussed but always evanescent concept of Joint Doctrine and, more important for purposes of this book, the reestablishment of a vital, powerful SOF system.

The Goldwater-Nichols Act had a revolutionary effect upon the defense organization, accomplishing five distinct tasks, all of which would have benefited Operation EAGLE CLAW. These were (1) defining the role of the Chairman of the Joint Chiefs of Staff (CJCS) as the principal advisor to the Secretary of Defense, the National Security Adviser, and the President; (2) creating and defining the position of the Vice Chairman of the JCS to develop doctrine and assist in procurement; (3) determining that the JCS would be a vital factor in developing Joint Doctrine; (4) empowering the commanders in chief (CINCs) of the unified commands to be the war fighters, concerned with their own designated theaters but able to have a greater say in both budget and acquisition, the chain of command defined to run from the President to the Secretary of Defense to the responsible CINC; and (5) creating a Joint Specialty Officers (JSO) program to bring about a cultural revolution in regard to joint operations. The value of fourth task has since been demonstrated in each of the Balkan and Middle East conflicts, perhaps with the greatest success in Operation IRAQI FREEDOM.

In effect, the Goldwater-Nichols Act made Joint Doctrine law rather than an option for all the military services. The JCS is responsible for developing Joint Doctrine, to create a joint war-fighting system to co-ordinate activities against the enemy. The Goldwater-Nichols Act was reinforced in 1987 by the Cohen-Nunn Amendment, which brought SOF to the unified command level in the United States Special Operations Command (USSOCOM). This new organization directed the joint efforts of SOF units from each service. With these changes, the enhancement of SOF became a reality, with increases in budget, personnel, and mission. The Army was given the lead role with the creation of the United States Army Special Operations Command (USASOC).

Perhaps even more important from an operational point of view than the Goldwater-Nichols Act was the earlier establishment of what became the 160th Special Operations Aviation Regiment (Airborne) in 1980. This came as a direct result of the failure of Operation EAGLE CLAW. Under the direction of President Carter, Admiral Holloway was instruct-ed to find out how the U.S. military could mount another, more effective way to rescue the hostages being held in Iran. As there were no special, designated helicopter units trained for such Special Operations missions, the U.S. Army took the 158th, 229th and 159th Aviation Battalions as a source for a new unit named Task Force 160.

Pilots from these units, all part of the 101st Aviation Group, received intensive training, including instrument and night flying. Before a sec-ond rescue attempt could be made, however, the Iranians released the hostages on the very day President Ronald Reagan was inaugurated, an obvious and direct reproof of President Carter. The new unit was offi-cially established on October 16, 1981, as the 160th Aviation Battalion. It went into combat for the first time in Operation URGENT FURY, the invasion of Grenada, and subsequently participated in numerous special operations, including Operation DESERT STORM. Over the years, it naturally received the usual series of re-designations, becoming the 160th Special Operations Aviation Regiment (Airborne) in May 1990. Members of the organization relish the unit's name, the "Night Stalkers," because it represents so well what they do.

The mission statement of the 160th Special Operations Aviation Regiment calls for the Night Stalkers to equip, train, resource, and employ Army special operations aviation forces worldwide in support of contingency missions and war-fighting commanders. They use highly modified Chinook, Black Hawk, and assault and attack configurations of Little Bird helicopters and, after decades of continuous engagement in combat, today operate from multiple locations in Afghanistan and Iraq, as well as providing support in other parts of the world. Other commands similar in function include the U.S. Naval Special Warfare Command, U.S. Marine Corps Special Operations Command, and U.S. Air Force Special Operations Command (AFSOCOM).

The rebirth and advancement of SOF brought about complete changes of attitude toward special operations after the Vietnam War. Sadly, while the failure of Operation EAGLE CLAW revealed the importance of new technological advances and, indeed, provided some—such as vastly improved night vision equipment—it did not prove to be the spur required to get new helicopters into production. The Sikorsky Model 65 UH-60 was developed in many variations, and the saga of the Boeing/Vertol V-22 began, but despite their relative and sometimes controversial success, the overall development of helicopters has lagged. Unfortunately, the demand for helicopter capability and achievement continued to go up with each passing conflict in the next three decades.

Great Opportunities Squandered

The failure to fund helicopter R&D adequately and the concomitant failure to place new types of helicopters into production has been previously mentioned. The numbers are mind-boggling, with fixed-wing tactical air receiving approximately nine times the development money from 1973 to 2004 as did rotary wing. To be fair, it must be acknowledged that long periods of time and huge amounts of money were spent on the development of helicopters of great promise, only to see delays, changes in perceived requirements, and politics result in their cancellation. A weary and uneasy cycle developed in which new helicopters were specified, competed, chosen for production, and then rejected without ever becoming operational. The following pages will briefly cover the best known of these dreary cycles of hope and despair within the chopper community.

The Lockheed AH-56A Cheyenne

Few failed aircraft are as celebrated and mourned as the Lockheed AH-56A Cheyenne. It was a revolutionary step forward in many ways but found itself overtaken by time, cost, requirements, and some, its fans insist, solvable technical problems.

The Cheyenne attack helicopter was created in response to the U.S. Army's need for a fast, armored, and heavily armed helicopter to supplement the escort-attack role. It was in fact to be an all-weather, close-air-support aircraft. The Vietnam experience and the specter of the Fulda Gap invasion made the Army want a helicopter that could do armed escort, long-range interdiction, LZ fire support, and antitank operations, by day or night in all weathers, and it was to this expensive specification that the Cheyenne was designed.

Sadly, the Robert S. McNamara conception of contracting, the Total Package Procurement (TPP), was in effect, virtually guaranteeing financial failure. Under TPP, the contractor and the services had to commit to a project, covering it from design through development, test, purchase, and service use, even though the costs implicit in such a process could never be accurately determined. McNamara came from the automobile industry, where a change in yearly styling might involve a new bumper and creating a new model took years. The TPP concept might have worked there, but in an advanced technological industry bent on pushing frontiers, it was simply unworkable.

A competition was held for the Advanced Aerial Flight Support System (AAFSS), and twelve companies submitted entries. The specifications called for a top speed of 220 knots, the ability to hover at 6,000 feet on a ninety-five-degree day, and a ferry range of 2,415 miles. This was formidable performance, for the contemporary UH-1 had a top speed of 120 while the Chinook was topped out at 170.[3] Two entries were selected for development, the Sikorsky Model S-66 and the Lockheed Model CL-840.

Lockheed's previous helicopter development had been slight but adventuresome. The Lockheed CL-475 had debuted under the leadership of the brilliant if unorthodox Irving Culver in 1959, a two-seat helicopter with a rigid rotor coupled to a gyroscopic system. Lockheed had devoted a small but talented engineering crew to its development, including Willis Hawkins and Culver. Under Lockheed chairman Robert Gross's direct orders, they were to create a helicopter that would be easy to fly. And so the CL-475 proved to be in time, as did the succeeding four prototypes. One of them, the XH-51A Compound, reached 302.6 mph, an unheard-of speed for helicopters.

Their competition winner, the CL-840, designated AH-56A Cheyenne by the Army, set the stage for the initial Lockheed contract of $12,750,000, a figure that would seem laughable by the time the program ended. The AH-56A retained the rigid rotor but instead of the gyroscopic compensator featured three weighted arms mounted directly above the four-blade rigid rotor. The AH-56A was a compound helicopter, in that it had stub wings of twenty-seven-foot span and an additional propulsion element. Its most unusual feature for the time was the combination of a four-blade anti-torque propeller and a three-blade pusher propeller. The latter was driven by a running shaft from the main Kelsey-Hayes transmission that drove the main rotor to a gearbox in the tail, and its pitch was determined by a motorcycle-like twist-grip on the controls in each of its tandem cockpits. In addition, the Cheyenne was among the first helicopters to be fitted with an integrated avionics suite that included weapons, communication, and navigation systems. The pilot was equipped with a helmet with night vision and gun aiming capability.

The landing gear was retractable, adding to its hungry, snake-slim appearance. The configuration provided an impressive performance. During vertical and hovering flight, the rotor and the anti-torque propeller absorbed all the power; in flight, this shifted, as the rotor was unloaded and all but about 700 shp was given to the pusher propeller. This feature, unique to compound helicopters, allowed the wind-milling main rotor to minimize drag and accounted for the sea-level high speeds of better than 240 mph. It also enhanced the Cheyenne's remarkable agility. The first flight took place on September 22, 1967, with veteran test pilot Donald Segner flying it for twenty-six minutes and lauding its performance after landing. Lt. Col. Emil "Jack" Kluever accompanied him in a still-unfinished front cockpit.

Further testing saw a total of ten Cheyennes built, but there were three crashes. One of these involved the third prototype. The main rotor malfunctioned, oscillating out of control and striking the cockpit and the tail rotor. The malfunction killed test pilot David Beil on March 12, 1969. Stability problems rose at speeds in excess of 184 mph. After the third crash, the production order was placed on hold. Lockheed worked hard and, by 1972, believed the stability problems to be for the most part solved. Performance was excellent, with a maximum speed of more than 240 mph, a climb rate that approached 3,300 feet per minute, and a range of 1,300 miles.

Unfortunately, over the previous five years, the Army perceived changes in requirements and the USAF emphasized its alarm over the traditional roles and missions arguments. The compound helicopter was simply too close to fixed-wing performance not to concern the Air Force. These factors, coupled with the history of stability problems, to led to the cancellation of the program on August 9, 1972, after an expenditure of more than $400 million.[4] The Cheyenne program was a disappointment to Lockheed in many ways, moving them out of the helicopter business and, under the basically unfair rules of TPP, incurring a loss of $150 million.[5]

The Army next did what was done too often, given the limited R&D funding: cancel a program that was experiencing cost increases but nearing its goal in order to launch another program with reduced requirements and a new development period to contend with. This was the Advanced Attack Helicopter (AAH) program, intended to improve on the performance of the HueyCobra but with less performance capability than the Cheyenne. Two engines were specified for reliability but the expected top speed was lowered to only 145 mph. The engines were to be the General Electric T700 turbo-shaft engines that produced 1,500 shp. They were also selected for the new utility helicopter competition that ultimately resulted in the Sikorsky UH-60 Black Hawk.

Given the combat conditions expected in Europe, the new helicopter was to have the capability to fly "nap-of-the-earth" missions. Five manufacturers competed in the contest, which was won by the Hughes YAH-64 in December 1976, nine long years—and to many a backward step—after

Originally developed by Hughes, the Apache was designed to replace the Bell AH-1 Cobra. It has since been continually improved with modern equipment. *(Courtesy of Zaur Eylanbekov [Foxbat])*

the first flight of the Cheyenne. The further history of the Apache will be included in the following chapters.

The second helicopter of interest here is the Sikorsky Comanche. Sikorsky had begun an experimental light helicopter project in 1981, and the Army expressed interest in a fleet-modernization plan in which a single type would replace fleets of four veteran helicopters, the OH-6, UH-1, AH-1, and OH-58.

The new helicopter was to have two engines and feature an all-composite, low-observable airframe to avoid enemy radar detection. In 1988, it was decided to add the armed reconnaissance role to the aircraft. A very sophisticated electronic suite was to be used primarily for reconnaissance but also incorporated the necessary equipment for attack and even air combat missions. The stealth characteristics imparted by the composite construction were aided by the design of the fuselage, the retractable landing gear, and careful attention to shaping details. One major stealth advance was the use of a ducted fan as a tail rotor rather than the conventional anti-torque rotor.

Sikorsky won the competition with the AH-66, and the first flight took place on January 4, 1996, some fifteen years after the first experiments had begun. The Army was impressed, and an order for 1,200 Comanches was ultimately given to begin the multiple-fleet replacement process. Operational RAH-66s were expected to be in service ten years later, in 2006. The Comanche's performance would have been good, with a maximum speed of just faster than 200 mph, an unremarkable tactical range of 302 miles, and a less than spectacular service ceiling of just less than fifteen thousand feet. However, the Comanche possessed network-capable communication links and sophisticated flight systems that promised a real advance in utility.

The program encountered the inevitable problems, and costs began to rise. In 2002, the Army reduced the number to be procured to 650, increasing the unit cost for the Comanche from $12 million to almost $60 million. This resulted in the customary congressional astonishment that the unit price on a reduced number of aircraft would go up because the development costs had to be amortized across the smaller number. This happens with every weapon system and, quite amazingly, seems to surprise Congress and its staffers each time.

And here we arrive at the crux of our current problem with our fleet of aging helicopters. On February 23, 2004, the Army cancelled the Comanche, essentially "to provide funds necessary to renovate the existing fleet that the Comanche was intended to replace." Cancelling programs is costly, and the expected price to close the Comanche program was up to $680 million. At the same time, a program to buy new manned helicopters was announced, some with whatever remained of the $1.2 billion already slated for the Comanche in the following year. Lt. Gen. Richard Cody, the Army's deputy chief of staff for operations, talked about a "new start" for 368 armed reconnaissance helicopters.

Somewhat predictably, given the long scenario of failed attempts, this program also resulted in delay. The Bell ARH-70 was designed for the new Armed Reconnaissance Helicopter Program (ARH) and was intended to replace the veteran OH-58D Kiowa Warrior. Called the Arapaho, the new helicopter went from a Request for Proposal in December 2004 to Bell's winning the contract for 368 helicopters on July 29, 2005, to a first flight on July 20, 2006, to cancellation on October 28, 2008. The reasons cited for the cancellation were a failure to meet performance requirements and the rising program costs from an estimated $8.5 million to $14.5 million per unit.

This litany of frustrated helicopter acquisitions would not be complete without a brief mention of the highly controversial situation surrounding perhaps the most famous helicopter fleet in the world, that used by the president of the United States. The presidential fleet was aging, and a replacement was deemed necessary. There followed an intense competition between the traditional supplier, Sikorsky, and a foreign firm that made marketing agreements with well-known American counterparts.

The prototype of the later EH 101 competitor first flew on October 9, 1987, the result of cooperation between the British firm Westland and the Italian firm Agusta. These firms merged in 2000 to become AgustaWestland and were successful in selling their new helicopter to Great Britain, Italy, Canada, Japan, Portugal, Denmark, and elsewhere. The aircraft was manufactured at the AgustaWestland factory in Yeovil, England, home of many famous helicopters (most derived from Sikorsky origins) and World War II fighter planes.

In 2001 two U.S. manufacturers, Lockheed Martin and Bell Helicopter Textron, signed an agreement with AgustaWestland to market the aircraft in the United States, using the road-sign-like designation US101. This combination became the prime contender against Sikorsky in heated competition to supply the next generation of presidential helicopters. In this scenario, the US101 was to be built in the United States, equipped with General Electric turbo-shaft engines and other American equipment. It was recognized from the start that it would be difficult to overcome the long tradition of Sikorsky helicopters being used as Marine One to carry the president of the United States.

This was particularly true because the Sikorsky S-92 entrant was already quite successful. Based on the S-70 heritage, the twin-engine S-92 made its first flight on December 23, 1998. Sikorsky subsequently formed a team with top U.S. contractors, including FlightSafety International, L-3 Communication Integrated Systems, Northrop Grumman, Rockwell Collins, Vought Aircraft Industries, and General Electric Aircraft Engines.

To the surprise of some and indignation of others, the U.S. Navy selected the US101 as the winner of the competition, awarding a $1.7 billion contract for the system development and demonstration phase of what was to become Marine One. However, the costly requirement to add equipment and fittings and, no doubt, the political reaction to purchasing a fleet of twenty-eight "foreign helicopters" for presidential use brought about the cancellation of the contract in 2009. The unit cost almost doubled over time, rising from about $220 million to $400 million. A new program is still being pursued.

The list of starts and stops does not end with Marine One. An even more necessary aircraft is a new CSAR helicopter. The current fleet of Sikorsky HH-60G Pave Hawks has demonstrated its capability all over the world since it was first deployed in 1982. In October 2003, the CSAR mission was passed (temporarily) from the Air Combat Command (ACC) to AFSOCOM. AFSOCOM determined that it needed at least 132 medium-lift helicopters to replace the aging Pave Hawks, with deliveries beginning in 2010. It is a tragedy that this program was also cancelled, this time because two of the contesting contractors, Sikorsky and Lockheed Martin, had registered protests with the General Accounting Office over the conduct of the competition.

In this age of asymmetric warfare, the USAF's Pave Hawk's role as transport for SOF and for CSAR make it invaluable. *(Courtesy of Zaur Eylanbekov [Foxbat])*

Thus sadly, despite some good intentions, conceptually advanced helicopter designs have cost the government and the industry billions of dollars since the 1960s. The services have been left with aircraft that have to be "recapitalized," which in the current jargon means remanufacturing old airframes that are costly to maintain, have to be equipped with new systems, and possess roughly the same limited performance capabilities that were considered inadequate in the Vietnam War.[6]

Using unmanned aerial vehicles is now being waved as a matador's cape to deflect attention from the dreadful lack of progress. The Army has started new programs with the recaptured Comanche funds, including a Light Utility Helicopter (LUH), the "Sky Warrior" Unmanned Aircraft System, and the Joint Cargo Aircraft. It also has proceeded with the delivery of a series of competent aircraft derived from older designs including the Sikorsky UH-60M and the Boeing CH-47H Heavy Lift Cargo Helicopter (and a nostalgic salute to the genius of Frank Piasecki, who originated the configuration) and improvements in even older programs such as the H-1 and OH-58.[7]

Few helicopters have ever been as useful, adaptable, and efficient as the CH-47 Chinook. *(Courtesy of U.S. Army Museum, Fort Rucker)*

There is folly in the current system of overstated requirements, career advocacy, congressional influence, and the tendency of program offices to pursue hobby-shop special interests. The American public and the armed services have been shortchanged by budgets that did not add money to the R&D effort. Even assuming there would have been more projects with perhaps more waste, the money should have been authorized, appropriated, and spent to achieve what was needed: better, more effective, and far more survivable new helicopters in the field. We should have done this at any cost that might have been required, because the current high casualty rate of our helicopters is unacceptable.

A starting point would be a reform of the current Department of Defense system to its very roots, but this is probably an impossible dream given the formidable political and bureaucratic opposition that would occur. Yet in truth, the new system could be created in relatively simple terms. The services and the industry would meet and decide the differences between what the services wanted and what the industry could produce. A firm schedule would be settled on, with penalties for failure to meet it. Once these decisions were made, the industry would be left alone to deliver the agreed-upon item at the agreed-upon price at the agreed-upon time. The result would perhaps not be ideal, but it would mean new equipment, produced in perhaps five-year cycles, rather than no new equipment produced over forty years of delays.

What Might Have Been

Since the 1960s, if there had been adequate investment in the science and technology as well as the R&D of helicopters, there might have been significant developments in a number of vital areas that would have contributed greatly to both helicopter performance and safety. These include the development of new and better rotors, the adequate streamlining of the rotor head, a decrease in basic structural weights, improvements in fuel consumption, and of course increases in speed, range, and hover altitude capability. It would be interesting to see exactly what new levels of performance might have been achieved in such a radically revised situation. However, an examination of the most advanced helicopters in the world today might signal that there are inherent limitations in conventional rotary-wing flight that can be overcome only by totally new technologies, including the controversial tilt-rotor.

After the rather depressing series of failed programs, it is worthwhile to point out that variations on older designs continue to do yeoman work throughout the world, particularly in combat. The great leap forward in technology occasioned by the Vietnam War, and then sustained by improvements in the following decades, brought the helicopter's effect on modern warfare to its current height. A discussion of the major wars since 1990 will highlight these effects—and in some instances the corresponding counter-effects of ever-changing warfare.

Chapter Ten

Other Wars and the Growth
of Foreign Helicopter Technology

Although Soviet tanks never came rolling though the Fulda Gap, there was a continuing requirement for helicopters since 1980 to not only conduct but affect modern warfare in combat action all around the globe. While the total number of helicopters declined, as did the sortie rate, the importance of the mission rose, for warfare had changed. Where MEDEVAC and CSAR once had been the primary missions of the helicopter, changing conditions now dictated that choppers first fulfill their nickname and become the cutting edge of the SOF sword. Then they become the workhorses, a combination of firepower and resupply that is essential.

The reason for this was the fundamental change in warfare over an extended period of time and with the experience of several conflicts. The probability of a nuclear exchange was discounted (even though to this day it remains a genuine danger by means of accident or a rogue launch), and there was no longer a Soviet threat to overrun Europe. Even wars on the scale of the Vietnam War became less probable. American air superiority was so great that fighter combat was almost absent, reducing the requirement for CSAR operations.

The reckless Iraqi invasion of Kuwait in 1990 initiated what would become the last major war of the twentieth century. It became accepted that future wars were going to be "low-intensity conflicts" or "regional insurgencies"—until September 11, 2001. Then events took on a whole new character with what was initially called the "global war on terror" but has since been politically sanitized to less warlike titles.

Instead of a national adversary, the major threat to the United States and the rest of the world came from a small but virulent group of Muslim fanatics, spearheaded by Osama bin Laden and the infamous al-Qaeda but buttressed by other Muslim extremist groups around the world and generally given passive (if denied) support by almost the entire Muslim community. This passive acceptance is all the more difficult to understand because the Muslim extremists have killed far more Muslims than they have their declared "infidel" foe. Dealing with this new enemy meant that helicopters had to adopt new missions in the far reaches of the world, most of them hundreds or thousands of miles from adequate staging bases. As had been hard-learned in the Vietnam War, many of these operations had to be conducted in concert with fixed-wing aircraft that ranged from the Lockheed Martin MC-130 Combat Talon to the Boeing A-10 to the Northrop B-2.

Over the previous three decades there had been a number of vividly named operations in which helicopters played important roles, including such widely dispersed places as Grenada (Operation URGENT FURY, 1983), Libya (Operation EL DORADO CANYON, 1986), Panama (Operation JUST CAUSE, 1989-90), Kuwait and Iraq (Operation DESERT SHIELD, 1990, and Operation DESERT STORM, 1991), Somalia (Operation RESTORE HOPE, 1992-93), Haiti (Operation UPHOLD DEMOCRACY, 1994-95), the Balkans (Operation DELIBERATE FORCE, 1995, and Operation ALLIED FORCE, 1999), Afghanistan (Operation ENDURING FREEDOM, 2001-present), and Iraq (Operation IRAQI FREEDOM, 2003-present, but renamed Operation NEW DAWN in February 2010). And it should never be forgotten that American military helicopters have responded brilliantly by providing aid to nations beset by national disasters ranging from earthquakes to tsunamis all over the world.

Nonetheless, for the purposes of this book, it must be noted that the effect of the helicopter on warfare has been diminished since the Vietnam War era, even as the effect of warfare on the helicopter has been extended. This will be related primarily by investigating operations in the Middle East, with emphasis on the brilliant introduction of SOF action in Operation DESERT STORM. There and in the subsequent Middle Eastern conflicts, the helicopter has continued to perform splendidly despite adverse weather, aging equipment, primitive basing, and a hostile countryside.

The Helicopter in Operations DESERT SHIELD and DESERT STORM

What has become known as the Gulf War began on August 2, 1990, with Iraq's invasion of Kuwait, using special forces flown in Soviet-built helicopters to seize the capital city. The Kuwaiti forces were quickly overcome by the 120,000 troops and 850 tanks, part of the highly publicized Iraqi army, which had become vastly experienced in the bloody, atrocity-filled eight-year Iran-Iraq war. In time, Iraq formally annexed Kuwait, conforming to its long-held contention that the country always belonged to Iraq and was an artificial entity created by Great Britain to ensure control of the Gulf. The Iraqi presence in Kuwait represented an immediate and ominous threat to Kuwait's biggest creditor, Saudi Arabia, to whom it owed some $26 billion.

To defend American interests, Pres. George H. W. Bush responded to a request for assistance from the Saudi King Faud and announced Operation DESERT SHIELD on August 7. The U.S. Navy quickly sent carriers to the area, and forty-eight Boeing F-15s made a brilliant nonstop flight from Langley Air Force Base, Virginia to establish immediate air superiority in Saudi Arabia.

There followed six months of diplomatic activity within the United Nations, as the United States and its coalition of thirty-four allies built up a formidable force approaching one million personnel in Saudi Arabia. Even as the diplomatic possibilities offered by the United Nation were being ceaselessly exercised, five months of arduous air- and sea-lift effort had created a massive coalition force ready to wrest Kuwait from Iraq when commanded to do so. The five months also revealed deficiencies in U.S. air- and sea-transport capabilities.

The command came on January 17, 1991, and unleashed a furious air campaign in which coalition forces flew more than one hundred thousand sorties and dropped almost ninety thousand tons of bombs. The air campaign, unlike any in the past, featured a "jointness" and an "interoperability" that stemmed from the leadership of its commander, the USAF's Lt. Gen. Charles Horner. His goal was to establish air superiority, destroy the Iraqi integrated air-defense system, and eliminate the enemy command and control capability. There was also an imperative political need to keep Israel out of the war in order to preserve the membership of Arab nations within the coalition. The most dangerous threat was that Iraq's vaunted Scud missiles might so damage Israel that it would enter the war on its own.

Horner had a wide choice of weapons that ranged from the Navy's barrage of BGM-109 Tomahawk missiles (TLAMs) to the AGM-86C conventional air-launched cruise missiles (CALCMs) to the precision-guided munitions equipping other coalition attack planes. In discussions with Gen. H. Norman Schwarzkopf, commander of the coalition forces, it was decided not to attempt to pave the way for the attack by inserting SOF on the ground within Iraqi territory. Instead, it fell to the helicopter, exercising its newest and most significant effect upon modern warfare, to initiate this massive DESERT STORM air campaign, in the form of Task Force Normandy. The goal of this specialized operation was to clear a way for coalition bombers, including the new and virtually untried Lockheed F-117A Nighthawk stealth fighters, to bomb Baghdad without being detected or intercepted.

A decision was made that Task Force Normandy should carry out what could have amounted to the most important—or most disastrous—mission of the war. Task Force Normandy consisted of eight missile-firing Army Boeing Apache helicopters of the 101st Army Air Assault Division, with one additional AH-64 serving as a spare. The Air Force contingent was part of the 20th Special Operations Squadron from Hurlburt Field, Florida and consisted of two USAF Sikorsky MH-53J Enhanced Pave Low III aircraft and a Sikorsky UH-60A Black Hawk to serve in the CSAR role. (Fortunately, no CSAR was required for elements of Task Force Normandy, but the crew of Moccasin 05, commanded by Capt. Tom Trask, would win the 1991 McKay Trophy for its rescue of a downed Navy Grumman F-14 pilot, the first American CSAR activity since Vietnam.)

The USAF Pave Lows were needed to provide the exacting navigation to reach, undetected, two key Iraqi air-defense positions some 380 nautical miles inside Iraq. These were a vital part of the Iraqi integrated air-defense system and provided overlapping coverage of the routes that U.S. warplanes would have to take to bomb Baghdad from bases in Saudi Arabia.

Originally designed as a Super Jolly Green, the Pave Low was later used prima-rarily for Special Operations missions. *(Courtesy of Zaur Eylanbekov [Foxbat])*

The Sikorsky UH-60 Black Hawk gained its greatest fame in the 1993 "Black Hawk Down" incident in Mogadishu, Somalia. *(Courtesy of Zaur Eylanbekov [Foxbat])*

Once the two radar installations were destroyed, opening an eighty-mile-wide, radar-free pathway, the following wave of USAF Grumman/General Dynamic EF-111A Raven electronic warfare aircraft would pave the way for the Lockheed F-117A Nighthawk stealth fighters to destroy key targets in downtown Baghdad and elsewhere. This progressively opened the envelope of the Iraqi defenses, permitting less stealthy warriors such as the B-1 and B-52 to bring their power to bear.

Unlike the Iran hostage fiasco, the mixed force had time to train together. It was divided into two teams, the White and the Red. The White team was led by the operation's commander, Army Lt. Col. Richard A. "Dick" Cody, while the Red team was led by Capt. Newman Shufflebarger. (Cody later became the Vice Chief of Staff of the Army, one of the very few Army aviators to reach such an important position.) The Air Force contingent was commanded by Lt. Col. Richard L. Comer. Comer and Cody hit it off from the start, both being experienced helicopter pilots and aware of the vital importance of planning and training.

The two target radar installations were about seventy miles apart. The navigating Sikorsky MH-53Js brought them to within about thirty miles of the targets, then stood by to let the Apaches attack. Each team of Apaches split into two-ship elements about half a mile apart.[1] At precisely 2:38 A.M. on January 17, 1991, the Apache crews struck their designated targets, using their infrared night-vision equipment to fire their weapons. The helicopters selected the electrical generating systems as the first targets, followed by the communication facilities and then the radar units themselves. In a furious blast of fire, the Apaches unleashed 4,000 rounds of 30-mm ammunition, almost 100 70-mm rockets, and 27 of the devastating Hellfire missiles.[2] During the operation, the 1st Special Wing Pave Low and Pave Hawk helicopters provided navigation and fire support, using flares to decoy any heat-seeking missiles being fired at the force.[3] The well-tested terrain-following and global-positioning navigation system (GPS) was operated by experienced Air Force crews and removed the uncertainty (if not all of the hazard) that had caused the Operation EAGLE CLAW debacle. With the radar stations destroyed, the aerial passage in the waves of Lockheed F-117A Nighthawks was ensured, along with the follow-on bombers.

During DESERT STORM, the Army and Marine helicopter forces were

Apache reliability is sometimes contested, primarily by those who do not under-stand just how advanced and complex the aircraft is. *(Courtesy of U.S. Army Museum, Fort Rucker)*

pitted against an enemy that was formidably armed with tanks but lacked the will and training to fight. Their major defensive weapons were the MANPAD missiles and the heavy antiaircraft installations on their tanks, but the aggressive tactics of both Army and Marine helicopters were more than adequate for the task.

The Apaches had gained a reputation for poor reliability and a low in-commission rate prior to the Gulf War. This was overcome during the DESERT SHIELD buildup period, and a readiness rate in excess of 85 percent was sustained for DESERT STORM. However, the talcum-powder quality of the desert sand proved disastrous to the electronics and even the rotor blades of the Apaches, requiring five hours of maintenance time for every hour flown.[4] Fine sand would be a continuing problem in the decades to come in the Middle East.

Nearly three hundred Apaches were deployed, and they indeed "ruled the night" as they claimed. Typically, the Apaches would fly armed reconnaissance missions, sometimes as deep as ninety miles into hostile territory, seeking out profitable targets such as a supply convoy or column of armor. They were also intended to destroy fortifications and attack enemy strong points, clearing the way for advancing allied armored forces.

When a target was located, an attack would be made by one of the three companies of an Apache battalion. A second company would be standing by to attack about twenty miles away, while the third company could be at a FARP (Forward Area Refueling Point) some thirty miles distant, refueling and rearming. The enemy could thus be engaged continuously. Each company usually operated in two teams, one of two helicopters and one of four. The two-helicopter team would engage first and then be followed into the attack by the four-ship element. A common technique was to take out the lead and trailing vehicles of the convoy with Hellfire missiles, then use the Apaches' 30-mm guns to devastate the vehicles trapped in between.[5]

The ferocity of the Apache attacks, often combined with those of tactical fixed-wing aircraft, intimidated the Iraqi ground forces, and as many as five hundred surrendered to the helicopters. The Apaches were supported by the CH-47D Chinook, which came in to pick up the prisoners, and by the UH-60V Black Hawk, which conducted the traditional MEDEVAC missions. AH-64s were credited with destroying more than five hundred tanks during Operation DESERT STORM, plus hundreds of additional armored personnel carriers, trucks, and other vehicles.

The lethality of the Apache was never questioned, but over the previous years it had been grounded no fewer than five times, and the Army called upon hundreds of Boeing technicians to help solve problems in Iraq. The very capability of the aircraft to follow the terrain, in any weather, day or night, is an inherent danger that can cause a crash in combat or in training.

The traditional "vertical envelopment" role of the helicopter was carried out on February 24, 1991, when the allies began their "Hail Mary" offensive against three points along the front. The idea was to avoid the carefully prepared fixed defenses of the Iraqis by making a wide slashing

The tremendous versatility inherent in the basic Sikorsky Model 71 design is evident in the vast number of competent variations that have been based on it. (*Courtesy of Zaur Eylanbekov [Foxbat]*)

attack deep to the left (west). The allied forces then enveloped the Iraqis from the west, taking out Saddam Hussein's only really reliable force, the Republican Guard.

A key to the success of this effort was the largest helicopter operation in history, with more than two thousand men of the 101st Airborne Division using almost four hundred helicopters to carry it out. Among the force were Apaches, Sikorsky UH-60A/L Black Hawks, and UH-60V "DUSTOFFs," plus Boeing CH-47D Chinooks and CH-46E Sea Knights. Their first task was to take Salman airfield, fifty miles inside Iraq, and use it as a key base to fuel and rearm the troop-carrying helicopters that were leapfrogging ahead to cut off the main Iraqi highway between Baghdad and Basra.

The Marine helicopter forces had already distinguished themselves early in the war, first in helping to break up the surprise Iraqi raid on the Saudi Arabian town of Khafji on January 29 and then in support of the 1st Marine Division's advance into Kuwait City. In both cases, the Marine Bell AH-1W "Whiskey" Super Cobra gunships slaughtered attacking

The CH-46 Sea Knight's longevity is matched only by its ability to adapt to new missions. *(Courtesy of U.S. Marine Corps History Office)*

Iraqi tanks. The gunships used both TOW and Hellfire missiles to deadly effect. They supported the Hail Mary offensive incursion in a similar manner, with CH-53s and CH-46s airlifting supplies and the gunships suppressing Iraqi armor.

There was one area of helicopter operations in the Gulf War that was disappointing in the extreme—that of CSAR. The CSAR mission was the victim of budget cuts and reorganizations. CSAR involves a three-phase process, each of which has its own hazards. The first phase is locating personnel down in enemy territory; the second is authenticating the personnel, that is, making sure it is an American in need and not an enemy trap; and third is the actual combat recovery.[6] During the Gulf War, CSAR fell under the control of the Special Operations Command Central (SOCCENT), and all of the United States CSAR forces were placed under the control of Air Force Special Operations Command Central.[7]

In the competition for funds, the Super Jolly Greens, the Sikorsky HH-53 helicopters, had been diverted from rescue work to the support of

The addition of a third engine to the Sikorsky Sea Stallion enabled the Super Stallion to become the largest, heaviest, and perhaps most useful helicopter in the service of the United States. *(Courtesy of Zaur Eylanbekov [Foxbat])*

special operations. They had been replaced by the earlier HH-3s, which were regarded as only marginally combat capable in a high-threat area such as Iraq. There were too few of them, however, and despite the excellence and devotion of their crews, they were unable to cover the vast areas of Iraq. As a result, only seven CSAR missions were launched, and only three out of sixty-four downed aircrew members were picked up.[8]

While the CSAR mission suffered from deficiencies in the number and the type of equipment, the DUSTOFF operations functioned relatively well using new procedures. In Vietnam, the MEDEVAC helicopters had flown under fire directly into the LZ to land and pick up patients. In the 1980s, the Sikorsky UH-60 Black Hawk was introduced to the MEDEVAC role. Bigger and more powerful than the Bell Hueys it replaced, the Black Hawk could carry more wounded faster, but was also a more valuable target. As a result, the Army no longer sent it in under fire to the LZs. Wounded soldiers were brought back out by the helicopters that had carried them in or, rarely, by dedicated SAR aircraft. The wounded were then flown to a staging area where MEDEVAC helicopters would transport them to a field hospital.

The events in Iraq now formed the pattern reflecting the effect of the helicopter on modern warfare. It was now apparent that dedicated, specially equipped helicopters could intervene on clandestine missions behind enemy lines to great effect. These missions involved specially trained crews and, inevitably, a high degree of risk. In addition to these specialized missions, the helicopter also performed its usual roles of providing invaluable fire support and resupplying troops in the field.

Before recounting the less dashing nature of subsequent helicopter employment and development over the next ten years, it is worth noting that the controversial former Chief of Staff of the United States Air Force, Gen. Merrill A. "Tony" McPeak, characterized the air war in DESERT STORM as being "the first time in history that a field army was defeated by air power." Helicopters were responsible for a major share in this victory.

War in the Balkans

Over the next decade, no fewer than three major operations were fought in the Balkans. They were wars that provided few victories yet managed to insinuate serious errors into the American way of warfare. They are worth discussing here for their failure to use helicopters to good effect and their deleterious impact on the political conduct of wars.

They began with a completely ill managed Operation DENY FLIGHT in 1993 and 1994 against Bosnian Serbs who were carrying out ethnic cleansing of former Yugoslav citizens of Muslim extraction. The results of DENY FLIGHT were negligible. The eighteen allied air forces involved in the NATO effort, begun in April 1993, conducted twenty-four-hour operations to enforce a no-fly zone over Bosnia. Over two years, only four close-air-support attacks were approved and carried out, meaning that 99.9 percent of the flights had simply been boring holes in the sky to the amusement of the Serb fighters.

Ironically, the ground-bound Serbs managed to shoot down Capt. Scott O'Grady's F-16. O'Grady evaded for six days before providing the first uplifting helicopter incident of the war—his rescue by a force from the 24th Marine Expeditionary Unit. They dispatched two Sikorsky CH-53 helicopters from the USS *Kearsarge,* complete with forty-three tough Marines, to the area where a tired and hungry O'Grady was waiting. The helicopters were accompanied by two of the faithful AH-1W Cobra gunships and two McDonnell AV-8 Harrier jump jets.

The usual network of forty aircraft—tankers, jammers, command and control, fighters—provided additional coverage. The helicopters snaked through the mountainous countryside until they reached O'Grady's position, an area large enough for two helicopters to land. The first CH-53 discharged troops to form a defensive perimeter, and O'Grady was picked up by the second helicopter. Within five minutes, the helicopters were airborne, mission accomplished, except for the hazardous flight home.

The second major effort, Operation DELIBERATE FORCE, in September 1995, was led by future USAF Chief of Staff Lt. Gen. Michael Ryan and was more successful. It was the largest combat air operation in Europe since World War II and it saw the emergence of a philosophy that has crippled American war-making ability: the over-concern about avoiding "collateral damage" (civilian casualties among the enemy). This concern was so great that Ryan, the NATO commander for AFSOUTH, personally vetted each target, each weapon, each aim point, each run-in approach, and the possible secondary effects of each bomb.[9] However, this was the beginning of a philosophy that, no matter how well intended, has come to cripple American war-making ability. The nation has become so concerned about avoiding "collateral damage" that it now impedes many military operations. Worse, it is combined too often with restrictive rules of engagement that are debated by Judge Advocate General lawyers prior to strikes.

The NATO force succeeded, despite the artificial limitations placed on bombing. Peace talks in Dayton in November 1995 led to the eventual cessation of combat operations. Helicopters were important in DELIBERATE FORCE but in what was obviously becoming a more supportive role.

Parenthetically, it should be noted that the helicopter was inadvertently, and incorrectly, placed in a bad light in Mogadishu, Somalia on October 3 and 4, 1993. The mission is related very well in Mark Bowden's 1999 book, *Black Hawk Down.* Two UH-60 Black Hawk helicopters were shot down as they were supporting a team of U.S. Army Rangers and

Delta Force. While the American forces inflicted some five hundred casualties on the Somali militia, eighteen Americans were killed and another seventy-three injured in the attack. The helicopters were struck by unguided rocket-propelled grenades, apparently fired by Somali personnel who had been given training by al-Qaeda.[10]

Four years later, Operation ALLIED FORCE began in Kosovo and initially appeared to be an impending debacle along the lines of Operation DENY FLIGHT. There was strong disagreement at command levels as to how airpower should be employed. The incident gained far greater attention because it essentially pitted the top NATO commander, Gen. Wesley K. Clark, against the White House and the Joint Chiefs of Staff. Clark argued that the Apache was much better suited to destroy the small bands of Serbian troops than the jet fighters being used.

There were additional problems at headquarters. Clark planned on using drones, radar, and satellites to find targets for the Apaches, which were seen by the Air Force as being too vague and unconventional for their use. It was known that the Serbs were well armed with the Soviet-built SA-7 surface-to-air missiles.

The Pentagon ordered that the twenty-four Apaches on hand in Albania be grounded after a training accident on April 27, 1999. An Apache had experienced problems with its tail rotor and crashed. The incident prompted Maj. Gen. Dick Cody, commanding the 101st Airborne, to comment on the failures in Apache crew training and equipment. The grounding exacerbated concerns that the expensive Apaches would be too vulnerable to ground fire from the Serbs.

Fortunately for the conduct of the war, the intensive bombing ultimately decided upon caused the Serbian leader, Slobodan Milosevic, to choose to "surrender," in the NATO view, or survive with a maximum credibility, according to his supporters. In either event, it was airpower that forced the decision.

The decision not to risk the Apaches signaled an increasing awareness of the effectiveness of SAMs, including the ubiquitous MANPADS, as a defensive measure. Aircraft designed to fight tanks on an open battlefield, loaded with all sorts of offensive and defensive equipment, were still an easy target when landing, landed, or taking off from hostile territory, where roving bands of forces might be found at any time.

Perhaps the most interesting aspect of the changing rules of engagement was how they also affected tactical fixed-wing aircraft. Each of their remarkable advances—stealth, sophisticated jamming gear, stand-off precision-guided munitions—was diluted and offset by political considerations in which offending the enemy with collateral damage became the principal concern. The irony in this is overwhelming. Just when the tactical fixed-wing air force is given the weapons it has always sought, their proper use is denied, devaluing the huge sums of money spent in their R&D, production, training, and deployment. In the same intervening period, helicopters had received only a fraction of the sums devoted to fixed-wing tactical effort, but the emasculation of fixed-wing efforts by politically inspired rules of engagement left it to the helicopters to go in and do the dirty work first.

The War on Terror

At no time was this more evident than when, after the brutal attack on the United States by twenty-one Muslim fanatics, nineteen of them Saudi Arabians, on September 11, 2001, a decision was made to go after terrorist training camps in Afghanistan, then being cruelly ruled by the Taliban. Inevitably, SOF were tasked with the initial missions, and it is interesting to note how these were commanded and manned at the time.

As previously noted, Congress established the U.S. Special Operations Command (USSOCOM) in 1986 as an attempt to reduce expenses and duplication and provide a single line of command for what seemed certain to be joint and even combined operations. The commander in chief of USSOCOM (CINCSOC) was a four-star general or admiral from any of the services. The headquarters was established at MacDill Air Force Base in Tampa, Florida. The CINCSOC reported directly to the secretary of defense, with an assistant secretary for Special Operations and Low Intensity Conflicts providing immediate civilian oversight—read "worries about collateral damage." The CINCSOC may personally command SOF operations but typically provides command in the manner conventional to the regional theater CINC.

In Afghanistan, that command was passed to the U.S. Central Command (USCENTCOM), also coincidentally but providentially located at MacDill. CINCCENT has permanent subordinate command for Special Operations Forces, SOCCENT. United States SOF had in 1986 about 45,000 active and reserve personnel in the Army, Navy, and Air Force Special Operation Forces. The Army SOF (ARSOF) was represented by 26,000 soldiers organized into units such as the Rangers, Special Forces Groups (Airborne), psychological affairs units, civil affairs (which despite its innocuous name is one of the most frequently deployed units), and others. Army special operations aviation units feature pilots trained to fly the most sophisticated Army rotary-wing aircraft in the toughest environments, day or night. The previously mentioned 160th Special Operations Aviation Regiment (Airborne) is stationed at Fort Campbell, Kentucky. The regiment's aircraft include MH-47, MH-60, O/AH 6, and Mil Mi-17 helicopters. Stationed at Fort Bragg is the unacknowledged and unreported-on Special Forces Operational Detachment-Delta, often called Delta Force.

The Air Force Special Operations Command had about ten thousand people in 1986, headquartered at Hurlburt Field, Florida. The AFSOC units are trained for modern warfare against guerilla forces, The training includes that necessary for direct action, unconventional warfare, special reconnaissance, foreign internal defense, and counterterrorism.

AFSOC has three active-duty flying units with both fixed-wing and rotary-wing aircraft, including many sophisticated versions of the Lockheed Martin C-130. These include the MC-130E Combat Talon 1 and MC-130H Combat Talon II aircraft for infiltration, resupply, and exfiltration of SOF units under all conditions; and the MC-130P Combat Shadow aircraft, which fly clandestine low-level missions penetrating hostile territory to refuel other aircraft and deliver SOF and equipment. The AC-130H Spectre and AC-130U Spooky gunships provide close-air support. The EC-130 Commando Solo aircraft conduct psychological operations.

All of this fixed-wing equipment supports the MH-53J/M helicopters, which are now forced by history to be at the point of the fight, conducting low-level, long-range penetrations into hostile territory at any time, in any weather, for bringing troops in, taking them out, and supplying them while there. As will be seen in the next chapter, the MV-22 Osprey aircraft supplements this effort.

The Navy SOF consist of about 4,950 active and 1,200 reserve personnel, organized into SEAL (Sea, Air, and Land) teams, Special Boat Units, and SEAL Delivery Vehicle teams. SEAL commandos, operating in sixteen-man platoons, can be deployed from helicopters and submarines. Navy ships and Navy and Marine Corps aircraft can also be used to insert or recover SOF of other military services.[11]

By 2009, USSOCOM has grown to include 54,000 active-duty, National Guard, and reserve personnel from all the services and including some DOD civilians. It has also been given additional responsibilities in conducting the war on terror. The ARSOF has grown to 30,000, the Air Force SOF to about 13,000, and the Navy components of SOF to about 4,600. On November 1, 2005, DOD announced the creation of the Marine Special Operations Command (MARSOC), with four subordinate units as a component of USSOCOM. Two of the latter units maintain battalion strength.[12]

This seems like far too little growth in strength for these essential units. Since the 1986 reorganization and the 9/11 attacks, the SOF units have grown immensely in their importance, handling crises at any point around the globe. Like the rest of the military services, the SOF have been affected by declining budgets. Yet the decline in SOF funding has had none of the attention paid to it that has been given to other victims of budgets and future planning, with the Lockheed Martin F-22 fighter being a perfect example of the situation.

The same shift in emphasis forced an increasing reliance on helicopters beginning with Operation ENDURING FREEDOM (first called Operation INFINITE JUSTICE) in Afghanistan and continuing to this day. Enduring Freedom also included actions in other areas being used as terrorist bases, such as the Philippines, the Horn of Africa, and regions of the trans-Sahara.

Afghanistan had been controlled by the Taliban since the Soviet withdrawal and had hosted Osama bin Laden since 1996. On September 20, 2001, announcing that Osama bin Laden was behind the 9/11 attacks, the U.S. government gave the Taliban government a five-point ultimatum. It included delivering to the U.S. all al-Qaeda leaders, releasing all imprisoned foreign nationals, closing all prison camps, handing over all terrorists and their supporters, and giving the U.S. full access to all terrorist training camps. This was immediately rejected by the Taliban government. Pres. George W. Bush announced on October 7, 2001, that a preliminary bombardment operation in Afghanistan was part of a plan to destroy terrorist training camps, capture al-Qaeda leaders, and force an end to terrorist activities within the country.

Almost all initial ground operations were conducted by SOF, and the helicopter was absolutely vital to each one. The result was an outstanding success, with the sole disappointment perhaps being a breakdown of the system at the battle of Tora Bora, where it is believed that less reliance on the Afghan forces supporting the SOF might have resulted in the capture of Osama bin Laden. Sufficient control was established over Afghanistan by the end of 2001 to permit elections for a new centralized government, the restructuring of Afghan military forces, and general rebuilding of the infrastructure. All of these in turn required the incessant use of helicopters in support roles.

The victory in Afghanistan, tenuous as it might have been, also prepared the way for Operation IRAQI FREEDOM (OIF) in 2003. However, the Taliban was never entirely eliminated and remains a threat to this day. As recently as June 2009, the U.S. representative for Afghanistan and Pakistan, Richard Holbrooke, announced that changes would be made in the attempts to cut off Taliban funding. While his remarks were principally related to reducing U.S. opium crop eradication efforts, they signaled the strength that the Taliban opposition still maintains.

In OIF, the massed, well-equipped forces of the United States and its allies quickly moved into Iraqi territory with the announced goal of changing the regime and removing the threat of weapons of mass destruction. The campaign was conducted with a massive number of air sorties, all using precision-guided munitions to reduce collateral damage. While there was intensive helicopter activity at all levels, it was not until the twelfth day of the war that the 101st Airborne Division (Air Assault) captured the An Najaf airfield, carrying out its role as blocking force and isolating enemy elements.

The vulnerability of the helicopter to small-arms ground fire was illustrated during an assault on Karbala on March 23. Of an attacking force of thirty-two Apaches, one was shot down, one was placed out of commission, and all of the others were damaged. The captured crew of the downed helicopter was exhibited on Iraqi television. Fortunately, there were few MANPAD missiles in the Iraqi defense of Karbala, or the losses would have been greater. On March 28, the Apaches returned to Karbala with more success. They destroyed tanks and trucks, with only two helicopters receiving damage.

The very recounting of these small-scale triumphs and setbacks frames the relative position of the helicopter in OIF. It remained an essential support item but was no longer tasked with being the point of the sword in a continuing offensive. The demands of the war required joint operations of UAVs (unmanned aerial vehicles), fixed-wing and rotary-wing aircraft, and the ground components. At present, it seems inevitable that rotary-wing UAVs will become an essential part of this mixture in the near future.

As the seemingly endless war in Iraq dragged on, fighting flared again in Afghanistan. After Pres. Barack Obama came into office in 2009, a specified date was set for the removal of American forces in Iraq. The war in Afghanistan was designated to be of primary interest, and the force levels were increased there.

Both Iraq and Afghanistan continued to require extensive support from helicopters, but in neither country could the helicopter be credited with reshaping the conduct of modern warfare. In essence, the continued use of the helicopter in combat and support roles was modern warfare, writ simple and clear. And the helicopters being used were almost all derivatives of the types introduced during or just after the Vietnam War.

Advances in Foreign Helicopters

In the United States, civilian helicopter availability has usually followed the development of a type by the military. In Europe, this was not always true, but there was a greater understanding of the mutual benefits that research backed by various European governments would have upon the marketplace. The net result was often the same—a military type being developed but translated into a civilian product. This sort of government-backed R&D is at the heart of the Boeing argument that its main Airbus opponents have received government subsidies that make their prices more attractive to customers.

Circumstances in Europe permitted advances in certain areas of helicopter design, offering a degree of improved performance. New rotors, more powerful engines, and new materials have allowed the European manufacturers to dominate the American commercial market and satisfy some American military needs. Evidence of the latter may be found in the U.S. Army's decision to adopt a militarized version of the Eurocopter EC145 as the UH-72 Lakota, for the Light Utility Helicopter (LUH) program. An initial contract for 345 aircraft was let to replace the venerable Bell UH-1H and OH-58A/C Kiowa helicopters.

An example of foreign improvements in helicopters is the Eurocopter NH-90. The NH-90 is typical of the long line of Eurocopter offerings that blanket the field and help account for the multibillion-dollar annual gross of the firm. The NH-90's design and development came about through a NATO agency that represented France, Italy, Germany, and the Netherlands, in a joint venture in which the member companies were Agusta, Eurocopter, and Fokker. The goal was to develop a new weapon system with features that were seen as adaptable to future wars. One of the newer features of the agreement for some participants was the equal weighting of such factors as reliability, maintainability, support in the field, and test results. As American companies had done so often in the past, consideration was given both to ground and naval employment but with the additional wrinkle of needing to comply with language differences and, to a degree, historical national precedents in such things are ergonomics. The ambitious goal was to achieve a basic model that would lend itself to the tactical transport task in all weather conditions, with the usual additional characteristics necessary for MEDEVAC, CSAR, airborne command and control, and other typical needs. The naval version would take into consideration the exceptional maintenance demands of shipboard operation, antisubmarine warfare, the insertion of SOF, plus the usual demands for a transport helicopter.

To achieve these goals, Eurocopter stressed the future. It created an all-composite fuselage to improve crash worthiness and reduce the radar signature. The large fuselage had a constant cross-section and two large sliding doors to facilitate loading and offloading. The fuel tanks and retractable landing gear were designed to resist damage in a crash, always a hazard in field operations. Special attention was given to reducing the drag of the titanium main-hub rotor, which was fitted with elastomeric bearings and four composite blades. The latest electronics, designed to be upgradable and replaceable, were fitted. The computer had the most modern approach for flight display and recorded the maintenance requirements as they occurred. All main systems were multiply redundant as a battle damage-control feature. The twin engines had thirty-minute "run-dry" features, another absolute necessity in a battlefield situation. Despite the complexity of the aircraft, it was specifically designed for one-pilot control under both VFR and IFR conditions. Controls were naturally fly-by-wire. The maintainability requirements were very high, with a mission reliability of 97.5 percent called for and only 2.5 maintenance hours per flying hour.

The reward for Eurocopter has been to achieve world dominance in the manufacture of helicopters. Its long-term track record in the United States is both astonishing and instructive. Figures from 2010 indicate an estimated $784 million that Eurocopter engaged in directly or introduced to its 1,000-vendor network. It has more than one million square feet of factory and assembly facilities in Grand Prairie, Texas and Columbus, Mississippi. It established its footprint with helicopters in the United States in 1957, and since then it has delivered more than 2,500 helicopters to U.S. operators. The firm established its first manufacturing partnership in 1969 and became a fully owned U.S. helicopter manufacturer in 1974. This positioned it to become the number-one producer of civilian turbine helicopters in the United States in nine of the ten years ending in 2009. This top position includes four market segments thanks to the broadest available product range, extending from the 4,000 pound EC120 to the 22,000-pound EC225.

According to American Eurocopter's president and CEO, Marc Paganini, the company's success can be attributed to three principles in its long-term business strategy: creating business stability through a wide sales mix of rotary-wing products, remaining a stable supplier to customers, and retaining a strong commitment to company employees.[13]

Other foreign producers include the association of Agusta and Westland (which was formalized into AgustaWestland under ownership of Finmeccanica, an Italian holding company). The firm fields a line similar in scope to Eurocopter but with more reliance on using an existing American design for its larger products. It produced the EH-101, already in services in nine countries. As previously noted, this provided the baseline for the Lockheed Martin winning entry in the Marine One competition.

With the exception of the Soviet Union and its successor states, foreign helicopter manufacturers often began operation by licensing a design from the United States. Westland, long a builder of such exotic fixed-wing aircraft as the Pterodactyl, Lysander, Whirlwind, and Wyvern, also dabbled in autogiros in the 1930s. In 1947 it bought the rights to produce the Sikorsky S-51. This led to the large-scale production of Westland versions of other Sikorsky models, including the S-55, S-58, and S-61, and ultimately to the acquisition of Fairey Aviation, Saunders Roe, and the Bristol Helicopter Division. Well established by its experience, Westland extended its cooperative agreements to include Agusta-Bell in producing the Sioux in 1965 and the Aerospatiale Gazelle and Puma in 1967. In the latter agreement, design authority remained with Aerospatiale, while Westland undertook production. The partnership resulted in a totally new design, the remarkable Lynx in 1971. It also led to Westland's participation in the design, development, and production of the EH-101, working with Agusta.

In contrast to Westland, French helicopter development was more nationalistic. Prior to World War II, the French aviation industry had been partially nationalized, resulting in the creation of small manufacturers such as SNCASE (*Société nationale des constructions aéronautiques du sud-est* [southeast]) and SNCASO (*Société nationale des constructions aéronautiques du sud-ouest* [southwest]). In the postwar years, these companies were merged over time, becoming first Sud and then Aerospatiale.

Thus it was that the Aerospatiale company had its foundations in the designs of Prof. Henry Focke, who assisted the Sud-Est in refining the basic Focke-Achegelis Fa 223. The first widely successful Sud-Est design was the S.E. 3120 Alouette, flown for the first time on July 31, 1952. Sud-Est did manufacture some Sikorsky helicopters under license. In 1992, Aerospace-matra and the German Daimler Chrysler Company formed the current Eurocopter group, now a subsidiary of the European Aeronautic, Defense and Space Company (EADS). As noted, Eurocopter, working with Agusta and Fokker, created the very successful NH-90 helicopter.

Aerospatiale had great success with the introduction of the jet-powered version of the Alouette II in 1955 and followed it with a series of indigenous designs that were fully competitive in the marketplace. A high point was the selection of the Eurocopter EH-101 as the winner in the competition to replace Marine One, the presidential helicopter fleet.

In January 2005, the US-101 variant of the Eurocopter EH-101 was declared the winner of the $1.7 billion contract, beating out the previously favored Sikorsky S-92. The new Marine One received the designation of VH-71A. It was to be built by a Lockheed Martin/AgustaWestland team, working with Bell Helicopter Textron. An estimated 80 percent of the twenty-three aircraft called for in the contract were to be made by the primary team and its many American suppliers, including General Electric, ITT, Northrop Grumman, Kaman Aerospace, and more. The decision came at a time when the European helicopter industry was dominating U.S. commercial helicopter sales.

Purchasing foreign aircraft for U.S. military use is not new. The Coast Guard shocked the world when it purchased first the Dassault Breguet Falcon as its HU-25 Guardian and followed this with the purchase of the Aerospatiale SA365 as its HH-65A Dolphin, the Agusta A109 as the HH-68 Stingray, and the Agusta A139 as a search and rescue helicopter. The Navy elected to purchase the BAE Hawk as its primary training aircraft, the T-45 Goshawk, and opted, with the USAF, for the Swiss Pilatus PC-9 for its nostalgically named Beech T-6 Texan II trainer. The Army has long used the Shorts 330 Sherpa as its C-23 transport. However, purchasing a foreign aircraft for use by the president of the United States was new.

The decision to purchase the US101 was analyzed intensively, with no little heat being generated by partisan supporters. An objective analysis indicated the following:

1. The US-101 fuselage is 33 percent larger than that of the Sikorsky S-92 entry. This had plusses and minuses. On the one hand, it allowed for more comfort and for growth potential. On the other hand, the US-101 would not fit into one of the standard helicopter transporters, the Lockheed C-5 Galaxy, while the S-92 would. However, either aircraft fit inside the Boeing C-17 Globemaster III.

2. The US-101 was equipped with three turbo-shaft engines, versus the S-92's two. This afforded a margin of safety for engine failure. Three engines are more costly to maintain, of course, and use more fuel. In discussions of the relative costs, Sikorsky maintained that two engines saved 50 percent in operational costs, while Lockheed Martin insisted that it was only 20 percent.

3. While Lockheed Martin's price was higher, their proposal indicated that they were closer to achieving the competition design goals than Sikorsky.

4. While the EH-101's handling was praised, its "mishap" rate was significantly higher than that of the S-92. Sikorsky advocates also emphasized that the S-92 is a newer design than the EH-101, which made its first flight on October 9, 1987. The S-92 made its first flight on December 23, 1998.

5. Politics played an important role at the local, state, federal, and international levels, with major figures ranging from congressmen to the secretary of state making pronouncements on the relative value of the two types.

Once again, however, rising costs and delivery delays resulted in the cancellation of the program, and once again, the funds originally planned for new equipment were diverted to pay for updating the existing equipment, this time the aging Sikorskys of the presidential helicopter fleet.

In Russia, the Mil design bureau brought out the Mi-26, which, while broadly based on its highly successful 1970s technology, is capable of very large payloads exceeding forty-four thousand pounds. With about twice the cabin space and payload of the Mi-6 (previously the world's largest and fastest production helicopter), the Mi-26 reflected the traditional Russian taste for size. It was equipped with an eight-blade rotor, entering service in 1983.

The strikingly named "Night Hunter" (the NATO code name is "Havoc"), the Mil Mi-28NE is a development of the original 1980s Mi-28 assault helicopter, designed as a larger and heavier response to the American Apache. First flown in April 1997, the Mi-28NE seems over-encumbered with drag-inducing equipment, and its general performance falls short of the Apache's. Russia, in its economic turmoil, has not been able to fund a sizeable production of the Mi-28NEs, but it has had several sales to foreign countries. Total production is estimated to be fewer than one hundred to date.

Another, rather more elegant addition to the Russian stable is the Kamov Ka-52 "Alligator" (NATO calls it "Hokum"), which entered production in 2008. It has a maximum speed approaching 240 mph, and its performance

The Ka-52 "Alligator" is a multirole, all-weather combat helicopter. *(Courtesy of Zaur Eylanbekov [Foxbat])*

generally exceeds that of the Mi-28NE. To date only ten have been produced for Russian forces, and the proposed rate of production is projected to be very slow.

Around the rest of the world, one can confidently expect China, Japan, and India to do what they have done so well in the past: purchase foreign equipment and technology to build an indigenous industry, and from there go forward with their own native concepts to produce competitive products.

Despite the evident competition everywhere, there has been a marked difference in the interest in R&D between Europe and the United States. In a paper entitled *Vision 2020,* the European Commission declared an aim to dominate the aerospace industry by funding research. In the United States there has been a tacit submission to this goal, with NASA closing the important wind tunnels that contribute to rotary-wing research, especially those investigating individual blade control using "smart" materials.

In both the United States and Europe, there are five fundamental areas that require extensive R&D funding:

1. Concepts for innovative configurations can radically improve rotor-craft speed, affordability, and mission effectiveness while retaining superior VTOL and low-speed characteristics.

2. Applications of information and computing technologies will result in safer, more affordable, environmentally friendly rotorcraft and far more effective and survivable military systems. These technologies can enable safe, nearly all-weather operation in confined urban areas, particularly important for scheduled transport and public service operations.

3. Active and adaptive controls have demonstrated the potential to improve performance and reduce external noise, internal noise, vibration, and weight and mechanical complexity.

4. Noise-reducing design and operational methods have demonstrated noise reductions totaling 20 dB (a 75 percent reduction), but continued research is needed to achieve this for future rotorcraft configurations.

5. New design tools can reduce development cycle time by 50 percent, speeding up the application of technology improvements. These include physics-based models, such as advanced structural analysis and computational fluid dynamics, which lead to improved performance, noise, and vibration characteristics. These methods are needed to optimize designs and to "get it right the first time," avoiding costly redesigning and retesting, particularly for innovative aircraft configurations.

Deice and anti-ice concepts and certification methods are needed for affordable and reliable all-weather operation. Operation of rotorcraft in icy conditions currently requires complex (hence costly and sometimes unreliable) systems and is difficult and time-consuming.

Under the present outlook for funding, it is obvious that Europe and not the United States will lead the way in these vital areas, and Europe and not the United States will benefit from the resulting military and civilian sales.[14]

It is a curious fact that despite all the obstacles placed in its path, the helicopter developed into the needed instrument at the needed time for major conflicts. Then, by a strange confluence of aerodynamic principles, human ingenuity, and the demands of modern warfare, it has arrived at its present stage of development, which just happens to meet perceived service needs if not service wishes.

Chapter Eleven

The Helicopter Today and Tomorrow

The helicopter has unquestionably had great effect upon modern warfare, despite its troubled history of inadequate funding, inter- and intraservice rivalry, quests by advocates for too extravagant performance improvements, and many other obstacles. It has developed from a frail and unreliable machine, best suited to the recovery of nearby wounded personnel, to become a formidable hunter-killer. Its lift capacity has increased from pounds to tons, and through the years it has remained the most welcome sight in the world to survivors in distress.

Even more important than its engineering and design development, its backers have learned how to use the helicopter efficiently, getting the most from its capabilities and adapting to an ever-varying series of wartime scenarios. The helicopter reached the peak of its effect upon warfare in Vietnam, where in the hands of dashing, daring combatants, it shaped and controlled the battlefield. In later wars, its role, while not so dominant as in Vietnam, has been ever more essential to the conduct of conflicts, particularly in the difficult situations encountered in the Middle East. There, the suppression of enemy assaults, the resupply of outposts, and the delivery of special-operation forays make the helicopter invaluable.

In the long run, and quite inadvertently, the helicopter has arrived at an invaluable, if not optimum, point for most civil and military requirements. The term "inadvertently" is used because the helicopter's current performance standards in terms of speed, range, reliability, and maintainability have not reached the goals so earnestly sought in years past when advanced new designs were coming off the drawing board. Instead, in the United States we have seen the basic helicopter designs of the 1970s and 1980s benefit from a steady, moderate improvement in capability. In practical terms, the American helicopter of contemporary production is a combination of decades-old basic design and thoughtful improvements in equipment, reliability, and maintainability. The people operating them accept the existing standards of performance, understand the limitations, and use this as the basis for their planning.

In practical terms, there has been a symbiotic relationship between the industry and the user that has withstood, and offset, the problems caused by the tribal instincts and managerial mistakes noted in the first paragraph of this chapter. This has resulted in a seasoned, mature series of American helicopter designs that continue to serve their military users well on many traditional missions.

Despite declines in the total U.S. helicopter fleet since the Vietnam War, the demands placed upon it have been great. Rising costs have forced the services to examine methods by which the number of types of helicopters can be reduced, thus simplifying maintenance and logistic efforts. As an example, the U.S. Navy is developing a master plan that places helicopters at the forefront of standard operations. Part of the plan is to reduce the number of helicopter types in the force structure to just three, all CH-60 variants of the Sikorsky Black Hawk, to handle anti-submarine warfare, anti-surface threats, mine warfare, CSAR, special operations, and vertical replenishment missions. It is worthwhile here to examine briefly the history of the Black Hawk as an example of how an aging but capable type can be adapted for multiple uses over many years, especially when the obvious new replacement vehicle is controversial.

Two Sikorsky model lines, the S-65 and S-70, illustrate this situation very well and demonstrate how careful and deliberate improvements over time can offset the failure to achieve technological breakthroughs to totally new performance levels. Other helicopters, including the Boeing CH-47 Chinook and, as we have seen, the many Bell variants of the Huey, have maintained their value through the same process.

The S-65 became one of the Western world's largest and most versatile helicopters since its first flight as the twin-engine CH-53 Sea Stallion on October 14, 1965. Playing upon its own strengths, Sikorsky created a hybrid design using the fuselage, engine, and rotor system of the proven

Aircraft nicknames often reflect the esteem in which they are held, and Huey is an affectionate adaptation of the original UH-1 designation. *(Courtesy of U.S. Army Museum, Fort Rucker)*

and popular CH-54 Tarhe heavy lifter. The result was a large, fast assault transport capable of carrying thirty-seven fully equipped troops; it also created a platform from which many variants could be derived over the years. On March 1, 1974, a three-engine version, the CH-53E Super Stallion, appeared. (The CH-53E became the new heavy-assault helicopter, with its predecessor CH-53 models being reclassified as medium helicopters.) Among the more than twenty variants, the USAF used the S-65 as the basis for rescue and Pave Low helicopter programs.

Sikorsky next drew on its experience to create the S-70, smaller than the S-65 and intended to replace the Bell UH-1 series. The first example, the YUH-60A, was first flown on October 17, 1974, as the winner of the competition for the U.S. Army's Utility Tactical Transport Aircraft System (UTTAS). The UTTAS was to represent the "lessons learned" from the intensive wartime use of the Bell UH-1 Huey helicopters, which performed so many different duties in Vietnam. After much thought, a design specification was issued by the Army. The Sikorsky response was deemed better than the corresponding Boeing Vertol offer, and the Sikorsky YUH-60A prototype made its first flight on November 29, 1974. By mid-1979, the Black Hawk was beginning to replace the Hueys within the 101st Airborne Division.

The Black Hawks have a muscular, almost sinister appearance, with a large fuselage capable of carrying the two-man crew and eleven personnel. Two General Electric turbo-shaft engines sit atop the fuselage, driving a four-blade main rotor and generating sufficient power to allow the Black Hawk to cruise at 175 mph. The commodious fuselage can handle about three thousand pounds of freight internally, while up to

Military helicopter armament has increased in potency over the years to include powerful turrets linked to helmet-mounted sights. *(Courtesy of U.S. Army Museum, Fort Rucker)*

an eight-thousand-pound load can be carried externally. It can be fitted with 30-mm chain guns, machineguns, mini-guns, and Hellfire missiles. Extra fuel tanks, formed as part of the optional wing stubs, can be added. These variations have enabled it to survive and serve in combat operations since its debut in the 1983 invasion of Grenada.

Yet the Black Hawk, in all its almost fifty variations including export models, remains essentially a helicopter with a 1970s pedigree. It has been improved considerably over the years, and it teaches that in the world of rotary-wing aircraft, the expense of major performance improvements becomes insupportable after certain thresholds of range, speed, and hover altitude are attained. As desirable as further improvements in these and other areas may be, they come at a price too high to pay compared to an improved Black Hawk.

The next step in this linear process has seen the Black Hawk's multiservice stable mate, the CH-53, so severely stressed by the demands of the Middle Eastern wars that the supply of aircraft to be remanufactured is being exhausted. The best way to maintain the capability was to call for a "new" CH-53, the much larger, more modern, and more powerful CH-53K, now in the process of manufacture at Sikorsky. The Heavy Lift Replacement (HLR) program calls for the purchase of 156 new-built helicopters derived from the CH-53E, with an initial operating capability set for 2014-15.

With a program value of more than $4 billion, the CH-53K is perhaps the current pinnacle in the process of refining past designs for the future. Sikorsky promises a large increase in range and payload coupled with a 42-percent reduction in direct maintenance costs, a 68-percent reduction in maintenance hours per flight hour relationships, and much increased survivability. There is a 20-percent reduction in fuel consumption, despite having three General Electric GE28-1B turbo-shaft engines of 7,500 shp in place of the 4,380-shp engines of the CH-53E.

The CH-53K fuselage is obviously larger and bulkier than its predecessor. Composite construction is used for the fuselage and the rotors, and it features an elastomeric rotor head, with hydraulic blade folding. With the CH-53K, the Marine Corps has reached a point in helicopter development that carries it at least into the second half of the twenty-first century.

Yet even as the Marine Corps continues to rely on rotary-wing aircraft for many traditional tasks, it has, in a way unique among the services, pressed for advances beyond the helicopter with the MV-22 Osprey. And as we will see, the same essential question of expense versus performance improvement is a current problem facing the MV-22.

In Europe and Russia, attack helicopters are still advocated, with the formidable Westland Lynx, Eurocopter Tiger, and Mil Mi-28NE offering new capabilities. These, like the U.S. Army Apache helicopter, face a most demanding question in how well will such attack-type helicopters do in future military conflicts, where the intensity of combat is certain to increase substantially. Admittedly, the problem is more germane to the American situation, engaged as it is in the global struggle against terror, but ultimately the new criteria of combat will apply to all countries.

The real difficulty facing helicopters is that the hostile environment in which they must operate has become more and more lethal. In the years to come, the threat will grow from ragged attacks by rocket-propelled grenades to very much improved MANPAD SAMs. These will continue their rapid proliferation in all areas of the world. Helicopters are still very vulnerable to small-arms fire, and the traditional Kalashnikov-style weaponry will likely be augmented in the future by more powerful automatic weapons firing even more lethal projectiles.

Since Operation DESERT STORM, most American military operations have faced relatively primitive military opposition. This may still be the case in large part, but there are almost certain to be requirements in the future to fight more sophisticated enemies armed with more advanced weapons such as radar-aimed anti-aircraft guns.

Possibilities for Improvements

Before coming to a conclusion on the future role of helicopters, it might be well to examine the possibilities for improvements in the type, which will enable it to sustain itself in the conflicts to come.

No new military helicopter has been procured for the U.S. armed services since 1990. The Apache was the last "new" rotary-wing aircraft to come into service, and it has been followed only by the Bell Boeing V-22 tiltrotor. It seems pertinent then to ask, after all the R&D, production, and experience since the helicopter came into being as the Sikorsky VS-300 in the 1930s, what the wildest hopes might be about the helicopter of the future.

The ideal, if somewhat magical, new helicopter would have incredible new rotors that would be virtually noiseless, stealthy, and able to absorb tremendous battle damage. The rotors would be operated by a low-drag hub with a totally new mechanism, simple and effective, for transferring the power from the engines to the blades. The body would be a light-weight composite structure able to shrug off small-arms fire and even absorb a hit from a rocket-propelled grenade. Smaller but more powerful engines would propel it at high speeds (more than three hundred knots) over long ranges (1,000 miles) to the LZs.

Sadly, no such magic helicopter is foreseen in any predictions, simply because the basic characteristics of the helicopter impose drag and per-formance penalties that currently cannot be overcome. By far the most important of these is the fundamental feature of the helicopter itself—the rotor. The inherent aerodynamic conflict of the rotor's advancing blade and retreating blade has been modified to some degree by clever rotor design and the addition of trim control surfaces. However, as the rotor speed, size, and design changes, the problems grow more complex, and to most authorities it seems reasonable to assume that the maximum speed available to a helicopter is limited to about 250 knots (287.1 mph). As speed increases, the rotor transitions from being a pure lifting device to acting somewhat as a drag chute. If the rotor is to be retained, not stowed or somehow retracted, the 250 knots is generally conceded to be the achievable limit.

This putative maximum helicopter speed has already been attained. The current speed record for helicopters is held by the versatile and well-liked Westland Lynx. On August 11, 1986, a specially modified version, piloted by Trevor Egginton, set an absolute speed record for helicopters over 15- and 25-kilometer courses at 249.09 mph. This Lynx had spe-cially tuned engines and used the British Experimental Rotor Programme (BERP), which features sweepback of the rotor from a notch at the outer end of rotor blade.

There is always the future hope that if the designer can "unload" the rotor, so that it is not imposing any drag, and another means of propulsion is added, then the maximum speed might advance to more than 250 knots. Beyond this point, one has to design a retractable rotor, one that folds up and stows to minimize drag. The entire propulsion system would then provide power for thrust rather than turning the rotor, and you essentially would have a compound helicopter that uses its rotor only for vertical ascents and descents.

As noted previously, compound helicopters have been tried over the years, and none has reached production. The Department of Defense defines a compound helicopter as "a helicopter with an auxiliary propulsion system which provides thrust in excess of that which the rotor(s) alone could produce, thereby permitting increased forward speeds; wings may or may not be provided to reduce the lift required from the rotor system." There are currently proposals for compound helicopters in the marketplace. The Piasecki X-49 is a twin-engine experimental compound helicopter based on the Sikorsky YSH-60F Seahawk but has lifting wings and uses the proprietary Piasecki vectored thrust ducted propeller design (VTDP) for propulsion. The changes include a third engine, a forty-five-inch extension of the fuselage, wings with a forward sweep, a general drag reduction, and a fly-by-wire control system.

Company president John Piasecki believes that applying the Speedhawk conversion to the UH-60 fleet would essentially provide a new generation of capable helicopters at a minimum of R&D and production expense. The same system could be applied to other helicopters as well.

Sikorsky has experimented with its X2 technology demonstrator, an advanced compound helicopter that uses coaxial rotor blades and auxiliary propulsion. First flown on August 27, 2008, the X2 drew heavily on the experience Sikorsky gained in the Comanche program. The X2 has an integrated fly-by-wire system to coordinate its engine/rotor/propulsion systems. The rigid rotor blades are designed with a high lift-to-drag ratio, and drag has been minimized. Sikorsky achieved its goal with an unofficial speed record of 250 knots in 2010. With the two rotors turning in opposite directions to cancel torque, no rear-mounted anti-torque rotor is necessary. Instead, the power is channeled to a pusher propeller.

As no compound helicopter has been placed in production, it has become necessary to "remanufacture" existing proven helicopter types so that they can continue in service. In the remanufacture process, important incremental improvements are introduced. The UH-60 featured a titanium spar of immense strength and a strong, crash-resistant construction. The Apache has rotor blades designed to be resistant to gunfire. Payloads have been increased considerably on most. The new Sikorsky CH-53K can lift 40,000 pounds, about twice what the dedicated heavy-lift Sikorsky CH-54 Tarhe could do. There have been reductions in noise levels, helicopters are more maneuverable than before, and their reliability is much better. New night vision, navigation, and maintenance equipment has been introduced, and new flying techniques have evolved.

There is already considerable experimentation with the UAV helicopter, a rotary-wing development in the vein of the successful Predator and Reaper UAVs that have gained increasing prominence. Without the requirement for a crew and all the concomitant load of safety and comfort features, the UAV helicopter offers possibilities for moderate improvements in range and speed. However, it is ultimately limited by the same features as a full-sized manned helicopter—the inevitable rise in drag of the rotor as speed is increased. It is an alternate approach to using helicopters but not an adequate substitute for many of their missions.

So it remains that standard systems become by default the basic helicopter of choice: Black Hawk, Chinook, CH-53K. All of these are adaptable, have been built in many variations, and face increasingly competent weaponry. Improvements to these workhorse helicopters are often added externally, creating more drag rather than boosting speed and range.

One drastic solution always seems to spring so readily to the lips of military leadership when armament deficiencies are found: to "take it out of the hide of the troops." This has certainly been the case with the helicopter in the past, as the leadership accepted high casualties in exchange for its continued use on the battlefield. In combat, certain techniques were established to make the helicopter more survivable. It was found in Vietnam that some 80 percent of damage inflicted on helicopters occurred during an approach to the LZ. Pilots soon crafted special techniques for the approach, landing, and takeoff phases of their missions. In many respects, they are only Band-Aids, but they aid in survival. Experience has dictated new procedures, including the following:

1. Continuously vary takeoff and landing directions.

2. Continuously vary routes, altitudes, directions, etc.

3. Do not follow predictable landmarks, such as riverbeds, streets, etc.

4. Never fly over populated areas if they can be avoided.

5. Always seek to have fixed-wing protection and make sure that rescue forces are available.

6. Always be aware of the possibility of collision. Maintain 1,500 feet of distance.

7. Have a portfolio of tactics for insertion and extraction so that you can use different techniques on an unpredictable basis.

8. Always be aware that unprepared LZs in combat areas are filled with hostile possibilities, including rocket-propelled grenades, landmines, and other defenses. In addition, the helicopter rarely has surprise on its side, given its noise.

9. Always be aware of the reflective qualities of rotor blades at night. The slightest light will illuminate them and give the enemy a target.

10. To repeat, never be without overwhelming firepower and without rescue capability.[1]

Sadly, given the effort and expenditures made over the decades, only one brand-new type of vertical-lift aircraft has so far been introduced to the Middle East conflict, the Bell Boeing V-22 tiltrotor. The Osprey is unquestionably a tribute to the persistence of the United States Marines and the uncanny ability of that service to somehow insist on acquiring new equipment despite its small size, small budget, and modest place on the procurement chain. It had succeeded previously with a V/STOL (vertical/short takeoff and landing) jet lift fighter, the McDonnell Douglas AV-8B Harrier, and is now "all-in" on the development of the Lockheed Martin F-35 tri-service aircraft. In rotary-lift aircraft, it has backed successfully and against great odds the Bell Boeing V-22 Osprey.

The Bell Boeing V-22: Problem or Solution?

The tiltrotor aircraft development process has followed the same long and often difficult path of the helicopter itself since the 1920s. The tiltrotor goes beyond the compound helicopter in combining the features of fixed-wing and helicopter aircraft and improves performance by removing the dynamics and drag of a huge rotor. In the tiltrotor, the large proprotors (and there is some ongoing discussion about which is the more accurate term, tiltrotor or proprotor) are used just as helicopter rotors are used, to achieve vertical lift during takeoffs and landing. However, in horizontal flight, the proprotors are designed to tilt to a horizontal position, providing turboprop-like thrust to an aircraft-like design and removing the inherent large-rotor problem of the standard helicopter. This gives the tiltrotor the capability of a helicopter for takeoffs and landing, plus most of the range and speed of a conventional aircraft in normal flight.

The first flying example of a primitive tiltrotor was a design by the gifted inventor Henry Berliner in 1922, following in the footsteps of his father, Emile. (Some historians dispute whether the design really merits attention as a tiltrotor. Others maintain that although the degree of tilt was slight, it existed and pointed the way to the future.) In 1930, a patent was issued to George Lehberger for a tiltrotor aircraft, but no aircraft was built to his design.

While crude in appearance compared to modern helicopters, the Berliner was a great advance for its day. *(Courtesy of U.S. Army Museum, Fort Rucker)*

A brilliant English engineer/designer/flyer/inventor, Leslie E. Baynes, was also interested in the tiltrotor design. Baynes, whose later patents would include a variable-pitch propeller and a 100-passenger jet airliner, was also associated with the notorious "Flying Flea" light aircraft design. His 1938 tiltrotor concept featured both turbines and a swivel rotor and was configured in a manner strikingly similar to the V-22.

There was a flurry of interest in the tiltrotor over the years by Focke-Achgelis and the American firm that followed its concepts, Platt-LePage, but it resulted only in design studies and patent applications and not hardware. It remained for a smaller firm, the aptly named Transcendental Aircraft Corporation of New Castle, Delaware, to create a successful flying version, the Model 1-G tiltrotor. Founders Mario A. Guerrieri and Robert L. Lichten, veterans of Kellet Aircraft and Platt-LePage, teamed in 1954 to create a design of surprising elegance, given its experimental

Obviously derived from the Focke-Achgelis configuration, the Platt-LePage did not receive a production contract. (*Courtesy of U.S. Army Museum, Fort Rucker*)

nature. A three-bladed rotor was mounted at each wing tip for vertical lift, and these were swiveled forward for horizontal flight. A single 160-hp Lycoming piston engine drove the rotors through a gearbox, which provided rotor rotation at 633 revolutions per minute (rpm) and propeller rotation at 240 rpm.

The firm received contracts from the Air Force and two aircraft were built, one flying for a year before crashing and logging about sixty flight hours in more than one hundred flights.[2] The Transcendental had promise, as it was easy to control and did not have the vibration characteristic of big rotor helicopters of the time. It achieved transitions up to 90 percent of horizontal flight, but it arrived at a time when helicopter performance was continually improving, and there did not appear to be a need for the additional sophistication and risk associated with tiltrotors.

Further, Bell, with its already long and successful record, had entered

The Bell XV-3 successfully demonstrated the tiltrotor concept in 1955, decades before a tiltrotor would go into production. *(Courtesy of U.S. Army Museum, Fort Rucker)*

the tiltrotor scene with the 1953 debut of its XV-3 Convertiplane. First flown on August 11, 1955, the XV-3 made more than one hundred conversions between helicopter and aircraft modes of flight, with experimentation continuing until 1966. Powered by a single 450-hp Pratt & Whitney R-985 engine installed in the fuselage, the XV-3 featured a complex gearbox that drove the three-blade, twenty-three-foot-diameter rotors mounted at the tips of the wings.

The most important contribution of the XV-3 was that it led to the Bell XV-15, unquestionably the most successful tiltrotor—and the greatest tiltrotor promotional device—prior to the arrival of the V-22. Interestingly enough, the design team for the XV-3 and subsequently both the XV-15 and the V-22 included Robert L. Lichten, who had inspired the Transcendental. Lichten was chief of flight technology at the Bell Helicopter Corporation and was influential in the development of the successful Huey and Jet Ranger aircraft.

The Bell XV-15 won a competition funded by NASA and the Army, beating out a Boeing proposal primarily on the basis of a very advanced engine/rotor design. Rather than placing the engines in the fuselage and driving the rotors through extended shafts, Bell placed the engines into rotating wing-tip pods, with the rotors coupled directly to the engine as in a conventional turboprop installation. The requirement to prevent control loss in the event of failure meant that an emergency driveshaft had to be installed, but this shaft was not for regular use and could be built to a lighter standard.

Bell selected two of Anselm Franz's workhorse Lycoming T-53 turboshaft engines to power the XV-15. Connected by a cross shaft, each drove a three-blade rotor of twenty-five-foot diameter. The engines, transmission, and rotor tilted as a single unit.

In December 1981, after the cancellation of yet another replacement assault transport helicopter program (HXM), Deputy Secretary of Defense Frank C. Carlucci directed that the services review V/STOL technology with the goal of creating a rotary-wing aircraft that would meet the needs of all three services for a medium-lift aircraft. Tiltrotor technology was particularly recommended, and this led to the Joint Advanced Vertical Lift Aircraft (JVX) tiltrotor program. While such backing in high places is an enormous help in obtaining budget share, allocating program responsibility, and giving the program visibility with the public, it also presents problems. Joint programs (the notorious TFX that Secretary of Defense Robert S. McNamara insisted upon comes to mind) often bear within them the seeds of compromise and ultimately disappointment. While joint programs sound reasonable and even prudent upon announcement, it inevitably happens that as the program develops, totally unexpected problems emerge. These often relate not to the new joint system itself but rather to the means by which the services intend to employ it. As a single example, the rotor size and thus the lift capacity of the nascent JVX would ultimately be limited by such things as deck space on Amphibious Assault Ships and elevator size on carriers. Naval aircraft have used folding wings for years, but the JVX would be the first to require folding wings and folding rotors. In a sophisticated aircraft such as the Osprey, the need to fold wings and rotors adds many problems, such as additional weight, complexity, and maintenance.

The initial goal of the backers of the JVX program was to create a tiltrotor aircraft with helicopter V/STOL characteristics combined with those of a fixed-wing propeller-driven aircraft. The concept was also strongly supported by the dynamic if sometimes controversial Secretary of the Navy John Lehman.

It is impossible to overestimate the effect that the successful promotion of the XV-15 had in the ultimate decision to pursue a full-fledged tiltrotor aircraft in the form of the Bell Boeing V-22 Osprey. Many people were given the opportunity to fly the XV-15 when it appeared at air shows, and it received widespread favorable media coverage. It was, not incidentally, a very good looking, well proportioned aircraft, impressive in size, and performed on demand. With two upgraded T-53 Avco Lycoming turbo-shaft engines of 1,250 hp each, it weighed a bit more than 13,250 pounds on takeoff. With a wingspan of fifty-seven feet, two inches, the handsome XV-15 could carry a crew of two and a cargo of some 1,000 pounds at 343 mph, far faster than any other helicopter. The range was an adequate 515 miles and the service ceiling was estimated to be near thirty thousand feet. Perhaps most important, a hover altitude of almost nine thousand feet could be maintained.

One of the two XV-15s subsequently crashed, but the second version was retired to the National Air and Space Museum's Udvar-Hazy facility at Dulles airport, near Washington. Both had more than paid for themselves for Bell, NASA, and the service that wanted V/STOL capability the most, the U.S. Marines.

So successful was the XV-15 that there was now sufficient confidence in the concept to launch a full-sized military aircraft, the Bell Boeing V-22 Osprey. There was general optimism that the multi-mission V-22 would replace aging helicopters in the Marines, Navy, and Air Force, and an ambitious program of 1,086 aircraft was initially considered. These numbers were reduced in later years to 360 MV-22s for the Marine Corps, 48 MV-22s for the Navy, and 50 CV-22s for the Air Force Special Operations Command, as the V-22 struggled for twenty-seven years to reach its Initial Operational Capability (IOC).

The United States Marine Corps, always somehow in the forefront of equipment development, was designated the lead service and planned

The United States Marine Corps is the most prominent advocate of the Bell Boeing Osprey, but the United States Air Force uses it also. (*Courtesy Department of Defense via Bob Dorr*)

to use its version, the MV-22B, to replace its aging CH-46E and CH-53D helicopters in the assault transport role. The Navy expressed interest in a version to use for CSAR and for special operations. The United States Special Operations Command uses the CV-22 version for its many specialty missions. The Air Force also uses the CV-22 for special missions and CSAR and as a supplement to its MH-53 Pave Low helicopters. The Air Force has recently expressed interest in expanding its requirement for the type by another two dozen or so.

The Osprey was developed by Bell Helicopter Textron, which manufactures the wing, nacelles, rotors, drive system, tail surfaces, and aft ramp, integrating all into the basic airframe with the engines. Boeing Helicopters manufactures the fuselage, cockpit, electronic systems, and flight controls. The final aircraft is assembled in a factory in Amarillo, Texas.

In the spirit of jointness, the service secretaries agreed in June 1982 that the services would fund a common development program, the JVX program, with the Navy providing 50 percent of the funds, the Army 34 percent, and the Air Force 16 percent. And while the aircraft was going to be common to each service in the main, each service also had special requirements, those of the Army being most demanding. The Army's lift, speed, and range requirements dictated a large aircraft weighing at least forty thousand pounds, using more powerful engines than the other services required. The Marines, prudent as always, wanted the new aircraft to be equipped with the same engines being used by its CH-53 helicopters, to minimize logistic and maintenance efforts. Initial unit cost estimates varied with the service but ranged from $12 to $17 million.

The program received what appeared to be a setback, but was probably a saving grace, when in 1983 the Army withdrew from the development of the JVX to concentrate on helicopter development. It did maintain an agreement to buy 200 of the Marine version of the JVX, thus preserving for a while the unit-cost computations. With the Army's withdrawal, lead on the JVX passed to the far more passionately concerned Marine Corps. The Marines deemed it ready for full-scale development in May 1986, and a contract was signed with Bell Boeing for six full-scale development aircraft.

The Osprey Takes Flight

The first flight of the V-22 Osprey took place on March 19, 1989, straight into a sea of budgetary controversy. From this point on, there would also be development delays, shifts in priority, and tragic accidents. The overwhelming goodwill that had followed the XV-15 program was denied the V-22. Instead, the V-22 was met with a stream of articulate opposition that threatened the program at every stage.

Despite this, the V-22 emerged as a remarkable aircraft by any standards. Classified by the Federal Aviation Administration as a "powered-lift" vehicle, the V-22 initially had a maximum takeoff weight as a helicopter of 47,500 pounds. If permitted a short takeoff run, the V-22 could accommodate up to 60,500 pounds. The fifty-foot, eleven-inch wingspan featured tilting 6,150-shp Allison turbo-shaft engines driving thirty-eight-foot-diameter, three-bladed proprotors. The fuselage appeared conventional, with accommodation for a crew of three (pilot, copilot, and flight engineer) and up to twenty-four troops with full combat equipment. Estimated cruising speed as a helicopter was a sedate 115 mph; when the rotors tilted for forward flight, the speed rose to an amazing 361 mph. With one in-flight refueling, the V-22 could reach out for 2,100 nautical miles, giving it a unique self-deployment capability denied helicopters. In practical terms, the V-22 is intended to reach farther and faster behind enemy lines, which allows greater selection of LZ sites, extending the traditional utility of vertical envelopment. If used for MEDEVAC, the greater speed of the V-22 over existing helicopters would result in lives saved.

Working through the almost impenetrable forest of Department of Defense rules, tests, and regulations, by September 2000 the Bell Boeing team succeeded in delivering eighteen aircraft to the U.S. government, including two MV-22s remanufactured to Air Force standards and requirements as the CV-22. In November 2000, the improved system for folding rotor blades and wings (Blade Fold Wing Stow or BFWS) was demonstrated, and the aircraft seemed destined for full-rate production.

Unfortunately, the opposition to the V-22 based on its increase in costs was buttressed by a series of four accidents and thirty fatalities between

1991 and 2002. All advanced aircraft experience difficulties in their initial test programs, but few have had accidents with the public exposure of the V-22. On June 11, 1991, a mishap in the flight-control system caused the left nacelle of a hovering MV-22 to strike the ground, bounce, and catch fire. The incident was prominently featured in television newscasts across the country and is still getting multiple hits on YouTube. On July 20, 1992, before a waiting group of congressmen, sponsors, and Marines, a gearbox leaked oil into the right nacelle of an approaching—and perhaps hot-dogging—MV-22, causing a fire that led to a spectacular crash at Marine headquarters at Quantico. Seven crewmen were killed, and the MV-22 fleet was grounded for eleven months. The political effect of the crash was enormous, and the post-crash analysis did nothing to ease concerns.

During the next eight years, the program moved in fits and starts. On April 8, 2000, an MV-22 loaded with Marines attempted to land at Marana Northwest Regional Airport in Arizona. Flight operations were apparently unsynchronized and the pilot tried to compensate by descending at a faster than normal rate, said to be more than 2,000 feet per minute, but at a very slow ground speed of less than forty-five miles an hour. This flight-attitude condition turned the tiltrotor concept into a disadvantage, as the descent was too fast for a helicopter but the forward speed was too low for a fixed-wing aircraft. The right rotor malfunctioned at only 245 feet above the ground, rolling the MV-22 over on its back to crash, killing all nineteen men aboard.

This tragic accident called attention to the vortex ring state (VRS) phenomenon, which also applies to helicopters. In this case, however, there was concern that given their configuration, the VRS phenomenon might be a more serious worry for tiltrotor aircraft, particularly if operating in proximity to another V-22. Later analysis has offset these concerns and led to the conclusion that while the Osprey is prone, as helicopters are, to the VRS phenomenon, it is generally less susceptible to, and more easily recovers from, the situation.

The fourth accident occurred on December 11, 2000, when the pilot lost control of an MV-22 at 1,600 feet when a chafing wire bundle caused a leak in a hydraulic line. This led in turn to a failure in the Primary Flight Control System. The aircraft crashed, killing all four crewmembers. When the accident report was examined, it was revealed that the maintenance records contained changes that gave the appearance of greater reliability than experience had warranted. While none of these changes was directly related to the accident, it cast a pall over the entire program.

V-22 operations were monitored even more closely by the services, the media, the public, and especially the Osprey's inveterate opponents. The vigilance was rewarded over the next several years by a series of serious events that were classified as incidents rather than accidents. They caused millions of dollars in damage, but fortunately there were no deaths.

In general, proponents of the V-22 cite its range, flexibility, speed, and capacity as governing reasons for its continued procurement and employment. Its opponents cite its cost and complexity as the primary reasons to cancel it, adding miscellaneous facts such as its lack of pressurization (which precludes long-range flights at higher altitudes), relatively light armament, and high maintenance requirements. Left unsaid is the implicit danger that another fatal accident, always a possibility as a new aircraft enters service, would lead to the cancellation of the program.

The Marines, intent on exploiting the full capability of the MV-22, have employed it in combat and in humanitarian missions in Iraq and Afghanistan. It now remains to be seen if the ultimate effect of the helicopter on modern warfare is the development of the tiltrotor, a related, but different aircraft.

Critics maintain that the operating characteristics of the V-22 make it vulnerable to the hazards encountered in combat, particularly those of hot LZs. Furthermore, the same critics state that the avoidance procedures mentioned earlier, which have proven so useful to helicopters, do not apply equally to the V-22, with its current cautionary techniques that limit angles of bank, rates of descent, and so on.

In contrast, its backers insist that the Osprey is the inevitable replacement for the helicopter, given its speed, range, and carrying capacity. Just for the record, and the following arguments, let us restate the V-22 potential missions. The Marine Corps will task the MV-22 with transporting assault troops past beachheads to inland destinations; it will use the MV-22 to resupply weapons, food, and ammunition and for the recovery of equipment and personnel from the battlefield. The Air Force will use its CV-22s for the infiltration and exfiltration of special forces and in the CSAR role. The Navy will use the Osprey for carrier-on-board delivery

(COD) of supplies and personnel, as well as for rescue missions and for service as an aerial tanker.

Even those who support the Osprey in principle ask if it can be afforded in the required numbers to achieve these multi-mission goals, given its current approximate $100 million per unit price tag. The expense of the V-22 leads to the question as to whether it can be risked in the same sort of environment in which helicopters have operated over the years, particularly where the threat-avoidance techniques used by helicopters do not apply. (It says much that the decision over risking the equipment seems to depend more upon its cost than its hazard to the crewmembers. This perhaps results from the tradition of accepting grave risks that the crewmembers established in the Vietnam War and elsewhere.)

In addition, over the long twenty-seven-year road to IOC, there has developed a strong, vocal opposition to the Osprey among those who feel that it is simply too expensive, too complex, and too dangerous. These critics cite a number of admittedly contested arguments as genuine hazards to the Osprey and reasons for abandoning the program.

First and foremost among these is an inability to autorotate (la Cierva's fundamental goal). Particular concerns are raised about the inability to autorotate in the event of the failure of both engines. The second major focus is an alleged susceptibility to un-commanded rolling as a response to the VRS phenomenon. The V-22 is described as being too sensitive to pilot-induced oscillation when operating in the helicopter mode, particularly when engaged in a demanding landing situation such as on shipboard or at night under low-visibility conditions. The admittedly high level of vibration of the V-22 is cited as being a possible cause for future accidents such as the one in which wire cables frayed hydraulic lines and started a fire. The V-22 is supposed to be much more susceptible to uncontrolled rolling due to the effect of either wake or wing-tip vortices from other aircraft, fixed or rotary wing. In desert or open-ocean operations, the V-22 rotors are alleged to create much more disturbance than the rotor of a conventional helicopter. The downwash from rotors over the ocean is claimed to be so extreme that it would make rescue of a downed airman virtually impossible.

The more vociferous opponents state that the very design of the tiltrotors, which are at the heart of the V-22's ability to function as either a helicopter or an airplane, has been compromised to a dangerous point. (In these discussions, critics also challenge "tiltrotor" as a descriptor, stating that given its shape and size it is more properly a "tiltprop.") To maximize the V-22's high-speed flight capability, its rotor blades are very stiff and have a forty-seven-degree-high twist design. Unfortunately, this is not the right combination of characteristics for a rapid vertical descent and compromises the V-22's potential in combat.

There are further concerns, including the sheer complexity of the structure; the net effects of the conflicting requirements inherent in any "multiservice" aircraft; the lack of cabin pressurization, which limits operating altitudes and reduces range capability; malfunctioning heating and cooling systems; inadequate visibility because of the size and placement of viewing ports; inadequate armor; inadequate offensive armament; the absence of a personnel hoist; and the inability to make field repairs to composite portions of the fuselage. Inevitably, all of these arguments are marshaled against the backdrop of the four major V-22 accidents and the prospects of another such tragedy in the future.

A cover story entitled "V-22 Osprey: A Flying Shame" by Mark Thompson in the October 8, 2007, issue of *Time* magazine recapitulated all the arguments against the Osprey in a vivid if perhaps not evenhanded manner. It provoked a response from M. E. Rhett Flater, the executive director of the American Helicopter Society. In brief, Flater noted that since the V-22's return to flight status on May 29, 2002, it had flown 25,929 accident-free hours and probably had more testing than any previous aircraft in the military industry. He emphasized that the V-22 was 50 percent more productive than the CH-46 helicopter it was designed to replace. Flater pointed out that the tiltrotor V-22 is not a helicopter and has never had a specific requirement for autorotation. However, he noted that it can perform single-engine autorotation with ease. He closes with this sentence: "In sum, the Osprey is a mature, fielded technology that will change the ways wars are waged."[3]

Other proponents of the V-22 argue that it has, since November 2007, proved itself in combat. Marines flew the Osprey on three tours in Iraq, accomplishing more than 2,500 missions supporting bases in Anbar Province. Replacing the aging CH-46 Sky Knight medium-lift helicopters, they mainly resupplied cargo and troops but also carried out MEDEVAC, scouting, and air-assault missions. No damage from insurgents' machine-guns and rocket-propelled grenades was recorded, thanks to the typically higher cruising altitude and higher ground speed. Lt. Gen. George Trautman, the Marine Corps's deputy commandant for aviation, stated that the Osprey had exceeded all expectations for reliability and performance and required only nine and one-half hours of maintenance per flying hour, compared to the twenty-four-hour requirement of the CH-46.

On November 6, 2009, ten MV-22s flew from the USS *Bataan* to join the Marine Medium Tiltrotor Squadron 261 (VMM-261) at Camp Bastion in Afghanistan. Within a month, the MV-22s entered combat, placing an eighty-person reconnaissance force in position in northern Helmand, with the mission of shutting down a Taliban line of communication. The operators of the MV-22 take pride in the fact that it is twice as fast as the helicopters it replaces, carrying twice the payload. For protection from ground fire, the MV-22s launch and land in a vertical "corkscrew" mode that keeps them well within the boundaries of the field until they reach a safe altitude.

Some Open Questions on the Osprey

There are nonetheless open questions about the Osprey, as highlighted in the May 2009 GAO-09-692T report to the Committee on Oversight and Government Reform in the House of Representatives.[4] The report, presented in testimony by Michael J. Sullivan, is done in an evenhanded manner, although it unquestionably disturbed advocates of the V-22. It pointed out that the rise in the Osprey's program cost estimates, in concert with the reduced number to be procured, had resulted in a 148 percent increase in unit cost. It also noted that the current cost per flying hour of $11,000 is twice the previously estimated target amount.

Perhaps the most delicate and insightful of the comments confirmed that the twelve MV-22s deployed to Iraq had successfully completed all missions assigned to them in what was considered an established, low-threat theater of operations. "Low threat" was defined as including sporadic small-arms fire from random locations. The deployment determined that the MV-22's enhanced speed and range enabled it to carry personnel and internal cargo faster and farther than the helicopters it was designed to replace, effectively, in the words of one commander, "cutting the battlefield in half." It was regarded as being two to three times as effective as the legacy helicopters it was replacing.

However, the question was raised as to whether or not the MV-22 can do the full mission repertoire of helicopters, especially over shorter distances or when transporting external cargo.

The report also noted that the mission capability (MC) of the V-22 fell significantly short of the level expected of it and of that routinely reached by helicopters. The discovery of faults in the V-22's Ice Protection System was of particular concern, given the weather to be expected in Afghanistan. The Osprey was prohibited from flying into known or forecast icing conditions.

Other maintenance problems included an unexpected requirement for spare parts of key items and the fact that V-22 engines' service life was fewer than four hundred hours, compared to the anticipated five hundred to six hundred hours.

Perhaps the most important of the report's comments concerned the fact that the Osprey had not yet demonstrated its ability to operate in a high-threat environment, defined as an environment that includes mobile and/or stationary SAM systems, early warning radars, integrated fire control systems, and interceptor aircraft. The Osprey is limited in its ability to perform defensive maneuvers and lacks adequate defensive weaponry to suppress threats when it approaches or leaves an LZ. In addition, the V-22 can accommodate only twenty fully equipped Marines, not its full combat load of twenty-four. Other problems include the inability to carry large loads of external cargo at high speeds.

The report concluded with the recommendation to reexamine available alternatives to the V-22 program and to require the Marine Corps to develop a strategy to improve system suitability and reduce operational costs. The Department of Defense did not fully agree with Sullivan's first recommendation, stating that such analysis is done routinely in the annual Marine Aviation Plan. However, it did concur with the second.[4]

An Air Force CV-22 was lost in Afghanistan in 2010, with two crewmembers killed. While the Taliban immediately claimed responsibility, the Air Force has not yet announced the probable cause of the incident. However, this event, and any other that may subsequently occur, will probably have important negative effects upon future Osprey development and procurement.

The cost effectiveness of the current inventory of helicopters, and the introduction of the Sikorsky CH-53E, will likely be of extreme, perhaps decisive, importance to the future not only of the Osprey but all subsequent replacement vehicles. The fact is that while the MV-22 demonstrated in Iraq that it could complete missions in a low-threat environment with an efficiency enhanced by its speed and range, it was challenged to complete the full repertoire of missions that had been the province of helicopters. This raised the immediate question as to the degree to which the MV-22 can replace helicopters.

It might therefore be concluded that the helicopter imposed many changes on modern warfare and that to date it remains irreplaceable in the very roles where it made those changes. There is some irony that this is so despite there having been no radical advancements in helicopter performance that materialized in production aircraft. Even more startling is the concept that in the not-too-distant future, the improvements in anti-helicopter weaponry may create a situation in which the helicopter will only be able to engage in combat when enemy defenses are fully suppressed by other means, such as fixed-wing attack aircraft, manned or unmanned, using precision-guided munitions.

It may just be that the pioneers in the field—Sikorsky, Piasecki, Bell, and others—had the genius to create a weapon with a level of performance that could be gradually improved not only to serve well for more than half a century but to change how modern warfare was conducted. Then, faced with a proliferation of weaponry specifically designed to exploit its performance characteristics, it may be that that helicopter designers came to recognize that their specialty product had already exerted its greatest effect upon modern warfare and would in the future prove to be more valuable in utilitarian roles.

In either case, the helicopter has significantly changed the face of modern warfare. It has done so despite restrictions placed on its performance by its inherent design features. And perhaps more than anything else, it has done so because of the brave, talented aircrews who flew the helicopter in the most intensely dangerous conditions of warfare that have ever been seen.

Appendix One

From Before Leonardo da Vinci to 1939: The Development of the Helicopter

It has yet to be determined whether or not animals dream of flight, but one can be certain that humans have always done so, in their sleep and in their imagination. Even the recently discovered "Omo I," perhaps the very earliest member of our family tree, must have looked up into the sunny Ethiopian sky and enviously watched birds soar effortlessly over the rough landscape.[1]

And one can be sure that Omo I did not envision entering flight by galloping into a long takeoff run followed by a slow climb to altitude. He must have seen, as so many later inventors did, that the best way to fly would be to move straight up and then maneuver freely in all directions. This goal, however desirable, proved to be the most challenging of all to pursue in the difficult quest for flight. Nonetheless, all through the centuries, a direct liftoff to flight has been sought everywhere, not least because there was already considerable evidence that this was possible. Most of the evidence was natural, as in the swift movement of a bird from its perch, but there were some mechanical clues as well.

One such clue is still evident today. It is the "Chinese top," a version of which was described as early as the fourth century A.D. This early concept featured rotary wings of wood with leather straps as the source of power. Later versions incorporated a wing-shaped device, remarkably similar to a modern propeller, placed at the top of a stick. The stick could be spun rapidly by rubbing one's hands, and the wing-shaped device would create sufficient lift to raise the toy straight up.

It is well known that a version of this toy helped inspire the Wright brothers to conduct their experiments. Their father, Bishop Milton Wright, customarily brought small toys home to the boys when returning from a trip. One of these was a helicopter powered by a twisted rubber band and designed by Alphonse Penaud (now fondly known as the "Father of Flying Models"). The Wrights attempted to copy the toy but failed.

As valuable as it was to the Wrights, the flying top had influence even earlier in history, especially on the development of the helicopter. While the myth that Marco Polo brought pasta to Italy has been given the lie, it is not improbable that he did bring examples of the Chinese top, and copies of these might well have inspired his famous countryman, Leonardo da Vinci. Leonardo began his series of designs for a helicopter in about 1493. They did not use a rotating wing, as had the Chinese top, but instead featured a continuous helical surface that, swiftly spun, would literally screw the device into the air. The concept derived from the Archimedes screw, famous for its use in transferring water from a lower level to a higher one. (Archimedes is said to have suggested that the same principle might be used to achieve flight.)

In some of da Vinci's drawings, the lifting element was about thirteen feet in diameter and constructed of reeds covered by taffeta and caulked with starch. Raw human power was provided by four men pushing on poles connected to the shaft. A drawing of another model depicts an energetic pilot using both arms and legs to power Nordic Track-like mechanical devices that turn the helical surface. And while da Vinci never attempted to build or fly a helicopter himself, there are now toy kits of his slightly modified designs, which do in fact fly.

There was a problem in the basic physics of helicopters that was not obvious to da Vinci but would be felt by everyone trying to create a vertical-lift machine down through the centuries. The problem is that the rotating blades cause a torque that forces the fuselage to turn in the opposite direction. To control the helicopter and move in the desired direction, that torque must be countered. Most early attempts at a helicopter would feature some form of counter-rotating blades to offset the torque effect. A more efficient solution, the use of an anti-torque tail rotor, would not see its first practical application until adopted by Igor Sikorsky in his famous VS 300 of 1939.

More than four hundred years passed between da Vinci's first recorded design and the 1907 design of Paul Cornu, which is generally (but inaccurately) considered to be the first man-carrying helicopter to fly. During those four-plus centuries, countless others undoubtedly sought a means to vertical flight, but only a relative few are known to history. One of the best documented of these is Mikhail Lomonosov, with his 1754 design.[2] With a clock spring for power, Lomonosov demonstrated his idea to the Russian Academy of Sciences, founded by Peter the Great thirty years earlier. The model was designed to indicate principle but is reported to have flown. It is perhaps most remarkable for the use of coaxial propellers to offset torque, a formula that design teams at the Russian Kamov helicopter company later used so successfully.

In 1784, it was the French Academy of Sciences' turn to be astounded, this time by the naturalist Christian de Launoy and his mechanic, Bienvenu (sadly relegated to history without a first name). The two men followed up on the coaxial theme with a vastly improved version of the Chinese top. Rotors about one foot in diameter were formed using four featherlike blades. These were mounted at each end of a central stick, which served as a shaft. A piece of spring steel in the shape of a bow had a hole in its center through which the shaft passed. A cord was fastened to the tips of the bow so that when the bow was rotated, the cord was tightened around the shaft, pulling the ends of the bow upward. When released, the bow straightened, pulling the string, rotating the shaft, and spinning the rotors. The two sets of blades, made of silk, revolved in opposite directions, cancelling torque and allowing the generated lift to take the device straight up into the air.

Further powered models would eventually lead to the helicopter. First among these was a product of a true "father of aeronautics," Sir George Cayley (1773-1857). Born to a life of relative ease, Cayley had wide-ranging scientific interests that led him to experiments in flight at the age of nineteen. His discoveries were pivotal yet often overlooked by subsequent investigators. Perhaps foremost among them was his recognition of the four basic forces of flight: lift, drag, thrust, and gravity. He also discovered that a rotated inclined plane generated lift, leading him to observe that the application of power to a surface would use the resistance of air to support a given weight.

While better known for his conventional aircraft, which included a full-scale piloted glider, Cayley built several helicopter models. A 1792 effort was a vastly improved version of the Launoy-Bienvenu device.[3] using wound rubber bands in lieu of the string and bow. In 1843, Cayley designed a much more complex example. Intended to be powered by a steam engine, it featured four eight-bladed rotors for vertical lift and two propellers for forward movement. The rotors were mounted in "biplane" fashion on booms that connected them to the boat-like fuselage, which featured a prow decorated with a bird's head. The steam engine drove the propellers and the contra-rotating rotors via a belt drive. Cayley was immersed in his glider experiments at the time, and his helicopter design drew on them by featuring a broad, horizontal surface to move the aircraft up and down, and a smaller vertical rudder for directional control.

Cayley had one more helicopter contribution to make. In 1853, at age eighty, he designed a single-rotor helicopter toy with three blades powered, as the Chinese toy had been, by a string wound around the stick. With it he obtained flights estimated to be as much as ninety feet in altitude.[4]

Another Englishman, W. H. Phillips, investigated helicopters and in 1842 created a steam-powered machine that anticipated future practice. Phillips' design allowed steam from the boiler to flow through the rotor and out the tips, much in the manner demonstrated 100 years later by the German *Weiner-Neustadt Flugzeugwerek* (WNF) 342. Designed by an Austrian, Baron Friedrich von Doblhoff, in conjunction with Theodor Laufger and August Stephan, the Wn 342 was the first jet-powered helicopter.

Phillips' model flew well, with the tiny steam engine delivering enough power to lift the twenty-pound helicopter swiftly into the air. One flight (which will be familiar to most modelers) saw the helicopter take off and fly across two fields before crashing. Phillips' success immediately encouraged some dreamers to think of steam-powered helicopters to transport passengers. Unfortunately for the helicopter, as for the airplane, the translation of a model into a full-scale aircraft brought about weight and structural problems that were not to be solved until the advent of the internal combustion engine.

An unlikely entrepreneurial event occurred in 1863 when four giants of the French cultural scene—Felix Tournachon, Gabriel de la Landelle,

Vicomte Gustav Ponton d'Amécourt, and Jules Verne—formed the world's first firm intended to promote heavier-than-air flight. They represented the cream of French intellectual society, each being famous in his own right.

Tournachon, a huge, well-built man with brilliant red hair and mustache, was truly larger than life. A writer, caricaturist, publisher, and photographer who "elevated photography to art," he was perhaps the first to capitalize on his celebrity by choosing to be known by a single name, the pseudonym "Nadar." His fame was so great that when Victor Hugo chose to write him, he addressed his letter with the one word, "Nadar," with complete confidence that it would reach him. Nadar took the first aerial photograph, a beautiful view of Paris. He later used artificial lighting to photograph the sewers and catacombs of underground Paris. Among his later achievements was carrying airmail when flying a balloon from Paris to Normandy in 1870, passing over the surrounding Prussian forces. And despite a series of financial setbacks after 1871, he held the very first exhibition for impressionist artists in 1874, a clear indication of his pioneering spirit.

Tournachon's previous balloon experience led him in 1863 to build the world's largest balloon, *Le Géant* (*The Giant*). The enormous, 6,000-cubic-meter balloon was not a success but did serve as inspiration for Jules Verne's novel *Five Weeks in a Balloon*. The failure of *Le Géant* convinced Tournachon and Verne that flight would ultimately be accomplished by a heavier-than-air machine and led to the establishment in 1863 of the "Society for the Encouragement of Aerial Locomotion by Means of Heavier than Air Machines." They were joined by two other equally gifted men, la Landelle and Ponton d'Amécourt, who previously had built a prototype of a steam engine intended for use in a helicopter.

The diverse backgrounds of these four men aided their imagination if not their ultimate success. La Landelle was a gifted naval officer turned novelist. Ponton d'Amécourt was a versatile scholar who combined Lomonosov's spring power and "biplane" coaxial propellers into a model helicopter. He used what was then a new material, aluminum, to build the small steam engine to power a larger twenty-pound helicopter. The steam engine drove two rotors, each of two blades, mounted one above the other. While this model did not fly successfully, the inventor exhibited and patented the idea in both France and England.

Perhaps of more lasting importance, Ponton d'Amécourt coined the term "helicopteres" from two Greek words meaning "turning wing." The adjective "turning" was *helix/helik-* (Ἕλικ-) while the noun "wing" was *pteron* (πτερόν). He established the term in a brochure he published in 1853 in which he stated, "The mechanism able to make a machine fly can be divided into two groups to which I have given the generic names of ornithopters [i.e., birdlike flapping-wing machines] and helicopters."[5] Twenty-five years later, his colleague Jules Verne incorporated the helicopter theme into his novel *Robur, the Conqueror*. In it, the protagonist, Robur, uses thirty-seven rotors to power a flying ship, the *Albatross*.

The *Albatross* drew heavily upon a design from the society that the four men founded and that ultimately boasted more than six hundred members of scientific repute. This design featured a ship-like hull, complete with the masts and rigging. The masts were topped with four lifting rotors and provided the attachments for the rigging to secure the large rectangular wings to the hull. In essence, it forecast the compound helicopter. As might be expected of an imaginative group of sailors, inventors, and novelists, they did not stop with mere flying devices but included parachutes and lifeboats as safety measures, along with a variety of creature comforts.

In spite of the relative slow means of communication at the time, word of the helicopter experiments of Cayley, Phillips, and others was transmitted around the globe. Other inventors came forward with paper designs or models, most of which had a single thing in common, their failure to fly. The future military potential of helicopters was foreseen in the world's first attack helicopter, designed by a Confederate soldier, William Powers. In 1862 he built a model of a steam-powered helicopter that he hoped would rise up to strike the Union ships blockading Southern ports. However impractical the design was, it provided a metaphor for the fate of helicopters in general, for all through their development and employment, they were always tasked with challenges far greater than whatever their current capability happened to be.

In the 1870s, Alphonse Penaud, a sensitive and probably depressive man, built the famous twin-rotor rubber-band-powered helicopters that inspired the Wright brothers. Penaud also built remarkable flying models

that foreshadowed future airplanes and in 1876 created with Paul Gau-
chot a very advanced concept of an amphibian that featured a retractable
landing gear. Sadly, when his work was rejected by his peers, Penaud, at
age thirty, committed suicide, unaware that his models and his correct
basic concepts would be honored in later designs.

An Italian inventor, Enrico Forlianini, was more famous for his pioneering series of hydrofoils, but in 1878 he demonstrated a steam-powered
helicopter model in Milan. It was quite successful, achieving flights for as
long as twenty seconds and as high as forty feet. Unfortunately, like all others based on the use of steam power in a helicopter, the idea was doomed
from the start by the combined weight of engine, fuel, and water required.

By 1880, the potential beginning to be seen in the helicopter was sufficient to interest a person as busy as Thomas Alva Edison. He conducted
some minor research on helicopters, using an electric motor to test a variety of propellers (rotors). Edison saw immediately that helicopter success would require a lightweight power source more powerful than a steam
engine and more reliable than the gunpowder engines he had blown up in
his studio. His tentative experiments also led him to believe that a large-
diameter rotor would be required to use the generated power effectively.

All previous pursuit of the helicopter had clearly indicated the need
for more power, but Edison's observations came at a time when such a
source was about to be available. It should be noted here that helicopter
development can be divided into three eras. The first is that prior to the
development of the internal combustion engine, the second, after that
development, and the third, after the debut of the jet engine. Therefore,
it is useful to look briefly at the chronology of the development of the
internal combustion engine as a part of the chronology of the helicopter.

Somewhat surprisingly, these two chronologies are relatively parallel,
in that successive steps were taken in each one over the course of several
centuries. While the chronology of the internal combustion engine does
not extend as far back as the Chinese top, it does antedate the helicopter
experiments of Leonardo da Vinci. In 1206, the Arab scholar Abū al-'Iz
Ibn Ismā'īl ibn al-Razāz al-Jazarī wrote a book entitled *Book of Knowledge of Ingenious Mechanical Devices* and in it described two essential
elements of the internal combustion engine: the double-acting recipro-

cating piston pump and a crank-connecting rod mechanism for converting rotary to linear motion.

The Enabling Effect of the Piston Engine

Many inventors approached the problem of an internal combustion engine over the next six centuries, and the middle of the nineteenth century saw a series of successes by Eugenio Barsanti and Felice Matteucci in Italy, Jean Joseph Lenoir in Belgium, Nikolaus Otto in Germany, Siegfried Marcus in Austria, and three names still famous today, Gottlieb Daimler, Wilhelm Maybach, and Karl Benz. By the turn of the twentieth century, internal combustion engines obtained a weight-to-power ratio that permitted their use first in a lighter-than-air vehicle, as Alberto Santos Dumont demonstrated. They were just efficient enough to power some of the early aircraft but were still unable to give the helicopter, with its greater demands, what was needed.

Fortunately, twentieth-century helicopter advocates were not entirely certain of this and thus pursued their efforts, each adding a bit to the necessary research. In 1905, two famous brothers, Louis and Jacques Bréguet, began collaborating with Prof. Charles Richet. This was a combination of genius equal to that of Nadar and his colleagues forty-two years earlier. Richet was a distinguished physician whose talents would ultimately be awarded a Nobel Prize. He had earlier worked with the aviation pioneer Victor Tatin and was so close a friend to Antoine Bréguet, father of Louis and Jacques, that he undertook the care of the two boys when Antoine died in 1882 at the age of thirty-one. Richet and the two Bréguet boys worked with Tatin for years on the latter's handsome but unsuccessful projects. Richet then advised and financed the Bréguets in their efforts to build a helicopter.

Louis Bréguet is well known for the prosperous aircraft firm he founded. He also deserves credit for a less famous 1914 flight in a plane of his own design during which he discovered and reported the advance of the German army on Paris. Jacques Bréguet's talents were apparently of a lesser order, but he was influential in the design and testing of the 1907 Bréguet-Richet Gyroplane No. 1.

Primitive but immensely complex, the Gyroplane No. 1 had a 45-hp Antoinette engine and four rotors. Each rotor was about twenty-five feet in diameter and consisted of four sections of biplane airfoil, thirty-two in all. It made a vertical ascent, hovering some two feet off the ground in the late summer of 1907. A "pilot" named Voulmard, deliberately chosen for his small size, was really more of a passenger, as there was no effective means to control the craft. The craft was stabilized on its short hops by a courageous man standing under each rotor. Jacques Bréguet subsequently claimed that the four men were holding the Gyroplane No. 1 down, but they themselves joked that they were in fact "pushing up."[6] In general, historians have assessed the Bréguet-Richet Gyroplane No. 1 as a test bed rather than being the first rotary-wing aircraft to lift a man from the ground. As will be seen below, that honor has been accorded, almost certainly in error, to Paul Cornu.

The Bréguets were encouraged, and the following year came closer to success with their second helicopter, the Gyroplane No. 2. Powered by a 55-hp Renault engine, it employed a more sophisticated layout. There were two rotors of about 26 feet in diameter and biplane wings that added 538 square feet of lifting area. It flew on July 22, 1908, rising to a height of about 13 feet and operating under some control. Landing a helicopter was as difficult then as it is now, and the craft crashed on one attempt. It reportedly was repaired and flown again the following year. During World War I, Bréguet warplanes became noted for their structural strength, but both Gyroplane No. 1 and No. 2 were intrinsically fragile aircraft, built as lightly as possible. Because of the nature of their structure, they have an airy, difficult-to-define look and one only wishes that motion pictures had been taken of them during their short lives.

The Bréguets came close, but the honor of having flown the first successful helicopter has long been accorded to Paul Cornu. One of thirteen children, Cornu worked in his father's shop, which made and repaired bicycles, à la the Wright brothers. Cornu's inventive nature was revealed early on in his work on bicycles. His interest in aviation was awakened by one of the great incentive programs of the era, one that corresponds to the Raymond Orteig Prize of 1919 for the first aircraft to fly nonstop between New York to Paris or the current X-Prize Foundation, which encourages innovations in everything from civilian space flight to genomics.

Like so many others of his era, Cornu was determined to win the 50,000-franc *Grand Prix d'Aviation* offered by Henri Deutsch de la Meurthe for the first person to fly a circular one-kilometer course in a heavier-than-air craft. Deutsch de la Meurthe was a wealthy French oilman who knew exactly what he was doing with his philanthropy. Aware that the expansion of the oil business depended upon the expansion of the use of internal combustion engines, he sought to stimulate growth in the industry by offering prizes to the inventors working on aviation and automobile projects. He had, with Ernest Archdeacon and Gustave Eiffel, founded the *Aéro-Club de France*, and the prizes he offered were often called the Deutsch-Archdeacon awards.

To win the prize, Cornu decided to use the light but strong structure of bicycles as a basis for a flying machine that would use rotors rather than wings for flight. His experiments began in 1904, and by 1907, at the age of twenty-three, he produced a lightweight helicopter powered by a 24-hp Antoinette engine. The "fuselage" was a box of steel tubing, supported by four wheels. Cornu was no lightweight himself, being a stocky, well-built, well-mustachioed man, and he sat directly behind the engine, which drove the two rotors. The rotors were formed of two large-diameter hubs and each was fitted with two blades. Huge belts drove the hubs in counter-rotating directions, just as the Wrights' chain drive had done for their propellers. A rectangular panel intended to provide a measure of control was installed just in front of each rotor.

History and convention have long held that on November 13, 1907, at Lisieux, Cornu became the first man ever to lift off the ground in a rotary-wing aircraft, not in a test rig. The flight was reported as being both low (one foot) and short (twenty seconds) but while it was uncontrolled, the machine was not stabilized by anyone holding on, as the Bréguet-Richet Gyroplane No. 1 had been. It is reported that slightly higher flights reaching about three feet in altitude were made the same day, and the wheezing Antoinette also is said to have lifted not only Paul Cornu but his two brothers into the air, making them the first helicopter passengers. Cornu himself said that complete success eluded him not because of a flaw in principle but "by a manufacturing detail: the belt transmission, which was mandatory considering the dimensions and lightness of this machine."[7]

The Deutsch-Archdeacon prize was won by Henri Farman for his famous skidding-turn flight of January 13, 1909, removing Cornu's main incentive. Over the next year, he improved his invention with an early form of variable-incidence rotor blades, calling it the "Helicoplane," but soon abandoned his efforts. Cornu maintained his interest in aviation in the years that followed only to die in a Paris bombing attack in 1944.

Somewhat sadly, the advances in technical analysis in aeronautics have permitted doubts to be cast on Cornu's claim. Prof. J. Gordon Leishman of the University of Maryland has made an in-depth study of Cornu's aircraft and concluded that the Antoinette engine could not have lifted Cornu and his aircraft off the ground. Leishman, having conservatively estimated the inevitable transmission losses of the belt-drive system even when offset by a generous estimate of the positive aspects of "ground effect," believes that an engine of at least 30 hp would have been required, six more than was available to Cornu. Leishman stipulates that "hops" might have been made, thanks to a sudden engine overspeed or some other factor, but he believes that the lift necessary to cause the machine to actually rise vertically from the ground was not available to Cornu.[8]

If Professor Leishman is correct, and other engineers support his view, then the honor of being the first to fly a helicopter, so long accorded to Cornu, must necessarily pass to someone else. The matter was honorably concluded in France in 2006. A group of well-known experts that included Jean Boulet, René Mouille, and Bernard Bombeau, plus all of the concerned French institutions (*Académie de l'air et de l'Espace, Association Aéronautique et Astronautique de France, Aéro-Club de France, Musée de l'Air et de l'Espace*), studied the possibility of a first helicopter flight taking place in 1907. They reported on the work of Cornu, as well as that of Louis Bréguet and Maurice Léger, concluding that none of the aircraft actually flew. They also wrote that the first actual helicopter flight was that of the Bréguet Gyroplane Laboratoire, which took place in 1935.[9]

Perhaps it would be less disturbing to history and convention to give Cornu the benefit of the doubt and assume that somehow his Antoinette engine was particularly vigorous on that November day and managed to squeeze out an additional 7 or 8 hp. Then the record books could be left intact.

While Cornu perhaps was not the first rotary-wing pilot to get into the air, he was in the forefront of a whole series of inventors eager to apply the growing benefits of internal combustion engine technology to their ideas on achieving vertical lift. One of these would ultimately achieve success and create a practical helicopter—but not until thirty years after his first experiments. Igor Ivanovich Sikorsky (1889-1972) began his experiments in 1908 with an earnest search for a means to achieve vertical flight. Well educated as an engineer, Sikorsky went to France that year to consult with Capt. Ferdinand Ferber, who told him, "Do not waste your time on a helicopter; the airplane will be far more valuable."[10] Given Ferber's inability to copy the Wright brothers' designs with any accuracy, it is just as well that the young Russian aristocrat ignored his advice.

Sikorsky built his first helicopter in 1909, using a 25-hp motorcycle engine to drive two counter-rotating propellers. No control system was installed, and after several attempts to lift vertically, Sikorsky ultimately realized that his "Machine No. 1" did not generate sufficient lift. The following year, he built No. 2, with much-improved rotor blades. While lift was improved slightly, Sikorsky recognized that he would not be able to afford to run sufficient tests to overcome the problems he faced. He went on to a highly successful career in the aviation industry, triumphantly returning to the rotary-wing field in the 1930s.

A single thread linked the many inventors who now chipped away at the problem of vertical flight—a basic error, one that the Wright brothers had *not* made in their pursuit of heavier-than-air flight. It was the erroneous assumption that power rather than control was the most difficult challenge. In the next three decades, an inability to define control requirements would defy the attempts of most helicopter investigators. During this period, some of the greatest progress would be made by a close relative of the helicopter, the autogiro.

Typical of many of the intuitive inventors of the time was Jacob C. H. Ellehammer, who would labor long in the vineyard of vertical flight. Just prior to World War I, Ellehammer created a tiny helicopter with its engine mounted in a tubular structure, driving two circular surfaces to which were appended rotors. While the surface/rotor layout was not unlike Cornu's design, they were superimposed upon each other and featured the first appearance of a cyclic-pitch device. The lower surface was covered with fabric, which Ellehammer intended to balloon up and become a sort of parachute. The safety device was unnecessary, as the aircraft reportedly rose only four feet off the ground. Ellehammer's machine is unusual among those of his peers in that photographs of it actually in flight survive. Even rarer is the fact that a candid comment from Ellehammer's test pilot, Eric Hildes-Helm, survives: "Although the aircraft could lift up on several occasions during the test, I could never accomplish a free flight."[11]

Ellehammer also built fixed-wing aircraft, one of which was reported to have flown in 1906 and thus contends with the aircraft of Traian Vuia for the honor of being the first to fly in Europe. Ellehammer continued with his helicopter work, retaining the idea of mounting rotors on a circular surface in a compound helicopter design of 1935.

World War I had tremendous effect upon aircraft and engine design but very little upon that of the helicopter, with a single exception. In Hungary, Theodore von Kármán, a man destined to become a commanding presence in aviation, worked with an Austrian army lieutenant, Stefan Petróczy, on a design by Wilhelm Zurovec.[12] They created the PKZ-2, a three-engine helicopter that was lifted vertically by two huge counter-rotating wooden propellers. The innovative craft was intended to replace the observation balloon and carry an observer and a machinegun. Designed for tethered flight, the PKZ-2 was test-flown successfully on many occasions but was cancelled after crashing during an official demonstration flight on June 10, 1918.

In the United States, Emile Berliner, a prolific inventor and leading light in the nascent audio industry, worked with John Newton Williams to build a coaxial rotor helicopter using two engines designed by Berliner. Berliner had anticipated European practice by designing the first production rotary aircraft engine. This lightweight, 36-hp engine was also used in the Adams-Farwell line of motorcars. The helicopter reportedly left the ground in 1920, piloted by Emile's son Henry, but was probably stabilized, à la the Bréguet-Richet, by ground personnel. Berliner was also one of the first to advocate the use of a vertically mounted auxiliary tail rotor.

He is more famous for the later work done with his pilot son. They created two more helicopters, this time using two large propeller-like rotors mounted outboard of the fuselage. The most successful example flew in 1923. With a Nieuport 23 fuselage and narrow-chord triplane wings, it might be considered a forerunner of the compound helicopter. It was capable of hovering flight and a speed of 40 mph but could reach only about fifteen feet in altitude, probably still in ground effect. This aircraft also featured a smaller tail rotor, not for longitudinal directional control but to lift the tail up or down as required.

Henry Berliner abandoned his helicopter efforts but founded the Berliner Aircraft Company, which transmuted into the Berliner-Joyce Corporation before merging with the giant North American Aviation Company. He went on to establish the Engineering and Research Corporation, which designed and built the very popular Ercoupe light airplane.

In the development of the helicopter, structural simplicity was almost as elusive as maintaining control, as the eccentric and demanding Georges de Bothezat found. He was of Rumanian birth but emigrated from Russia to

The complexities of helicopter design and construction reached a high point with the de Bothezat helicopter of 1922. *(Courtesy of U.S. Army Museum, Fort Rucker)*

the United States after World War I. Using a single 180-hp Le Rhone rotary engine (later upgraded to a 220-hp Bentley), de Bothezat, working with the less cantankerous Ivan Jerome, constructed a tubular X-shaped frame with twenty-four-foot rotors mounted at each extremity. The inventor made a successful first flight at McCook Field on December 18, 1922, and the helicopter was subsequently flown by the intelligent, efficient, and sometimes hard-nosed McCook Field commander, Col. Thurman H. Bane. The de Bothezat pilots were among the world's busiest, for each rotor had its own collective-pitch control.[13] The de Bothezat helicopter went on to make numerous flights, once carrying four people, but it never exceeded fifteen feet in altitude and was, by inspection, too complex for service work. In perhaps an excessive burst of enthusiasm, Bane told de Bothezat, "It is my sincere belief that your helicopter is the biggest aeronautical achievement since the first flight of the Wright brothers."[14]

In France during the same time period, Etienne Oehmichen began development of a long series of increasingly complex helicopters. An engineer with the Peugeot automobile firm, Oehmichen constructed six different machines, the first of which he fitted with a hydrogen-filled balloon when it failed to lift off the ground. He indicated that the balloon was primarily for stability and not lift, but he much later returned to the idea, terming the hybrid design a "heliocostat."

Like de Bothezat's, Oehmichen's designs consisted of X-shaped tubular structures with rotors mounted at the end of each arm. The two-blade rotors were driven by rotary engines through an intricate, power-consuming drive mechanism. His second machine proved to be both flyable and reliable, making more than one thousand short flights and exhibiting control in all directions. It continually improved its ability to stay airborne and in 1924 established the first *Fédération Aeronautique Internationale* (FAI) distance record for helicopters by flying 360 meters. A whole series of FAI records followed, including a 1-kilometer circular flight in about seven minutes—a blistering pace of just a bit more than 5 mph.[15] Despite these successes, Oehmichen's design was flawed by complexity and an inability to rise out of ground effect.

A move toward more simple structure in a helicopter was found in the work of Raúl Pateras Pescara de Castellucio, an Argentine-born aristocrat and prolific inventor. Among Pescara's many patents were designs of coaxial-rotor helicopters. He is perhaps even more famous for his series of 1919 experiments in which he erased one of the most troublesome contemporary questions of helicopter flight: what happens when the engine quits? He demonstrated that a helicopter could auto-rotate to the ground and thus land reasonably safely even after engine failure.[16] In 1924, Pescara departed from the almost standard use of a rotary-type engine, installing a 180-hp Hispano Suiza in his helicopter. This aircraft featured counter-rotating rotors, each consisting of four sets of biplane blades, making even an engine run-up resemble a dogfight. Pescara broke Oehmichen's record by flying for .8 kilometer in four minutes and eleven seconds or about 7.12 mph. He did not rise above six feet, but he flew under control, and his primitive but effective pitch-control mechanism worked.

All around the world, other inventors were pursuing the dream of vertical flight, with varying degrees of slight success. Control and stability remained the major challenges, and only a few were able to go higher than the helping hand of ground effect allowed. As late as 1937, Etienne Oehmichen stated, "With more than two thousand flights accomplished with helicopters of totally different designs, all of which I built and flew myself, my conclusion is not really optimistic. The helicopter taking off during ground runs is and remains a dangerous aircraft."[17]

The Contributions of the Autogiro

Ironically, the helicopter would not be successful until the way was paved by a far less ambitious rotary-wing discipline termed the "autogiro" by its inventor, Don Juan de la Cierva Codorníu (1895-1936). Strictly speaking, the term "autogiro" should be applied only to aircraft built by the Cierva firm or its licensee. For other unpowered rotary-wing aircraft, the generic term "autogyro" should apply. It may be stretching biology a bit to make the comparison, but Cierva's ideas proved to be the fertilizing agent that enabled the rotary-wing to give birth to the modern helicopter.

It is convenient here to discuss briefly some of the differences between the two aircraft types under discussion, the helicopter and the autogiro. The most important of these is the way in which the rotary-wing element is used. The helicopter uses a powered rotor to push air downward and thus can rise vertically. The autogiro obtains forward propulsion from an ordinary propeller. Its unpowered and freewheeling blades work like wings, gaining lift from the passage of air over them. This property conveyed a safe descent rate in case of engine failure. The autogiro initially required a short takeoff run to ascend, but later developments allowed the rotor to be brought up to speed, shortening the takeoff roll substantially. The efficient use of the rotor and the means of effecting control vary greatly between the two types and will be discussed separately.

As Cierva's biographer, Peter W. Brooks, notes, the inventor's interest in rotary wings began and ended with crashes in fixed-wing aircraft.[18] Cierva progressed from models to gliders to building the first Spanish aircraft to fly. This was followed by two more ambitious projects, including a tri-motor bomber. The bomber crashed on its first flight as a result of the inexperienced pilot turning too low and too slow. The crash inspired Cierva to begin a study of how to achieve mechanical flight that was not dependent on flying speed. Sadly, as Brooks wrote, his life ended in a crash at England's famous Croydon airport on December 19, 1936. He was flying as a passenger in what was considered to be one of the safest and most advanced transports in the world at the time, a Douglas DC-2.

An engineer and mathematician, Cierva was, as were so many others, inspired by a toy helicopter. Spurred by the crash he witnessed, he evolved the theory of a freely revolving wing (in other terms, an autorotating rotor), which would serve both as a wing to provide lift and as a device to enable safe landings after engine failure.

A systematic experimenter, Cierva created a series of experimental aircraft that eventually led him to the idea of flapping hinges on the blades to overcome the imbalance in lift between advancing and retreating blades. The idea of articulated blades was not entirely new, having been patented by Bréguet in 1908, but for another purpose, that of reducing stress in the blades. The idea was incorporated in Autogiro No. 4, which used a four-blade rotor of twenty-six feet three inches in diameter. After a long and troublesome development, the C.4 made the first fully controlled gyroplane flight in history on January 17, 1923.[19]

There followed a long series of increasingly refined autogiros in which

Cierva's basic concept was improved with new ideas that proved critical to helicopter development and, ironically enough, relegated the autogiro to a less important role in aviation history. His innovations included the 1931 introduction of the cantilever rotor, in which external rotor bracing was eliminated and the relative size of the rotors to the area of the disc they swept reduced. In 1932 he demonstrated a vitally needed direct control of his autogiros at low speeds by tilting the rotor. He reportedly conceived the idea after witnessing long lines of umbrellas on a rainy night in London. Cierva achieved the desired results by creating a universally mounted rotor hub that could be tilted in all directions by the pilot. Two push-pull rods linked the control column to the tilting head of the rotor. This eliminated the need for auxiliary surfaces (wings and horizontal stabilizer) for control, which not only produced drag but were ineffective at low speeds.

In 1935, Cierva announced the successful development of a direct ("jump-start") takeoff system that he had debuted in 1933. The jump-start was achieved by a long series of rotor-blade hinge designs that were combined with a clutch-drive system, enabling the engine to spin the rotors up to takeoff speed while sitting on the ground. When the appropriate blade speed was reached, the engine was declutched and the blade angle set for a vertical ascent.

Cierva had moved from Spain to England in 1925 to establish the Cierva Autogiro Company. In addition to being an inventor, test pilot, record-setter, engineer, mathematician, and opera fan, he was an excellent businessman. He licensed his invention for production in France, Germany, Spain, and the United States. He also inspired pirated versions in the Soviet Union, while Japan sublicensed production from his American licensee, Kellet.

In the United States, the names of his licensee firms, Pitcairn and Kellet, became famous from flights at air shows, air races, and association with great names such as Amelia Earhart and Richard Byrd. The military services of many countries were interested in the use of the autogiro for reconnaissance and liaison purposes, and they service-tested small quantities. Unfortunately, autogiros were generally found to be unable to carry sufficient fuel and equipment and still perform adequately in the field.

Cierva's work inspired many others to contribute new ideas to the rotary-wing field. These ranged from the dedicated engineers of the Soviet Union's TsAGI research establishment to the sometimes flamboyant inventors of other countries. Among these may be found Scotland's David Kay, Great Britain's Raoul Hafner and James Weir, Germany's Anton Flettner and Heinrich Focke, as well as America's Burke Wilford and Gerard Herrick. All of these men offered new insights and possible routes to rotary-wing success. Their work, like Cierva's, would be subsumed by the arrival of successful helicopters in the 1930s. These incorporated the many contributions of autogiro development into their own helicopter heritage.

The groundwork was laid for the helicopter in modern warfare by the keen interest of the military all around the world in the autogiro. In the United States, the Navy signaled its enthusiasm by the purchase of three Pitcairn PCA-2 autogiros, assigning the designation XOP-1 and giving each one a specific role. Perhaps more spectacularly, one was almost certainly flown by David S. Ingalls, the Navy's only World War I ace and then assistant secretary of the Navy for aeronautics.[20]

Lt. (later Adm.) Alfred M. Pride made three takeoffs and landings from the first U.S. aircraft carrier, the USS *Langley*, in the XOP-1. The second version of the Pitcairn was fitted with pontoons for use as a seaplane, while the U.S. Marines got its first taste of what would become a principal air arm with the third XOP-1. Unfortunately, in tests during the 1932 Nicaraguan campaign, the autogiro did not do well. It was competing against Vought O2U-1 biplanes, and while they had equally short takeoff runs, of vital importance in a jungle campaign, the autogiro could not carry a sufficient load and was deficient in both speed and climb. The U.S. Army, having tested the Kellet A-2, ran tests on a borrowed XOP-1 and came to identical conclusions on both: interesting but vastly underpowered.[21]

In Great Britain, despite the enthusiasm of the highly regarded Brig. James H. "Jimmy" Weir, autogiros suffered a similar fate, although they served one unique role. The RAF had purchased ten Cierva C.30A helicopters, with the name "Rota I" assigned, while two more were acquired by the Royal Navy as the "Rota II." Service trials were unsatisfactory, and the duty passed to liaison aircraft. However, there came a time when the autogiro was essential in calibrating the super-secret "Chain Home" radar complex, which would be essential in winning the Battle of Britain. A Rota I, flown by Squadron Leader Reginald "Reggie" A. C. Brie (who later led the postwar Fairey Rotodyne test program), showed that the autogiro could serve as the precise instrument to calibrate the still-new radar stations. The RAF's first operational rotary-wing unit, Number 529 Squadron, ultimately operated seventeen Cierva C.30s and was not disbanded until October 1945, after flying more than nine thousand hours.[22]

France had enthusiastically embraced the autogiro, building Ciervas under license beginning in 1929, leading to autogiro construction by several companies. More than one hundred were acquired by the French military, and they were used in minor roles until their surrender to the Germans in 1940. In the Soviet Union, as elsewhere, efforts with the autogiro began by copying Cierva but soon advanced to indigenous studies under the TsAGI design bureau, where the most successful Soviet autogiro, the TsAGI A-7, was developed. The A-7 was actually the first rotary-wing aircraft designed as a full-fledged combat aircraft, armed with machineguns and bombs. A big aircraft at more than five thousand pounds gross weight at liftoff, the A-7 was powered by a 480-hp M-2 engine, a Soviet standby. Five A-7-bis production aircraft were used in combat with the Germans during 1941. They were too vulnerable in daylight action and ineffective in nighttime warfare, suffering a high accident rate.

The always observant Japanese military attachés had witnessed autogiro demonstrations in the United States and ordered two Kellet K-3 models for testing. Two Cierva C.19s were already being tested by the Imperial Japanese Navy, and a third was in use by the forward-thinking, aeronautically minded *Asahi Shimbun* newspaper. Although a total of ninety-five autogiros were manufactured in Japan, all were, in Dr. Bruce Charnov's phrase, "Kellet clones." Eight were deployed for antisubmarine work on the *Akitsu Maru*, a merchant ship converted into a light escort carrier. Unfortunately for Japan, the *Akitsu Maru* was sunk by the famous USS *Queenfish* submarine before it could begin operations.[23]

Numerous other nations experimented with the autogiro, but while all found them interesting, and even crowd-pleasing at demonstrations, none found a viable economic or military application. During the 1923-44 development of the "original generation" of autogiros, forty-six distinct individual types appeared. These generated 48 experimental and 454 production auto-giros.[24] Despite their relatively small numbers, it must be remembered that autogiros sustained the quest for vertical flight while making absolutely vital contributions to it. Their basic appeal can still be seen in modern experimental variations of the theme.

The First Practical Helicopters

The 1930s saw the return of three remarkable men to the scene of their first aviation love, the helicopter. Now a patrician industrialist, Louis Bréguet teamed with Rene Dorand to fly the Bréguet-Dorand 314 *Gyroplane Laboratoire* on June 26, 1935. A bit of a heavyweight at 4,500 pounds, the Bréguet-Dorand was rapidly improved over the next year, achieving a speed of 65 mph and an altitude of 518 feet. The new helicopter featured superimposed coaxial two-blade rotors with cyclic and collective pitch control.[25] The Bréguet-Dorand 314 is now considered by many to have been the first true successful helicopter, twenty-eight years after Paul Cornu's efforts. It continued in test work through 1939.

The Bréguet-Dorand's success was vastly overshadowed one year later when Heinrich Focke's pioneering Focke-Wulf Fw 61 made its first flight on June 26, 1936, piloted by Ewald Rohlfs. After considering many variations of helicopter design, Focke opted for twin side-by-side rotors to cancel torque effect. (As noted earlier, torque is the inherent tendency of a single-rotor helicopter to twist the fuselage in the opposite direction of the rotor, causing obvious control problems.) The Fw 61 designation was subsequently changed to Fa 61 when Focke founded the Focke-Achgelis firm with test pilot Gerd Achgelis on April 27, 1937. Focke, a cofounder of the Focke-Wulf aircraft company, had been ousted from that firm for political reasons.

The Fa 61 immediately set about demolishing all helicopter records for speed, distance, and altitude. It also reaped a whirlwind of publicity from favorable public comments by Charles Lindbergh and a dazzling display by Hannah Reitsch. The famous young woman test pilot flew the Fa 61 inside the *Deutschlandhalle* sports arena in Berlin in February 1938, thrilling the crowds with a series of carefully choreographed landings, takeoffs, and maneuvers. The Fa 61 was large, with two three-blade rotors positioned on outriggers from the fuselage, using cyclic/collective pitch control hubs licensed from Cierva. It led directly to orders for a larger, six-passenger version that was ultimately known as the Fa 223. Twelve of these large and efficient aircraft were built, and one made the first crossing of the English Channel by helicopter—but only after WWII had ended.

There were other innovators in the helicopter field, but the most important of these was Igor Sikorsky, who returned to his first love. "Returned" is probably a misnomer, for Sikorsky never truly abandoned his ideas on vertical flight. He began development in 1929, which led to a patent in 1935 of a single-rotor helicopter using collective and cyclic pitch and having a small anti-torque tail rotor. The design was first flown on September 14, 1939, and after years of development made a flight in what came to be its definitive form on December 8, 1941, one day after Pearl Harbor. A development of the VS-300, the Sikorsky R-4, was ordered into production by the United States Army Air Corps, and it, with some German counterparts, would introduce the helicopter to modern warfare.

Appendix Two

Specifications

Bell OH-13 Sioux

The use of the names of Indian tribes for U.S. Army helicopters is a carefully monitored and considered program that pays a tribute to the selected tribe. *(Courtesy of U.S. Army Museum, Fort Rucker)*

Type: MEDEVAC, observation, liaison
Manufacturer's Type/Model Number: 47
Powerplant: One Lycoming TVO-435 of 260 hp
Dimensions:

Main Rotor Diameter	37 ft
Main Rotor Disc Area	1,018 sq ft
Length (rotor turning)	40 ft 2 in
Height	9 ft
Weight Empty	1,800 lb
Weight Maximum	2,952 lb

Performance:

Max Speed	106 mph
Range	275 miles

Armament (Typical): .30 machinegun fitted on some occasions

Bell UH-1D Iroquois (Huey)

The UH-1D Iroquois was informally called the "Army's flying truck" for its hauling capacity. *(Courtesy of Zaur Eylanbekov [Foxbat])*

Type: Assault, troop transport, supply, observation
Manufacturer's Type/Model Number: 204
Powerplant: One Avco Lycoming T-53 of 1,100 shp
Dimensions:

Main Rotor Diameter	48 ft
Main Rotor Disc Area	1,089 sq ft
Length (rotor turning)	57 ft 1 in
Height	14 ft 5 in
Weight Empty	5,190 lb
Weight Maximum	9,500 lb

Performance:

Max Speed	130 mph
Range	310 miles

Armament (Typical): Two 7.62 M60 or two 7.62 GAU-17/A machineguns; two 2.75-in rocket pods

Bell AH-1G HueyCobra

The HueyCobra demonstrated the skills of the Bell design department, for it imparted a lethal quality to an aircraft that had already proved itself in the field. *(Courtesy of U.S. Army Museum, Fort Rucker)*

Type: Assault, close-air support
Manufacturer's Type/Model Number: 209
Powerplant: One Lycoming T-53 of 1,400 shp

Dimensions:

Main Rotor Diameter	44 ft
Main Rotor Disc Area	1,520 sq ft
Length (rotor turning)	53 ft 11 in
Height	13 ft 10 in
Weight Empty	6,050 lb
Weight Maximum	9,500 lb

Performance:

Max Speed	170 mph
Range	360 miles

Armament (Typical): One M197 cannon in nose; option for XM-18 minigun pods, 70-mm rocket pods, other ordnance

Bell AH-1W SuperCobra

The USMC adapted the AH-1 HueyCobra to its special needs by purchasing a twin-engine version (for improved safety operating over water) with more powerful weapons. *(Courtesy of U.S. Marine Corps History Office)*

Type: Attack, close-air support
Manufacturer's Type/Model Number: 209
Powerplant: Two General Electric T-700 turbo shafts of 1,625 shp
Dimensions:

Main Rotor Diameter	48 ft
Main Rotor Disc Area	1,810 sq ft
Length (rotor turning)	53 ft 4 in
Height	13 ft 8 in
Weight Empty	10,200 lb
Weight Maximum	14,750 lb

Performance:

Max Speed	205 mph
Range	500 miles

Armament (Typical): One M-197 20-mm cannon; option for minigun pods, rocket pods, other ordnance

Bell OH-58D Kiowa Warrior

With a more powerful engine and transmission and a four-blade main rotor, the OH-58D Kiowa Warrior also features a Mast Mounted Sight over the rotor. *(Courtesy of Department of Defense via Bob Dorr)*

Type: Observation, attack, transport, training
Manufacturer's Type/Model Number: 206
Powerplant: One Rolls Royce T703 turbo shaft of 650 shp
Dimensions:

Main Rotor Diameter	35 ft
Main Rotor Disc Area	1,483 sq ft
Length (rotor turning)	48 ft 2 in
Height	12 ft 11 in
Weight Empty	3,820 lb
Weight Maximum	5,500 lb

Performance:

Max Speed	144 mph
Range	350 miles

Armament (Typical): .50-caliber machinegun; Singer, Hellfire missiles; 70-mm folding-fin aerial rockets

Bell Boeing MV-22 Osprey

Type: Troop carrier, transport
Manufacturer's Type/Model Number: MV-22
Powerplant: Two Rolls-Royce Allison T406 turbo shafts of 6,150 shp
Dimensions:

Main Tiltrotor Diameter	38 ft
Main Rotor Disc Area	1,133 ft each
Length	57 ft 4 in
Height	22 ft 2 in
Weight Empty	33,200 lb
Weight Maximum	60,500 lb

Performance:
    Max Speed   351 mph
    Range   890 miles
Armament (Typical): M240 machinegun installed on ramp

Boeing CH-46E Sea Knight (Vertol, Boeing Vertol)

Type: Transport, supply, rescue, MEDEVAC, assault
Manufacturer's Type/Model Number: Vertol 107
Powerplant: Two General Electric T-58 turbo shafts of 1,900 shp
Dimensions:
    Main Rotor Diameter   51 ft each
    Main Rotor Disc Area   1,962 sq ft each
    Length (rotor turning)   83 ft
    Height   16 ft 9 in
    Weight Empty   15,500 lb
    Weight Maximum   24,450 lb
Performance:
    Max Speed   160 mph
    Range   250 miles
Armament (Typical): Varied but included .50-caliber machineguns

Boeing CH-47C Chinook (Vertol, Boeing Vertol)

The faithful Chinook continues in service, continually being modified with new equipment to meet the new demands of combat. *(Courtesy of U.S. Army Museum, Fort Rucker)*

Type: Assault, transport, MEDEVAC
Manufacturer's Type/Model Number: V.114
Powerplant: Two AVCO Lycoming T55 turbo shafts of 3,750 shp
Dimensions:

Main Rotor Diameter	60 ft each
Main Rotor Disc Area	2,828 sq ft each
Length (rotor turning)	99 ft
Height	18 ft 8 in
Weight Empty	21,500 lb
Weight Maximum	38,500 lb

Performance:

Max Speed	178 mph
Range	250 miles

Armament (Typical): Varied; some versions carried cannon and machinegun armament

Boeing AH-64 Apache (Hughes, McDonnell Douglas)

One of the most famous helicopters of modern times, the AH-64 Apache has received both plaudits and criticism over the years. *(Courtesy of U.S. Army Museum, Fort Rucker)*

Type: Assault

Manufacturer's Type/Model Number: H-77, AH-64D

Powerplant: Two General Electric GE-700 turbo shafts of 1,820 shp

Dimensions:

Main Rotor Diameter	8 ft
Main Rotor Disc Area	1,810 sq ft
Length (rotor turning)	58 ft
Height	17 ft 2 in
Weight Empty	16,400 lb
Weight Maximum	23,000 lb

Performance:

Max Speed	182 mph
Range	370 miles

Armament (Typical): One M230 Chain Gun; Hydra 70 FFAR rockets; AGM-114 Hellfire, AIM-9 Sidewinder, AIM-92 Stinger missiles

Hughes OH-6 Cayuse (Loach)

Small, vulnerable, but always in the fight, the Hughes OH-6 Cayuse turned helicopter pilots into fighter pilots over Vietnam. *(Courtesy of U.S. Army Museum, Fort Rucker)*

Type: Observation, liaison, MEDEVAC, assault
Manufacturer's Type/Model Number: 369H
Powerplant: One Allison T63 turbo shaft of 217 shp
Dimensions:

Main Rotor Diameter	26 ft 4 in
Main Rotor Disc Area	545 sq ft
Length (rotor turning)	30 ft 4 in
Height	8 ft 1 1/2 in
Weight Empty	1,200 lb
Weight Maximum	2,700 lb

Performance:

Max Speed	140 mph
Range	400 miles

Armament (Typical): 7.62 machinegun; XM-75 grenade launcher

Kaman HH-43 Husky

The Kaman HH-43B Husky, with its distinctive counter-rotating blades, was continually modified to improve its performance. *(Courtesy of Zaur Eylanbekov [Foxbat])*

Type: Rescue
Manufacturer's Type/Model Number: K-600

Powerplant: One Lycoming T53 turbo shaft of 860 shp

Dimensions:

Main Rotor Diameter	47 ft
Main Rotor Disc Area	1,735 sq ft
Length (rotor turning)	32 ft
Height	17 ft 2 in
Weight Empty	4,800 lb
Weight Maximum	9,150 lb

Performance:

Max Speed	115 mph
Range	190 miles

Armament (Typical): Usually none

Kamov Ka-32 "Helix"

The "Helix" is used for a wide variety of duties, including SAR, transport, attack, and surveillance. *(Courtesy of Zaur Eylanbekov [Foxbat])*

Type: Assault, rescue, transport, antisubmarine warfare

Manufacturer's Type/Model Number: Ka-32

Powerplant: Two Klimov TV-3 turbo shafts of 2,200 shp

Dimensions:

Main Rotor Diameter	52 ft
Main Rotor Disc Area	2,122 sq ft
Length (rotor turning)	46 ft
Height	18 ft 6 in
Weight Empty	15,000 lb
Weight Maximum	24,200 lb

Performance:

Max Speed	150 mph
Range	400 miles

Armament (Typical): Torpedoes; rockets; depth charges; bombs

Kamov Ka-50 "Hokum"

NATO designations such as "Hokum" often don't do justice to the capabilities of the aircraft being named. The KA-50 is a formidable single-place attack helicopter. *(Courtesy of Zaur Eylanbekov [Foxbat])*

Type: Gunship, assault, anti-helicopter
Manufacturer's Type/Model Number: Ka-50
Powerplant: Two Klimov TV3 turbo shafts of 2,200 shp
Dimensions:

Main Rotor Diameter	48 ft
Main Rotor Disc Area	1,808 sq ft
Length (rotor turning)	52 ft 6 in
Height	16 ft
Weight Empty	17,000 lb
Weight Maximum	23,900 lb

Performance:

Max Speed	211 mph
Range	285 miles

Armament (Typical): 30-mm cannon; 20-mm gun pods; rockets; Archer air-to-air missiles; 500-kg bombs

Mil Mi6 "Hook"

The Soviet Union had a predilection for large aircraft, and the huge Mil Mi-6 "Hook" was not only big but effective. *(Courtesy of Zaur Eylanbekov [Foxbat])*

Type: Transport, assault, MEDEVAC

Manufacturer's Type/Model Number: Mi-6
Powerplant: Two Soloviev D-25 turbo shafts of 5,500 shp
Dimensions:

Main Rotor Diameter	114 ft 10 in
Main Rotor Disc Area	10,360 sq ft
Length (rotor turning)	136 ft 11 in
Height	32 ft 4 in
Weight Empty	60,000 lb
Weight Maximum	93,700 lb

Performance:

Max Speed	186 mph
Range	400 miles

Armament (Typical): Usually none installed but many ad hoc installations over the years.

Mil Mi-8 "Hip"

The Mi-8 has been built in greater numbers than any other helicopter and has been used by more than fifty countries. It is a true classic. *(Courtesy of Zaur Eylanbekov [Foxbat])*

Type: Transport, assault, command and control
Manufacturer's Type/Model Number: Mi-8
Powerplant: Two Klimov TV-2 turbo shafts of 1,480 shp
Dimensions:

Main Rotor Diameter	69 ft 10 in
Main Rotor Disc Area	3,830 sq ft
Length (rotor turning)	82 ft 10 in
Height	18 ft 6 1/2 in
Weight Empty	15,000 lb
Weight Maximum	26,500 lb

Performance:

Max Speed	160 mph
Range	325 miles

Armament (Typical): Varied in assault role; .50-caliber machineguns; rockets; missiles

Mil Mi-10 "Harke"

Type: Heavy lift
Manufacturer's Type/Model Number: Mi-10
Powerplant: Two Soloviev D-25V turbo shafts of 5,500 shp
Dimensions:

Main Rotor Diameter	114 ft 10 in
Main Rotor Disc Area	10,351 sq ft
Length (rotor turning)	110 ft
Height	27 ft 2 in
Weight Empty	60,000 lb
Weight Maximum	96,400 lb

Performance:

Max Speed	125 mph
Range	160 miles

Armament (Typical): None

Mil Mi-24 "Hind"

A powerful gunship, and able to transport small numbers of troops, the Mi-24 "Hind" demonstrates the capabilities of the Soviet design/production system. *(Courtesy of Zaur Eylanbekov [Foxbat])*

Type: Assault, troop carrier
Manufacturer's Type/Model Number: Mi-24
Powerplant: Two Isotov TV3 turbo shafts of 2,200 shp
Dimensions:

Main Rotor Diameter	56 ft 9 in
Main Rotor Disc Area	2,550 sq ft
Length (rotor turning)	70 ft 6 in
Height	13 ft

| Weight Empty | 18,000 lb |
| Weight Maximum | 26,500 lb |

Performance:

| Max Speed | 205 mph |
| Range | 310 miles |

Armament (Typical): .50-caliber machinegun turret; cannon pods; rockets; missiles

Mil Mi-28N Havoc

As lethal as its name, the Mil Mi-28 is designed to attack enemy armor exclusively. *(Courtesy of Zaur Eylanbekov [Foxbat])*

Type: Assault, gunship
Manufacturer's Type/Model Number: Mi-28N
Powerplant: Two Klimov TV3 turbo shafts of 2,200 shp
Dimensions:

Main Rotor Diameter	56 ft 5 in
Main Rotor Disc Area	2,500 sq ft
Length (rotor turning)	59 ft
Height	12 ft 6 in
Weight Empty	17,400 lb
Weight Maximum	23,000 lb

Performance:

| Max Speed | 220 mph |
| Range | 275 miles |

Armament (Typical): One 30-mm cannon turret; bombs, rockets, air-to-air missiles, antitank missiles

Piasecki H-21 Shawnee/Workhorse

Type: Transport, assault, rescue, MEDEVAC
Manufacturer's Type/Model Number: 46

Powerplant: One Wright R-1820 of 1,425 hp
Dimensions:

Main Rotor Diameter	44 ft each
Main Rotor Disc Area	3,050 sq ft each
Length (rotor turning)	91 ft
Height	15 ft 9 in
Weight Empty	8,900 lb
Weight Maximum	15,250 lb

Performance:

Max Speed	127 mph
Range	270 miles

Armament (Typical): Two .50-caliber machineguns

Sikorsky H-5

Type: Liaison, observation, MEDEVAC
Manufacturer's Type/Model Number: S-51
Powerplant: One Pratt & Whitney R-985 of 450 hp
Dimensions:

Main Rotor Diameter	48 ft
Main Rotor Disc Area	1,809 sq ft
Length (rotor turning)	56 ft
Height	12 ft 11 in
Weight Empty	3,600 lb
Weight Maximum	4,815 lb

Performance:

Max Speed	90 mph
Range	270 miles

Armament (Typical): None

Sikorsky H-19 Chickasaw

The workhorse H-19 was produced in the United States, the United Kingdom, France, and Japan. *(Courtesy of Zaur Eylanbekov [Foxbat])*

Type: Rescue, MEDEVAC, transport
Manufacturer's Type/Model Number: S-51
Powerplant: One Wright R-1820 of 1,200 hp
Dimensions:

Main Rotor Diameter	53 ft 6 in
Main Rotor Disc Area	2,290 sq ft
Length (rotor turning)	73 ft 6 in
Height	13 ft 4 in
Weight Empty	4,800 lb
Weight Maximum	7,300 lb

Performance:

Max Speed	110 mph
Range	400 miles

Armament (Typical): None

Sikorsky H-34 Choctaw

Type: Rescue, transport, assault
Manufacturer's Type/Model Number: S-58
Powerplant: One Wright R-1820 of 1,525 hp
Dimensions:

Main Rotor Diameter	56 ft
Main Rotor Disc Area	2,485 sq ft
Length (rotor turning)	72 ft
Height	15 ft 11 in
Weight Empty	7,850 lb
Weight Maximum	13,950 lb

Performance:

Max Speed	124 mph
Range	240 miles

Armament (Typical): None

Sikorsky CH-54 Tarhe

The huge Tarhe found employment as a firefighting aircraft after its service career ended. *(Courtesy of U.S. Army Museum, Fort Rucker)*

Type: Heavy lift
Manufacturer's Type/Model Number: S-64
Powerplant: Two Pratt & Whitney T73 turbo shafts of 4,800 shp
Dimensions:

Main Rotor Diameter	72 ft
Main Rotor Disc Area	4,072 sq ft
Length (rotor turning)	98 ft
Height	25 ft 5 in
Weight Empty	20,000 lb
Weight Maximum	47,000 lb

Performance:

Max Speed	150 mph
Range	240 miles

Armament (Typical): None

Sikorsky HH-3E

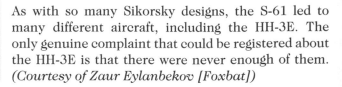

As with so many Sikorsky designs, the S-61 led to many different aircraft, including the HH-3E. The only genuine complaint that could be registered about the HH-3E is that there were never enough of them. *(Courtesy of Zaur Eylanbekov [Foxbat])*

Type: Rescue, transport, antisubmarine

Manufacturer's Type/Model Number: S-61R
Powerplant: Two General Electric T-58 turbo shafts of 1,400 shp
Dimensions:

Main Rotor Diameter	62 ft
Main Rotor Disc Area	3,018 sq ft
Length (rotor turning)	79 ft
Height	18 ft 1 in
Weight Empty	13,300 lb
Weight Maximum	22,100 lb

Performance:

Max Speed	165 mph
Range	750 miles

Armament (Typical): Varied, with different machinegun installations for defense

Sikorsky CH-53E

Few weapons of war have the longevity and the modifications accorded to helicopters. The Model S-65 CH-53 eventually served as the HH-53 Super Jolly Green and later as the MH-53 Pave Low. *(Courtesy of Zaur Eylanbekov [Foxbat])*

Type: CSAR, antimining, SOF, transport, inflight refueling
Manufacturer's Type/Model Number: S-65
Powerplant: Three General Electric T-64 turbo shafts of 4,380 shp
Dimensions:

Main Rotor Diameter	79 ft
Main Rotor Disc Area	4,900 sq ft
Length (rotor turning) 96 ft	
Height	28 ft 5 in
Weight Empty	33,236 lb
Weight Maximum	73,500 lb

Performance:

Max Speed	150 mph
Range	480 miles

Armament (Typical): Varied but includes .50-caliber machineguns, 7.62 miniguns

Sikorsky MH-53J Pave Low

Type: Long-range infiltration/exfiltration, resupply of SOF
Manufacturer's Type/Model Number: S-65J
Powerplant: Two General Electric T-64 turbo shafts of 4,330 shp
Dimensions:

Main Rotor Diameter	72 ft
Main Rotor Disc Area	4,070 sq ft
Length (rotor turning)	87 ft
Height	25 ft
Weight Empty	34,000 lb
Weight Maximum	46,000 lb

Performance:

Max Speed	165 mph
Range	480 miles

Armament (Typical): Three 7.62 miniguns or three .50-caliber machineguns

Sikorsky HH-60G Pave Hawk

Using improved communications, navigation, and other advanced equipment, the Pave Hawk is an upgraded version of the basic Black Hawk. *(Courtesy of Zaur Eylanbekov [Foxbat])*

Type: CSAR, insertion of SOF
Manufacturer's Type/Model Number: S-70
Powerplant: Two General Electric T700 turbo shafts of 1,890 shp
Dimensions:

Main Rotor Diameter	53 ft 8 in
Main Rotor Disc Area	2,262 sq ft

Length (rotor turning)	67 ft 1 in
Height	16 ft 10 in
Weight Empty	13,700 lb
Weight Maximum	21,700 lb

Performance:

| Max Speed | 157 mph |
| Range | 550 miles |

Armament (Typical): Two .50-caliber machineguns or two 7.62 miniguns

Sikorsky UH-60 Black Hawk

With more than 2,300 built over thirty years, the Sikorsky Black Hawk is one of the most important helicopters of its time. *(Courtesy of Zaur Eylanbekov [Foxbat])*

Type: CSAR, insertion of SOF, troop and cargo transport
Manufacturer's Type/Model Number: S-70
Powerplant: Two General Electric T700 turbo shafts of 1,890 hp
Dimensions:

Main Rotor Diameter	53 ft 8 in
Main Rotor Disc Area	2,262 sq ft
Length (rotor turning)	67 ft 11 in
Height	7 ft 2 in
Weight Empty	10,600 lb
Weight Maximum	22,000 lb

Performance:

| Max Speed | 181 mph |
| Range | 550 miles |

Armament (Typical): Two .50-caliber machineguns or two 7.62 miniguns; two GAU-19 Gatling guns; 70-mm Hydra 70 rockets; AGM-114 Hellfire missile

Notes

Chapter One

1. Roger Conner, curator, National Air & Space Museum, e-mail interview with author, March 29, 2009.

2. Rodney Propst, *Marine Helicopters in Korea,* http://www.popasmoke.com/korea/chronology.html.

3. Gen. Robert Magnus, USMC (Ret), e-mail to author, April 7, 2009.

4. Spencer C. Tucker and Priscilla Mary Roberts, eds., *Encyclopedia of World War II* (Santa Barbara: ABC-CLIO, 2004), 67.

5. Ibid., 68.

6. *Aeronautical Development at McCook Field,* http://www.ascho.wpafb.af.mil/birthplace/CHAP3.HTM.

7. The Australian Parachute Federation, *The History of Parachuting,* http://www.apf.asn.au/apf-history-parachuting.htm,

8. "Geronimo and the Red Army," *U.S. Army Intelligence Bulletin,* May 1946.

9. I. C. B. Dear and M. R. D. Foot, "Voroshilov, Marshal Kliment," in *The Oxford Companion to World War II* (Oxford: Oxford University Press, 2001).

10. Student, Kurt, http://www.spartacus.schoolnet.co.uk/GERstudent.htm.

11. Conner, e-mail interview with author, April 27, 2010.

12. Steve Coates with Jean-Christophe Carbonel, *Helicopters of the Third Reich* (Hersham, Surrey, United Kingdom: Ian Allen Publishing, 2002), 104.

13. Ibid., 186.

14. Jean Boulet, *History of the Helicopter as Told by Its Pioneers 1907-1956* (Paris: Editions France Empire, 1982), 90.

15. Ibid., 91.

16. Maj. Gen. John Alison, USAF (Ret), conversations with author, 1996-98.

17. Charles Gablehouse, *Helicopters and Autogiros* (New York: J. B. Lippincott, 1969), 124.

18. Robert F. Dorr, *Chopper* (New York: Berkley Books, 2005), 14.

Chapter Two

1. James W. Bradin, *From Hot Air to Hellfire: The History of Army Attack Aviation* (Novato, CA: Presidio Press, 1994), 70.

2. Walter J. Boyne, *Beyond the Wild Blue: A History of the United States Air Force, 1947-2007* (New York: St. Martin's Press, 2007), 34.

3. James H. Williams, *A History of Army Aviation: From Its Beginnings to the War on Terror* (Lincoln: Universe, 2005), 36.

4. Propst.

5. Frank E. Ransom, *Air-Sea Rescue, 1941-1952,* Numbered USAF Historical Studies 95 (Montgomery, AL: Maxwell Air Force Base, 1953), 161.

6. Ibid., 165.

7. Ibid., 166.

8. Propst.

9. Ibid.

10. George Galdorsi and Tom Phillips, *Leave No Man Behind: The Saga of Combat Search and Rescue* (Minneapolis: Zenith Press, 2008), 118.

11. Propst.

12. Galdorsi and Phillips, 136.

13. Propst.

14. Otto Kreisher, "The Rise of the Helicopter During the Korean War," *Aviation History*, January 2007.,

15. John Everett-Heath, *Helicopters in Combat: The First Fifty Years* (London: Arms and Armour Press, 1993), 17.

16. http://www.heliopsassn.co.uk/Helicopters%20in%20Malaya.htm.

17. http://ehistory.osu.edu/vietnam/essays/insurgency/0006.cfm.

18. Everett-Heath, 45.

19. Charles R. Shrader, *The First Helicopter War: Logistics and Mobility in Algeria, 1954-1962* (Westport, CT: Praeger, 1999), 24.

20. Everett-Heath, 56.

21. Ibid., 53.

22. Shrader, 48.

Chapter Three

1. Michael Hirschberg, briefing to the American Helicopter Society International, Bückeburg, Germany, July 7, 2000.

2. Gablehouse, 26.

3. Ibid., 40

4. Boulet, 11.

5. David Donald, ed., *The Complete Encyclopedia of World Aircraft* (New York: Barnes & Noble, 1997), 842.

6. Ibid.

7. Ibid.

8. Frank Piasecki, *The Piasecki Story of Vertical Lift*, brochure by Piasecki, circa 1990.

9. U.S. Coast Guard History, http://www.uscg.mil/history/webaircraft/Piasecki_HRP.pdf.

10. http://www.arthuryoung.com/about.html.

11. J. Gordon Leishman, *Principles of Helicopter Aerodynamics* (New York: Cambridge University Press, 2006).

12. http://www.cwa.ru/tsaginfo.htm.

13. Bruce H. Charnov, *From Autogiro to Gyroplane: The Amazing Survival of an Aviation Technology* (Westport, CT: Praeger Publishers, 2003), 200.

14. Robert Jackson, ed., *The Aviation Factfile: Helicopters, Military, Civilian and Rescue Rotorcraft* (San Diego: Thunder Bay Press, 2005), 153.

15. http://www.aviastar.org/people/kamov/index_2.html.

16. Donald, 543.

17. Coates, 128.

18. Paul Lambermont with Anthony Pirie, *Helicopters and the Autogyros of the World* (New York: A. S. Barnes, 1970), 315.

19. Donald, 21.

20. Walter J. Boyne, ed., *Air Warfare: An International Encyclopedia* (Santa Barbara: ABC-CLIO, 2002).

21. Rod Simpson, *Airlife's Helicopters and Rotorcraft* (Shrewsbury, United Kingdom: Airlife, 2008), 48-57.

22. http://www.globalsecurity.org/military/world/russia/klimov.htm.

Chapter Four

1. http://www.vhpa.org/heliloss.pdf.

2. Civilian helicopters are expensive and almost always evolve from previous military experience. Therefore there is a direct causal relationship between the failure of the American Congress to provide the necessary direction and funding to spur the R&D of military helicopters and the horrific increase in the fatalities occurring with civilian helicopters. As a single example, the number of U.S. medical helicopter crash deaths increased from four in 2006 to twenty-eight in 2008. One medical helicopter pilot was quoted as saying that "we have been killing ourselves the same way for twenty years," meaning that the technology has not changed, the helicopters have gotten older, and the flights have become more frequent. The jobs of medical helicopter crews are rated as the second most dangerous in the nation, behind only those of commercial fishermen.

3. Charles Tustin Kamp, "The JCS 99-Target List: A Vietnam Myth that Still Distorts Military Thought," *Aerospace Power Journal,* Spring 2001.

4. James M. Gavin, "Cavalry and I Don't Mean Horses," *Harper's,* April 1954, 54-60.

5. Ibid.

6. Bradin, 95.

7. Ibid., 114.

8. Ibid., 128.

9. Everett-Heath, 64.

10. http://www.quad-a.org/Hall of_Fame/personnel/kinnard.htm.

11. Williams, 162.

12. Philip H. Chinnery, *Vietnam: The HelicopterWar* (Annapolis: Naval Institute Press, 1991), 8.

13. John J. Tolson III, *Airmobility in Vietnam: Helicopter Warfare in Southeast Asia* (New York: Arno Press, 1981), 26.

14. Ibid., 31.

15. Ibid., 38.

16. Chinnery, 48.

17. Tolson, 72.

18. Chinnery, 50.

19. J. D. Coleman, *Pleiku: The Dawn of Helicopter Warfare in Vietnam* (New York: St. Martin's Press, 1988), 70.

20. Tolson, 91.

21. Ibid., 22.

22. Peter B. Mersky, *U.S. Marine Corps Aviation, 1912 to the Present,* 3rd ed. (Baltimore: The Nautical & Aviation Publishing Company of America, 1983), 211.

Chapter Five

1.Williams, 193.

2. Tolson, 26.

3. Ibid.

4. Walter J. Boyne, *Beyond the Horizons: The Lockheed Story* (New York: St. Martin's Press, 1998), 345.

5. Norman Polmar and Floyd D. Kennedy, Jr., *Military Helicopters of the World* (Annapolis: United States Naval Institute, 1981), 179.

6. For perhaps the most graphic portrayal of helicopter combat in the Vietnam War literature, readers are referred to the book *Low Level Hell*, by Hugh L. Mills, Jr. (New York: Bantam, 1992).

7. Williams, 133.

8. Everett-Heath, 112.

9. Robert G. K. Thompson, *No Exit from Vietnam* (New York: David McCay, 1969), 130.

10. Andrew F. Krepinevich, Jr., *The Army and Vietnam* (Baltimore: The Johns Hopkins University Press, 1986), 67.

11. Everett-Heath, 112.

12. Tolson, 102.

13. Williams, 157.

14. Peter Brush, *The Battle of Khe Sanh 1968*, http://www.library.vanderbilt.edu/central/brush/BattleKheSanh1968.htm.

15. Krepinevich, 178.

16. Bernard Nalty, *Air Power and the Fight for Khe Sanh* (Washington, D.C.: Office of Air Force History), 1986.

17. Ibid.

18. Tolson, 102.

19. Jeremiah S. Boenisch, *The Cambodian Incursion: A Hard Line for*

Change, http://www.militaryhistoryonline.com/vietnam/articles/cambod
ianincursion.aspx.

20. Tolson, 245.

21. http://www.a101avn.org/LamSon719.html.

Chapter Six

1. John L. Cook, *Rescue Under Fire: The Story of DUSTOFF in Vietnam* (Atglen, PA: Schiffer Military/Aviation History, 1998), 1-175.

2. Army Medical Department Regiment Oral History, March 27, 1987,
http://www.ameddregiment.amedd.army.mil/MOHOralhistoryBrady.asp.

3. Earl H. Tilford, Jr., *Search and Rescue in Southeast Asia, 1961-
1975* (Washington, D.C.: Office of Air Force History, 1981), 12.

4. Ibid., 13.

5. Galdorsi and Phillips, 165.

6. Tilford, 69.

7. Ibid., 76.

8. Ibid., 97.

9. http://www.specialoperations.com/Operations/sontay.html.

Chapter Seven

1. Robert Shisko, *The European Conventional Balance: A Primer*,
http://www.rand.org/pubs/papers/2008/P6707.pdf.

2. John M. Collins, *U.S./Soviet Military Balance* (New York: McGraw
Hill, 1980), 20.

3. Shisko.

4. Ibid.

5. Ibid.

6. James C. Slife, *Creech Blue: Gen. Bill Creech and the Reformation
of the Tactical Air Forces 1978-1984* (Maxwell Air Force Base, Montgomery, AL: Air University Press, 2004), 135.

7. Kenneth P. Werrel, "Did USAF Technology Fail in Vietnam?: Three
Case Studies," *Airpower Journal,* Spring 1998, 1.

8 Slife, 136.

9. Frank Boynton, briefing to the American Helicopter Society, Alexandria, VA, Oct. 7, 2007.

10. Ibid.

11. http://www.thefreelibrary.com/The+SA-7+grail:+man-portable+missile +packs+a+punch.-a0213402273.

12. http://www.globalsecurity.org/military/systems/aircraft/ah-64d-ops.htm.

Chapter Eight

1. Robert F. Baumann, *Compound War Case Study: The Soviets in Afghanistan* (Fort Leavenworth, KS: CSI Home Publications, 1990), 292.

2. Johnnie H. Hall, "To Save the Pilot's Life—Soviet Air Rescue Service" *Air University Review* (May-June 1982), 1.

3. Everett-Heath, 127.

4. David Isby, "Soviets in Afghanistan, Prepared for the Long Haul," *Defense Week* (February 21, 1984), 14.

5. Everett-Heath, 146.

6. Viktor Markovskii, *Zharkoe nebo Afganiatana* (Moscow: Tekhnika-Molodezhi, 2000), 68-101. My sincere thanks to George Mellinger, as most of this chapter's material concerning Soviet activities in Afghanistan derives from his translation of this book.

Chapter Nine

1. C. E. Holzworth, *Operation Eagle Claw: A Catalyst for Change in the American Military,* http://www.google.com/#hl=en&source=hp&q=Operation+Eagle+Claw++Global+Security&btnG=Google+Search&aq=f&aqi=&aql =&oq=Operation+Eagle+Claw++Global+Security&fp=a048890d3c90c6fc^.

2. Ibid.

3. Tony Landis and Dennis Jenkins, *Lockheed-56A Cheyenne* (North Branch, MN: Specialty Press, 2000), 19.

4. Ibid., 81.

5. Boyne, *Beyond the Horizons,* 342-45.

6. David A. Fulghum and Robert Wall, "Comanche Helicopter Program Killed," *Aviation Week & Space Technology* (February 29, 2004).

7. http://www.army.mil/aps/09/information_papers/restructuring_army _aviation.html.

Chapter Ten

1. Thomas Taylor, *Lightning in the Storm: The 101st Air Assault*

Division in the Gulf War (New York: Hippocrene Books, 1994), 131.

2. Stan Morse, ed., *Gulf Air War Debrief* (London: Aerospace Publishing, 1991), 48, 49.

3. Ibid., 80.

4. Stanley S. McGowen, *Weapons and Warfare* (Santa Barbara: ABC-CLIO, 2005), 209.

5. Morse, 160.

6. Darrel D. Whitcomb, *Combat Search and Rescue in Desert Storm* (Maxwell Air Force Base, Montgomery, AL: Air University Press, 2006), xviii.

7. Richard P. Hallion, *Storm Over Iraq* (Washington, D.C.: Smithsonian Institution Press, 1992), 246.

8. Ibid.

9. Lambeth, Benjamin S. *Reflections on the Balkan Air Wars.* Air Power History, Clinton, Vol 57, No 1, Clinton, MD Spring 2010, 35

10. http://www.globalsecurity.org/security/profiles/black_hawk_down.htm.

11. http://www.globalsecurity.org/military/library/report/crs/RS21048.pdf.

12. Andrew Feickert, *Congressional Research Service Report for Congress: U.S. Special Operations Forces, Background and Issues*, RS 221048 13 (August 3, 2009).

13. http://www.eurocopterusa.com/news_features/2010/02-22-10-heli-expo-2010-leadership.asp.

14. M. E. Rhett Flater, testimony to House Armed Services Committee, Subcommittee of Tactical and Land Forces, 108th Congress, in *Regarding Aviation Industrial Case: The Department of Defense Rotorcraft Investment Programs* (March 4, 2004), 9.

Chapter Eleven

1. Ralph Omholt, DefenseWatch 2003, http://www.military.com/NewContent/0,13190,Defensewatch_120303_Helicopter,00.htm.

2. Lambermont with Pirie, 396-97.

3. M. E. Rhett Flater, letter to *Time,* October 3, 2007, quoted in *Vertiflite Magazine* (Fall 2007), 6.

4. Michael J. Sullivan, "V-22 Osprey Aircraft Assessments Needed to Address Operational and Cost Concerns to Define Future Investments," GAO-09-692T (Washington, D.C.: Government Accounting Office, June 23, 2009).

Appendix One

1. Ian McDougall, Francis H. Brown, and John G. Fleagle, "Stratigraphic Placement and Age of Modern Humans from Kibish, Ethiopia," *Nature* 433, no. 7027 (2005): 733-36.

2. Gablehouse, 3.

3. Charles H. Gibbs-Smith, *Sir George Cayley, 1773-1857* (London: Her Majesty's Stationery Office, 1968), 4.

4. Warren R. Young, *The Helicopters* (Alexandria, VA: Time-Life Books, 1982), 20.

5. Boulet, 8.

6. Ibid., 20.

7. Ibid., 23.

8. http://terpconnect.umd.edu/~leishman/Aero/Cornu. pdf.

9. Phillipe Boulay, *Union Française de l'Hélicoptère,* e-mail exchanges with author, 2009.

10. Boulet, 25.

11. Ibid., 32.

12. http://www.aviastar.org/helicopters_eng/petroczy.php.

13. Gablehouse, 22.

14. Ibid.

15. http://www.centennialofflight.gov/essay/Rotary/early_20th_century/HE2.htm.

16. Boulet, 37.

17. Ibid, 44.

18. Pete W. Brooks, *Cierva Autogiros: The Development of Rotary Wing Flight* (Washington, D.C.: Smithsonian Institution Press, 1988), 19.

19. Charnov, 24.

20. Ibid., 92.

21. Ibid., 91.

22. Ibid., 189.

23. Ibid., 209.

24. Brooks, 356.

25. Boulet, 63.

Index